NARCISSUS REFLECTED

DAVID LOMAS

NARCISSUS REFLECTED

THE MYTH OF NARCISSUS IN SURREALIST AND CONTEMPORARY ART

DAVID LOMAS

NARCISSUS REFLECTED

DAVID LOMAS

Published by
The Fruitmarket Gallery
45 Market Street, Edinburgh, EH1 1DF
Telephone +44 (0)131 225 2383
Facsimile: +44 (0)131 220 3130
www.fruitmarket.co.uk

On the occasion of the exhibition
Narcissus Reflected
22 April – 26 June 2011
Curated by David Lomas and Dawn Ades

Exhibition supported by
The Terra Foundation for American Art
and The Art Mentor Foundation Lucerne

Exhibition conceived in collaboration with
the AHRC Centre for the Study of Surrealism
and its Legacies at The University of Manchester
Publication supported by the British Academy

ISBN 978-0-947912-99-4

Distributed for Reaktion Books Ltd in the USA
and Canada by the University of Chicago Press
1427 East 60th Street / Chicago IL 60637

Distributed in the UK and the rest of
the world by Reaktion Books Ltd,
33 Great Sutton St, London EC1V 0DX, UK

Publishing is an intrinsic part of The Fruitmarket Gallery's creative programme, with books published to accompany each exhibition. Books are conceived as part of the exhibition-making process, with the book extending the reach and life of each exhibition and offering artists and curators a second space in which to present their work.

The Fruitmarket Gallery is a not-for-profit organisation and a Scottish charity presenting world-class, challenging art made by Scottish and international artists in an environment that is welcoming, engaging, informative and always free.

The Gallery is Foundation Funded by Creative Scotland for up to 58% of its running costs and must raise additional funds to support its exhibitions, education and publishing programmes.

The Fruitmarket Gallery is a company limited by guarantee, registered in Scotland no. 87888 and registered as a Scottish Charity no. SC 005576
Registered Office 45 Market St., Edinburgh, EH1 1DF.
VAT no. 398 2504 21

Editor's note: All translations are the author's unless otherwise stated.

The Fruitmarket Gallery

CREATIVE SCOTLAND

TERRA
FOUNDATION FOR AMERICAN ART

ART MENTOR FOUNDATION LUCERNE

Arts & Humanities Research Council

CONTENTS

FOREWORD

FIONA BRADLEY

'Narcissus Reflected' is the latest in The Fruitmarket Gallery's series of group exhibitions and accompanying publications made by invited scholars, writers and artists. Its prime mover and chief curator is David Lomas, an academic and exhibition-maker known for his work in the fields of surrealism and contemporary art who has been researching the theme of narcissism in art at least since 1999, when he contributed an essay on Salvador Dalí's painting *Metamorphosis of Narcissus* (1937) to the catalogue of the exhibition 'Salvador Dalí: A Mythology'at Tate Liverpool. Lomas has been supported in his research for this exhibition by acknowledged Dalí expert Dawn Ades (who was co-curator of the Tate Liverpool exhibition) and by Silvia Loreti, a colleague at the Centre for the Study of Surrealism and its Legacies, in collaboration with which this Fruitmarket Gallery exhibition was conceived.

'Narcissus Reflected' grows from David Lomas's interest in and knowledge of Dalí's painting, and of the poem – also called *Metamorphosis of Narcissus* – that Dalí wrote to accompany it. Text and image intertwine in Dalí's treatment of Narcissus and 'Narcissus Reflected' celebrates this, enjoying the centrality of the written word to the myth: Narcissus comes to us from Ovid's *Metamorphoses* and, as Lomas shows, many pictorial treatments of the story make such explicit reference to it as to evoke the rhetorical device of *ekphrasis*, the written description of a work of visual art. Word and image similarly combine in 'Narcissus Reflected', as the book explores and amplifies the theme of narcissism through the work of more artists than can be presented in an exhibition.

'Narcissus Reflected' explores both Narcissus and narcissism. Narcissus is the beautiful youth from Greek mythology, turned by the gods into a narcissus flower as punishment for his self-obsession and inability to love anyone other than his own reflection. Narcissism was identified by Sigmund Freud as an early stage in his account of the formation of an individual's ego, at which point they begin to be aware of their sexual drives and desires, and seek a love object. The first love object they choose is their own body. In a 'normal' individual, according to Freudian psychoanalysis, narcissism should be only a passing phase.

In the developing tradition of The Fruitmarket Gallery's group exhibitions, 'Narcissus Reflected' is a scholarly yet also personal, passionate, speculative and eclectic journey into the realm of Narcissus. At its appropriately doubled heart lies Dalí's

Metamorphosis of Narcissus and *Narkissos* (1976–91) the masterwork of the San-Francisco-based artist Jess. Dalí's painting is one of the most famous, most well-travelled and most often reproduced works of modern art, although this exhibition and publication offer a rare chance to see the painting, poem and a wealth of preparatory material together. Jess's large, hand-drawn collage, by contrast, rarely leaves the San Francisco Museum of Modern Art and is published here together with all the material of its making for the first time.

These two great pictures are examined in some detail in 'Narcissus Reflected'. Lomas explores them in terms of both art and personal history, and weaves a web of connections around them. In the exhibition, he follows the thread of Narcissus through experimental film and photography in the 1920s and 1930s and in America in the 1940s and 1950s, winding up in the big, immersive contemporary environments of Yayoi Kusama's *Narcissus Garden* (1966) and Pipilotti Rist's *Sip My Ocean* (1996). In the book, he turns his gaze on art and artists as wide apart as Gustave Moreau and Jake and Dinos Chapman, Caravaggio and Mat Collishaw.

'Narcissus Reflected' examines Narcissus and narcissism as structural and theoretical, as well as narrative or illustrative impulses. Lomas discerns narcissism in Dalí's interest in stereoscopic vision and painting as well as in his carefully constructed narcissistic persona. In Jess he examines collage as an essentially narcissistic pursuit – an interest in doubles, copies, reflections – and reveals the picture to be structured around a similarly reflective axis. Narcissus has been seen as a symbol for the artist, and Lomas uses him as a figure through which to look at identity and identity politics with reference to gay art and queer theory from the *fin de siècle* to the present day.

We are grateful to David Lomas for bringing 'Narcissus Reflected' to The Fruitmarket Gallery. We are indebted to his scholarship, ideas and enthusiasm. We thank Dawn Ades and Silvia Loreti and other colleagues at the Centre for the Study of Surrealism and its Legacies, for their involvement with the project. 'Narcissus Reflected' is the fortunate recipient of funding from the Terra Foundation for American Art, the Art Mentor Foundation Lucerne and the British Academy, and we are profoundly grateful to them for their support. Finally, we thank the artists and art institutions who have collaborated with us on the exhibition and allowed their works of art to be seen in the context of 'Narcissus Reflected'.

OVID'S METAMORPHOSES

BOOK III: THE STORY OF ECHO AND NARCISSUS

Translation by Mary M. Innes
(Penguin, 1955)

The dark river nymph, Liriope, was the first to test his reliability and truthfulness. She was the nymph whom Cephisus once embraced with his curving stream, imprisoned in his waves, and forcefully ravished. When her time was come, that nymph most fair brought forth a child with whom one could have fallen in love even in his cradle, and she called him Narcissus. When the prophetic seer was asked whether this boy would live to a ripe old age, he replied: 'Yes, if he does not come to know himself.' For a long time this pronouncement seemed to be nothing but empty words: however it was justified by the outcome of events: the strange madness which afflicted the boy and the nature of his death proved its truth.

Cephisus' child had reached his sixteenth year, and could be counted as at once boy and man. Many lads and girls fell in love with him, but his soft young body housed a pride so unyielding that none of those boys or girls dared to touch him. One day, as he was driving timid deer into his nets, he was seen by that talkative nymph who cannot stay silent when another speaks, but yet has not learned to speak first herself. Her name is Echo, and she always answers back.

Echo still had a body then, she was not just a voice: but although she was always chattering, her power of speech was no different from what it is now. All she could do was to repeat the last words of the many phrases that she heard. Juno had brought this about because often, when she could have caught the nymphs lying with her Jupiter on the mountainside, Echo, knowing well what she did, used to detain the goddess with an endless flow of talk, until the nymphs could flee. When Juno realised what was happening, she said: 'I shall curtail the powers of that tongue which has tricked me: you will have only the briefest possible use of your voice.' And in fact she carried out her threats. Echo still repeats the last words spoken, and gives back the sounds she has heard.

So, when she saw Narcissus wandering through the lonely countryside, Echo fell in love with him, and followed secretly in his steps. The more closely she followed, the nearer was the fire which scorched her: just as sulphur, smeared round the tops of torches, is quickly kindled when a flame is brought near it. How often she wished to make flattering overtures to him, to approach him with tender pleas! But her handicap prevented this, and would not allow her to speak first;

she was ready to do what it would allow, to wait for sounds which she might re-echo with her own voice.

The boy, by chance, had wandered away from his faithful band of comrades, and he called out: 'Is there anybody here?' Echo answered: 'Here!' Narcissus stood still in astonishment, looking round in every direction, and cried at the pitch of his voice: 'Come!' As he called, she called in reply. He looked behind him, and when no one appeared he cried again: 'Why are you avoiding me?' But all he heard were his own words echoed back. Still he persisted, deceived by what he took to be another's voice, and said, 'Come here, and let us meet!' Echo answered: 'Let us meet!' Never again would she reply more willingly to any sound. To make good her words she came out of the wood and made to throw her arms round the neck she loved: but he fled from her, crying as he did so, 'Away with these embraces! I would die before I would have you touch me!' Her only answer was: 'I would have you touch me!' Thus scorned, she concealed herself in the woods, hiding her shamed face in the shelter of the leaves, and ever since that day, she dwells in lonely caves. Yet still her love remained firmly rooted in her heart, and was increased by the pain of having been rejected. Her anxious thoughts kept her awake, and made her pitifully thin. She became wrinkled and wasted; all the freshness of her beauty withered into the air. Only her voice and her bones were left, till finally her voice alone remained; for her bones, they say, were turned to stone. Since then, she hides in the woods, and, though never seen on the mountains, is heard there by all: for her voice is the only part of her that still lives.

Narcissus had played with her affections, treating her as he had previously treated other spirits of the waters and the woods, and his male admirers too. Then one of those he had scorned raised up his hands to heaven and prayed: 'May he himself fall in love with another, as we have done with him! May he too be unable to gain his loved one!' Nemesis heard and granted his righteous prayer.

There was a clear pool, with shining silvery waters, where shepherds had never made their way; no goats that pasture on the mountains, no cattle had ever come there. Its peace was undisturbed by bird or beast or falling branches. Around it was a grassy sward, kept ever green by the nearby waters; encircling woods sheltered the spot from the fierce sun, and made it always cool.

Narcissus, wearied with hunting in the heat of the day, lay down here: for he was attracted by the beauty of the place, and by the spring. While he sought to quench his thirst, another thirst grew in him, and as he drank, he was enchanted by the beautiful reflection that he saw. He fell in love with an insubstantial hope, mistaking a mere shadow for a real body. Spellbound by his own self, he remained there motionless, with fixed gaze, like a statue carved from Parian marble. As he lay on the bank, he gazed at the twin stars that were his eyes, at his flowing locks, worthy of Bacchus or Apollo, his smooth cheeks, his ivory neck, his lovely face where a rosy flush stained the snowy whiteness of his complexion, admiring all the features for which he was himself admired. Unwittingly, he desired himself, and was himself the object of his own approval, at once seeking and sought, himself kindling the flame with which he burned. How often did he vainly kiss the treacherous pool, how often plunge his arms deep in the waters, as he tried to clasp the neck he saw! But he could not lay hold upon himself. He did not know what he was looking at, but was fired by the sight, and excited by the very illusion that deceived his eyes. Poor foolish boy, why vainly grasp at the fleeting image that eludes you? The thing you are seeing does not exist: only turn aside and you will lose what you love. What you see is but the shadow cast by your reflection; in itself it is nothing. It comes with you, and lasts while you are there; it will go when you go, if go you can.

No thought of food or sleep could draw him from the spot. Stretched on the shady grass, he gazed at the shape that was no true shape with eyes that could never have their fill, and by his own eyes he was undone. Finally he raised himself a little. Holding out his arms to the surrounding woods: 'Oh you woods,' he cried, 'has anyone ever felt a love more cruel? You surely know, for many lovers have found you an ideal haunt for secret meetings. You who have lived so many centuries, do you remember anyone, in all your long years, who has pined away as I do? I am in love, and see my loved one, but that form which I see and love, I cannot reach: so far am I deluded by my love. My distress is all the greater because it is not a mighty ocean that separates us, nor yet highways or mountains, or city walls with close-barred gates. Only a little water keeps us apart. My love himself desires to be embraced: for whenever I lean forward to kiss the clear waters he lifts up his face to mine and strives to reach me. You would think he could be reached – it is such a small thing that hinders our love. Whoever you are, come out to me! Oh boy beyond compare, why do you elude me? Where do you go, when I try to reach you? Certainly it is not my looks or my years which you shun, for I am one of those the nymphs have loved. With friendly looks you proffer me some hope. When I stretch out my arms to you, you stretch yours towards me in return: you laugh when I do, and often I have marked your tears when I was weeping. You answer my signs with nods, and, as far as I can guess from the movement of your lovely lips, reply to me in words that never reach my ears. Alas! I am myself the boy I see. I know it: my own reflection does not deceive me. I am on fire with love of my own self. It is I who kindle the flames which I must endure. What should I do? Woo or be wooed? But what then shall I seek by my wooing? What I desire, I have. My very plenty makes me poor. How I wish I could separate myself from my body! A new prayer this, for a lover, to wish the thing he loves away! Now grief is sapping my strength; little of life remains for me – I am cut off in the flower of my youth. I have no quarrel with death, for in death I shall forget my pain: but I could wish that the object of my love might outlive me: as it is, both of us will perish together, when this one life is destroyed.'

When he had finished speaking, he returned to gazing distractedly at the same face. His tears disturbed the water, so that the pool rippled, and the image grew dim. He saw it disappearing, and cried aloud: 'Where are you fleeing? Cruel creature, stay, do not desert one who loves you! Let me look upon you, if I cannot touch you. Let me, by looking, feed my ill-starred love.' In his grief, he tore away the upper portion of his tunic, and beat his bared breast with hands as white as marble. His breast flushed rosily where he struck it, just as apples often shine red in part, while part gleams whitely, or as grapes, ripening in variegated clusters, are tinged with purple. When Narcissus saw this reflected in the water – for the pool had returned to its former calm – he could bear it no longer. As golden wax melts with gentle heat, as morning frosts are thawed by the warmth of the sun, so he was worn and wasted away with love, and slowly consumed by its hidden fire. His fair complexion with its rosy flush faded away, gone was his youthful strength, and all the beauties which lately charmed his eyes. Nothing remained of that body which Echo once had loved.

The nymph saw what had happened, and although she remembered her own treatment, and was angry at it, still she grieved for him. As often as the unhappy boy sighed 'Alas,' she took up his sigh, and repeated 'Alas!' When he beat his hands against his shoulders she too gave back the same sound of mourning. His last words as he gazed into the familiar waters were: 'Woe is me for the boy I loved in vain!' and the spot re-echoed the same words. When he said his last farewell, 'Farewell!' said Echo too. He laid down his weary head on the green grass, and death closed the eyes which so admired their owner's beauty. Even then, when he was received into the abode of the dead, he kept looking at himself in the waters of the Styx. His sisters, the nymphs of the spring, mourned for him, and cut off their hair in tribute to their brother. The wood nymphs mourned him too, and Echo sang her refrain to their lament.

The pyre, the tossing torches, and the bier, were now being prepared, but his body was nowhere to be found. Instead of his corpse, they discovered a flower with a circle of white petals round a yellow centre.

Narcissus from Pompeii, Roman fresco, 1st century

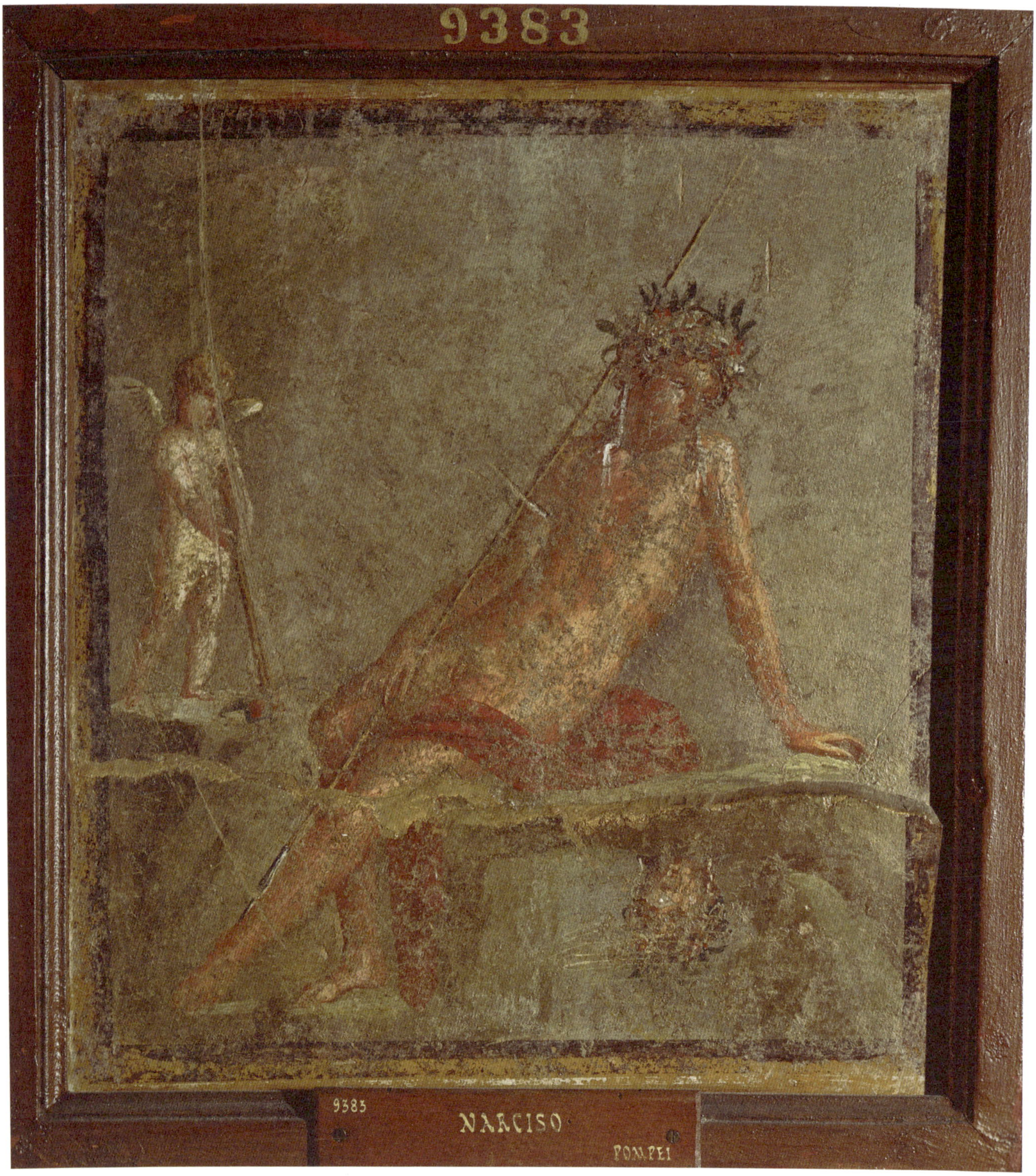

INTRODUCTION

> It is perhaps more interesting today to stress the originality of the narcissistic figure and the very particular place it occupies in the history of Western subjectivity.
>
> Julia Kristeva[1]

The fable of Narcissus – the story of a beautiful youth who, infatuated by his reflection in a pool, dies and is changed into a flower of the same name – is a simple but beguiling story susceptible to widely divergent interpretations that have accumulated from its first recording up to the present.[2] This book, and the exhibition it accompanies, examine the potency of the Narcissus myth in surrealist and contemporary art, including painting, drawing, sculpture, photography, installation, film and video. From Salvador Dalí's *Metamorphosis of Narcissus* (1937) to Pipilotti Rist's *Sip My Ocean* (1996), 'Narcissus Reflected' keeps in play the many meanings of the myth, exploring in depth, and seeking to explain, the enduring appeal of the Narcissus subject in art.

It would be hard to think of a myth with a richer tradition in literature and art. The danger of an exhibition on the Narcissus theme is that it truncates one half of this representational history. The way these two traditions echo (or mirror) each other, their intimate reciprocity, is epitomised in the classical genre of *ekphrasis* – textual commentary on real or imagined works of art. Philostratus the Elder and Callistratus produced notable examples of Narcissus *ekphrases* in the third century AD but the tradition is still going strong in the period covered by 'Narcissus Reflected', with evidence that artists like Dalí, who wrote a poem, also titled *Metamorphosis of Narcissus*, intended to be read in conjunction with the painting, thought about the alternate potentials of word and image for depicting this complex, ambiguous narrative. The theme was also favourite one with numerous symbolist and other more recent poets. Psychology and psychoanalysis are other sites of commentary on Narcissus, again intersecting with visual and literary representations of the Narcissus myth. The purpose of this publication, which serves as a complement to the exhibition, is to give a presence to these intertwined textual and visual histories and to expand on the necessarily selective presentation of works in the Gallery with further examples that show the potential richness of this Greek myth for artists, and its capacity to speak to contemporary audiences.

NARCISSUS IN ART AND LITERATURE

The story of Narcissus is a capacious myth, not least because it exists in several versions. *Metamorphoses* by the Roman poet Ovid, completed in 8 AD, is the most influential and also the most elaborate account. There are two earlier versions one by a contemporary of Ovid, Conon, and another, discovered only very recently, attributed to a Greek poet from the first century AD Parthenius of Nicaea, and both differ from Ovid's version in certain respects. They are shorter and neither includes the nymph Echo – she appears to have been Ovid's invention. Conon tells of a spurned lover called Ameinias, who kills himself with a sword on Narcissus's doorstep after beseeching the gods to punish Narcissus with the same fate. In this more bloody account, Narcissus commits suicide and the flower springs from his spilt blood, whereas in Ovid he simply fades away. Another variant of the myth from the second century is recorded by Pausanias who thinks it preposterous that anyone could fall in love with their reflection and fail to recognise themselves in it. Pausanias relates the story that Narcissus was reminded of a beloved twin sister who had died and it was she whom he chose to see in the place of his image. Twins or doubles of the same or another sex are encountered more than once in 'Narcissus Reflected'.

The myth undergoes a number of subsequent modifications and accretions. Plotinus, in the mid-third century, introduces the idea of drowning, asking: 'is there not a myth telling in symbol of such a dupe, how he sank into the depths of the current and was swept away to nothingness?'[3] The Neoplatonist philosopher considers Narcissus the dupe of images – 'copies, vestiges, shadows' – that are mere reflections of a higher reality. Throughout history, Narcissus has had quite a lot of bad press with the motif of error a recurrent theme.

Narcissus's metamorphosis into a flower that is reborn every spring was the assurance of his immortality. Another transformation that Narcissus underwent in its subsequent history which has implications for the artworks discussed in 'Narcissus Reflected', was the introduction of a gender switch with the appearance, and eventual dominance, of a female Narcissus. The figure of Eve in Milton's *Paradise Lost* (1667), engrossed by her own image reflected on the surface of a lake and thus led astray from contemplating the greater beauty of God, is recognised as deriving from the Ovidian Narcissus myth with a Neoplatonist overlay.[4] In Renaissance art this motif of the 'female Narcissus' could be seen to be taken up in the tradition of paintings of Venus at her toilet, shown gazing into a mirror assisted by Cupid. Perhaps the best-known example is Velázquez's *Rokeby Venus* (1649–51), but there are also paintings by Rubens and Titian, among others.

The persistence of this crossover between Narcissus and Venus is shown by Dalí's later installation in the window of the Bonwit Teller department store in New York in 1939, legendary due to an altercation in the course of which a bathtub went crashing through the window onto the pavement with Dalí following it. As it was *in situ* only for a short time, there are sadly no photographs of the installation but we are lucky to have Dalí's detailed recollection:

> In the 'Day' display one of the manikins was stepping into a 'hairy bathtub' lined with astrakhan [lamb's wool]. It was filled with water up to the edge, and a pair of beautiful wax arms holding up a mirror evoked the Narcissus myth; natural narcissi grew directly out of the floor of the bedroom and out of the furniture.[5]

Dalí's window decoration was prescient for making the connection between fashion and narcissism. One of the newspapers that reported on the incident described it as: 'Obviously a chamber for Narcissus himself, the handsome youth who was drowned while gazing in admiration at his own reflection in a pool and gave his name to a Freudian complex.'[6] None of the journalists seems to have appreciated that, for all its surreal jests, the work tapped into the august pictorial tradition of

Venus at her toilet. Some indication of how it might have looked can be surmised from Dalí's *Dream of Venus* pavilion at the 1939 New York World's Fair. Among a sequence of dioramas representing Venus's dreams was one with multiple mirrors reflecting a mannequin's face, titled 'The Lunatic Narcissus.'

Whenever Narcissus is invoked in art, it is often liable to be as a surrogate for the artist. The fifteenth-century Italian architect and writer Leon Battista Alberti lent his authority to this designation when he auspiciously proclaimed Narcissus the first artist:

> Consequently I used to tell my friends that the inventor of painting, according to the poets, was Narcissus, who was turned into a flower, for, as painting is the flower of the arts, so the tale of Narcissus fits our purpose perfectly. What is painting but the act of embracing by means of art the surface of the pool?[7]

Cultivated by Romanticism, the image of the poet or artist as a delicate flower, a solitary and self-absorbed Narcissus, reaches its apogee in symbolism. As one critic not so delicately put it: 'Narcissus … is the favourite god of symbolist mythology, god of solipsism, of aesthetic onanism.'[8] A counterpart to the artist's use of Narcissus as an identificatory figure is the conception of the artist as a poet. This notion is exemplified by French film-maker Jean Cocteau, who claimed to be a poet in everything he did, and it garnered support among writers and underground film-makers in the United States who were strongly influenced by his work. For Cocteau, the figure of Narcissus is on a par with that of Orpheus as a personal myth. Anticipating him, an affinity of Narcissus and Orpheus can be observed in the work of the nineteenth-century symbolist painter Gustave Moreau and is taken up again by German philosopher Herbert Marcuse in *Eros and Civilization* (1955), where the invocation of these mythic figures adds an aesthetic dimension to the book's anti-capitalist critique.

Narcissus is the first, but also the last artist. Moving forward from the mid-1990s cut-off of the works in the exhibition, the Narcissus theme continues to resonate in contemporary art. Coming after the postmodern 'death of the author', the conceptual artist Olaf Nicolai offers an ironic take on the Narcissus topos. The final chapter will consider the successive moments of the Narcissus narrative and their implications for artistic subjectivity: not just the specular reflection, but also a subsequent moment when Narcissus's tears falling into the water bring about the dissolution of his image. The combination of Narcissus with his generally much-less-distinct reflection on the water has allowed traditional artists to represent these temporally discrete moments. The Colombian artist Oscar Muñoz meditates on this latter moment in an ongoing work begun in 1994 titled *Narcisos en proceso* (Narcissi in Process), which artfully represents his own disappearance and brings the book to a provisional conclusion.

Further to this approach to Narcissus as a surrogate for the artist is the use of the myth as a vehicle for the expression of same-sex desire and identity. The homoerotic content of the myth is inescapable. As he lay beside the water's edge, 'admiring all the features for which he was himself admired,'[9] Narcissus at first did not recognise that the youth whose beauty aroused his ardent desire was himself. As described by Ovid, Narcissus is an androgynous youth on the cusp of manhood whose adolescent physiognomy is evoked in metaphoric terms that one reads as feminine: twin stars for eyes, ivory neck, a lovely face 'where a rosy flush stained the snowy whiteness of his complexion'. His flowing locks are like those of Apollo or Bacchus, gods who are generally represented as beardless. The classicist Rabun Taylor notes parallels with the story of Hermaphroditus, another youth with blushing cheeks the colour of ripe apples, from whom the nymph Salmacis endeavours to steal 'sisterly kisses'.[10] Taken together, these characteristics justify the late-nineteenth century depiction of Narcissus as a dainty youth of rather

John Waterhouse *Echo and Narcissus*, 1903, oil on canvas

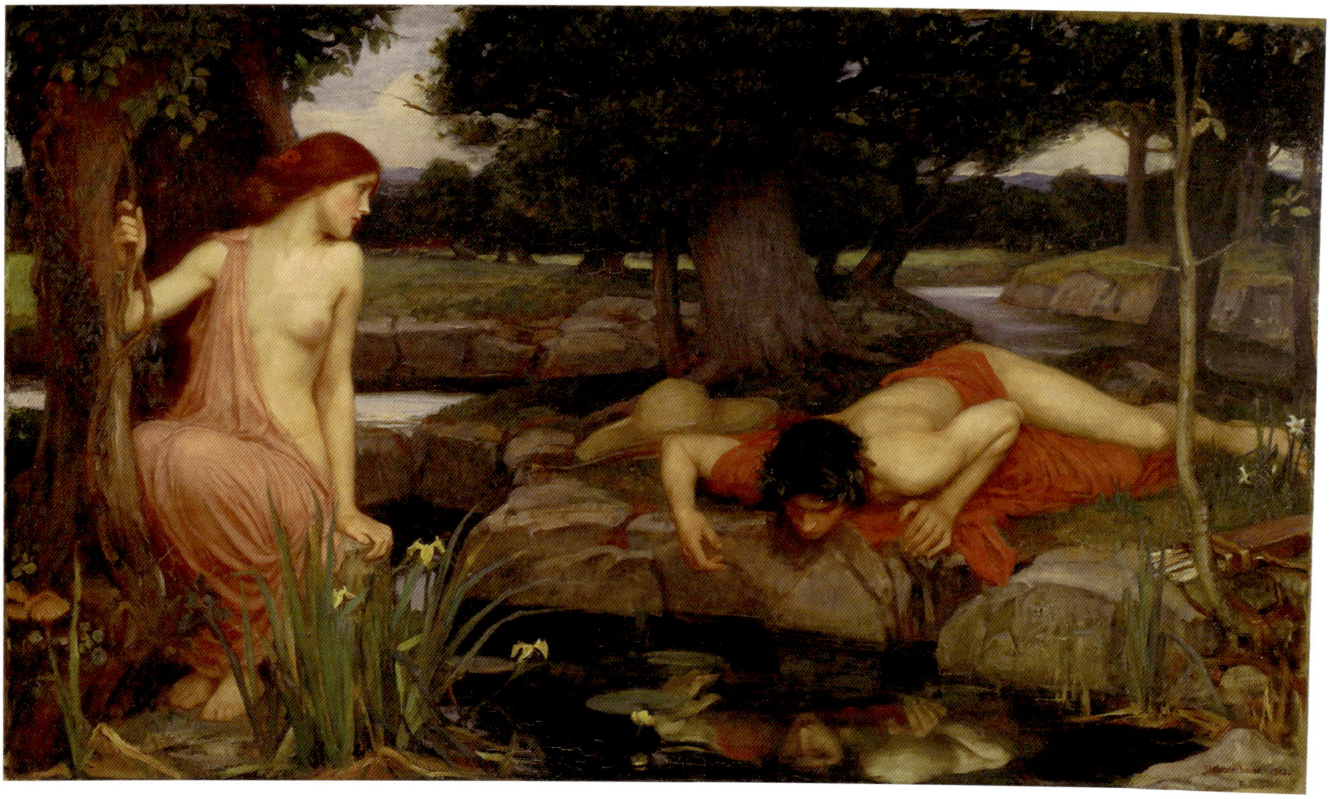

indeterminate gender by Moreau, an artist much admired by the surrealists. The figure of the androgyne, an artistic and literary construct of a body combining physical characteristics of both sexes, or neither, intersects with late-nineteenth century medical definitions of 'sexual inversion', which one psychologist deemed to be an embryonic form of hermaphroditism.

Accordingly the Narcissus myth functions as a barometer for anxieties about hetero-normativity. John Waterhouse's *Echo and Narcissus* (1903) is obviously based on Ovid but transfers the setting to a bucolic English landscape. Painted in the aftermath of the Oscar Wilde trials in 1895, which provoked a harsh backlash against homosexuality, anxiety about the sexual invert is embodied in the inverted pale and staring reflection that lures Narcissus away from a socially-mandated desire for the nymph Echo, whose charms are placed on display for the viewer as much as for Narcissus.[11] Looking carefully at the application of paint, it is evident that the artist has prevaricated over whether to cover or expose the rump of the prone Narcissus, a symptomatic indecision on his part. Waterhouse's ever-popular canvas is a Victorian morality tale about the dangers that lie in waiting for anyone who strays from the straight and narrow. Such considerations are far from irrelevant for Dalí who, while a student in the early 1920s in Madrid, conspicuously adopted the affectations of a Wildean dandy and kept company with the writer Federico García Lorca.

The notoriety of Narcissus as a cipher for dissident sexuality accelerated in the wake of Wilde's trial and the French critic André Gide's defence of homosexuality.[12] The theme of Narcissus permits one to track a strand of non-normative desire within surrealist and post-surrealist imagery. Omitted from a recent book on surrealism and myth, the Narcissus myth was crucial in enabling a subversive alliance to be forged between same-sex desire and surrealism – notwithstanding the homophobia of the surrealist leader, André Breton.[13] This was notably the case among the circle of surrealist writers and photographers involved with *View* magazine in the United States, who soon found themselves in conflict with Breton over the issue of sexuality. For a number of these latter-day disciples of the myth, a detour through the *fin de siècle* was an obligatory step to affirming their sexuality via Narcissus. Certainly that was true for the American artist Jess, whose *Narkissos* is subtitled 'a homage to Moreau'.

NARCISSISM IN PSYCHOLOGY

Paralleling the prevalence of the concept of narcissism in symbolist art and literature, the 1890s were also a crucial watershed as the point when the concept was introduced to psychology. Narcissus played a key role in the crystallization of notions of homosexuality in the emergent field of sexology and subsequently in psychoanalysis. Women were regarded as especially prone to it too. The English psychologist, Havelock Ellis, introduced the term 'a Narcissus-like tendency' in 1898 in a paper titled 'Autoeroticism: A Psychological Study'. The passage warrants quoting in full:

> I may briefly mention that tendency which is sometimes found, more especially perhaps in women, for the sexual emotions to be absorbed, and often entirely lost, in self-admiration. This Narcissus-like tendency, of which the normal germ in women is symbolised by the mirror, is found in minor degrees in some feminine-minded men, but seems to be very rarely found in men apart from sexual attraction for other persons, to which attraction it is, of course, normally subservient.[14]

This psychological approach validated negative stereotypes of femininity that circulated more widely in the culture at large. Images of female vanity, together with the mirror, its symbolic attribute, were ubiquitous in the *fin de siècle*.[15] The reference to 'feminine-minded men' is a euphemism for male homosexuals. Both are contrasted with a normative masculinity where egoistic self-love is subordinated to love of the other person.

The word narcissism ('Narzissismus') was first coined by Dr Paul Näcke, a German psychiatrist, in 1899 in a report on Ellis's article.[16] Subsequently, it was incorporated by Freud into psychoanalytic theory culminating in his 1914 paper 'On Narcissism', and thereafter the concept underwent major progressive expansion. No longer restricted to an unusual aberration, as it was for Havelock Ellis, it is given a role in the regular development of human beings. Freud reasons that a unified subject with a discrete ego cannot exist from the start. The inchoate impulses of the autoerotic infant must be transformed: 'there must be something added to autoeroticism – a new psychical action – in order to bring about narcissism.'[17] Jacques Lacan's mirror stage hypothesis was meant to elucidate a process left obscure by Freud. There is a clear allusion to the Narcissus myth in Lacan's contention that we become a unified subject by identifying with an externalised image of ourselves – not merely the image as seen in a mirror, but the more metaphorical image reflected back to us from our social interactions with others. In accordance with the longstanding motif of error, Lacan regards this 'alienating' identification, which is responsible for the formation of the ego, as leading the subject away from its essential truth, which he locates in the unconscious.

A later development of Freud's own thinking comes when he introduced a distinction between primary and secondary narcissism. The latter corresponds to a cathexis of the ego with the libido that has been secondarily withdrawn from an external love object. Freud considers mourning as a prime example of a state where interest is removed from the outside world in favour of a narcissistic preoccupation with the self. What is now termed primary narcissism is very similar to what Freud had earlier sought to distinguish narcissism from, namely autoeroticism. The contrasting, even quite contradictory, meanings of narcissism give rise to the varied appropriations of the myth by artists.[18]

In psychoanalysis, narcissism veers between specific accounts of femininity and homosexuality, and a universal account of the subject. The way it is accommodated within a developmental schema is as a provisional step on the path to mature heterosexual love. Women and male homosexuals are understood as evincing an arrested stage of development. Negative consequences follow from the fact that Narcissus stands for an illusory form of desire. When I *appear* to desire another individual of the same sex, I really only desire myself. This means that same-sex desire is deprived of an object.[19] It is, moreover, a false imitation of an authentic desiring relation. These connections are spelt out in Freud's psychobiography of Leonardo da Vinci (1910) in which the concept of narcissism was first introduced to psychoanalysis. According to the mechanism outlined by Freud, Leonardo identifies with his mother and then proceeds to imitate her love for him:

> The boy represses his love for his mother: he puts himself in her place, identifies himself with her, and takes his own person as a model in whose likeness he chooses the new objects of his love. In this way he has become a homosexual. What he has in fact done is to slip back to autoeroticism: for the boys whom he now loves as he grows up are after all only substitutive figures and revivals of himself in childhood – boys whom he loves in the way in which his mother loved *him* when he was a child. He finds the objects of his love along the path of *narcissism*, as we say…'[20]

Given that psychoanalysis was incredibly influential to surrealism, it behoves us to take note of the status of Narcissus in psychoanalytic theory. As an avid reader of Freud, Dalí would have been aware of the connection between narcissism and homosexuality from the Leonardo case study and this has implications for my treatment of the myth in *Metamorphosis of Narcissus*, a work that is laden with autobiographical references.

In parallel fashion, the evolution of Lacan's thinking shows that the problem of homosexuality is soon entirely subsumed within the topic of the imaginary. Paranoia, a subject that occupied Lacan when he was fraternizing with Dalí and the surrealists, is a larval or unconscious form of homosexuality. Within a Hegelian construct of desire to which Lacan and the surrealists both fundamentally subscribed, it seems that homosexual desire is inevitably posed as an imaginary (that is to say, unreal) modality of desire:

> The requirement of this style of desire can only be satisfied in an inexhaustible captation of the desire of the other … implying at each moment a complete abdication of the true desire of the other … the subject exhausts himself in pursuing the desire of the other, which he will never be able to grasp as his own desire, because his own desire is the desire of the other. It is himself whom he pursues. Therein lies the drama of this jealous passion, which is also a form of the imaginary inter-subjective relation.[21]

Though somewhat obfuscating, the general point is clear: same-sex desire is not a true relation to an other, which can only exist along an axis of sexual difference. Though Lacan did not share the prejudice against homosexuality that was rife in the French psychoanalytic establishment, the broad framework is one that discounts sameness. The defenders of Lacan point out that he goes on to deny the possibility of *any* sexual relation. However, by depriving the homosexual subject of a real object, we can see that the Narcissus myth as a model for homosexuality is double-edged. That could account for the ambivalence the photographer Claude Cahun displays towards Narcissus whom she chides for not going beyond the merely virtual image.

In the essay 'On Narcissism', Freud distinguishes between a so-called 'anaclitic' or 'attachment' type of object-choice and a narcissistic object-relation. The nurturing mother and protective father are the main avatars of the former. Here the libidinal bond reinforces another that serves to satisfy essential needs. In the case of the son, normally the bond to the mother is transferred to another woman, the love for whom is of the 'attachment' type. Contrasting with this is the kind of object relation discovered in homosexuality where the love object is not modelled on the mother but on the boy himself: 'They are plainly seeking themselves as a love-object, and are exhibiting a type of object-choice which must be termed "narcissistic".'[22] Freud struggles to maintain the distinction between an anaclitic object choice, an authentic model of a desiring relation, and a narcissistic object choice, which is an imitative copy of the former. Whether he succeeds in doing so is questionable. Even in 'complete object-love of the attachment type', which is properly speaking only found in the male, Freud observes 'the marked sexual overvaluation which is doubtless derived from the child's original narcissism and thus corresponds to a transference of that narcissism to the sexual object.'[23] When Dalí addresses his wife Gala as 'my new Narcissus' at the conclusion of his *Metamorphosis of Narcissus* poem, he exposes the narcissistic basis of surrealism's ideology of love. Narcissus's deluded love oddly resembles the core surrealist concept of mad love (*l'amour fou*).[24]

Since the time of Freud, the concept of narcissism has been extended into many different domains and been used for sometimes diametrically opposed purposes. Christopher Lasch's bestseller, *The Culture of Narcissism* (1979), tapped into a vein of self-doubt about the unbridled materialism of American consumer society. Lasch appeals to psychoanalytic theories of a narcissistic personality to describe narcissism as the correlate of a selfish society obsessed with consumption – a dead-end as he saw it, of the ethos of rugged individualism. The need to distinguish his use of the myth in a context where narcissism had become a byword for the American malaise was one of the reasons that caused the San Francisco-based artist, Jess, to revert to the Greek spelling 'Narkissos' as the title for his major work. Marcuse makes a positive appeal to narcissism, finding support for his attempt to broaden the notion of Eros beyond narrow procreative sexuality in the figures of Orpheus and Narcissus.[25] Drawing upon the connotations of both these figures, Marcuse dared to imagine an aestheticised existence in which man would no longer be divided from nature by a restrictive civilization. Citing the pantheistic and eroticised fusion with nature in the Ovidian myth, Marcuse writes: 'The love of Narcissus is answered by the Echo of nature.'[26] Based on Freud's distinction between pleasure and reality, Marcuse's critique of the 'production principle' of capitalism struck a chord with the counter-cultural generation of the 1960s and 1970s. As we shall see, it underpins Jess's secular hymn to Eros in *Narkissos*.

The Freudian concept of primary narcissism corresponds to Marcuse's utopian vision.[27] A crucial aspect for Marcuse is the experience of oneness with the universe of which an adult vestige is expressed in the 'oceanic feeling'. Concluding this exploration of the Narcissus myth will be consideration of the notion of primary narcissism as the basis of a reading of Pipilotti Rist's immersive video installation *Sip My Ocean* (1996). Rist gives an affirmative, feminist spin to the persistent belief that women have more immediate access to the autoerotic realm. Her recurrent imagery of the body submerged in water connotes the blissfulness of intra-uterine existence – a state of 'total narcissism', writes Freud, in which 'libido and self-interest, still united and indistinguishable, dwell in the self-sufficing ego.'[28]

NOTES

1. Julia Kristeva, *Tales of Love*, trans. Leon S. Roudiez (New York: Columbia University Press, 1987), p.105.
2. See Louise Vinge, *The Narcissus Theme in Western European Literature up to the Early Nineteenth Century* (Lund: Gleerups, 1967).
3. Plotinus, *The Enneads*, trans. Stephen MacKenna (Harmondsworth: Penguin, 1991), pp.1, 6: 8.
4. John Milton, *Paradise Lost*, (1667), book IV, (London: Macmillan, 1974), pp.460–473.
5. The idea for the bathtub came from a colloquial expression that caught Dalí's notice. Pointing out the absurdity of something, the speaker would say: 'that wins the fur-lined bathtub!' Dalí's outré installation pokes fun at itself. Salvador Dalí, *The Secret Life of Salvador Dalí*, (1942), trans. Haakon M. Chevalier (London: Vision Press, 1968), p.372.
6. 'Dalí, Surrealist, Has A Nightmare While Wide Awake', New York World Telegram (New York), 17.03.1939.
7. Leon Battista Alberti, *On Painting* (1436), book II, translated by Cecil Grayson (Harmondsworth: Penguin, 1991), p.26. I am grateful to my colleague Dr Silvia Loreti for bringing this to my attention.
8. Ramon Fernandez, *André Gide* (Paris: Corrêa, 1931), p.60.
9. Ovid, *Metamorphoses*, trans. Mary M. Innes (Harmondsworth: Penguin, 1955), book III.
10. Rabun M. Taylor, *The Moral Mirror of Roman Art* (Cambridge: Cambridge University Press, 2008), p.77ff.
11. For an account of the Wilde trials and their aftermath, see Alan Sinfield, *The Wilde Century: Effeminacy, Oscar Wilde and the Queer Moment* (London: Cassell, 1994).
12. See Steven Bruhm, *Reflecting Narcissus: A Queer Aesthetic* (Minneapolis and London: University of Minnesota Press, 2001).
13. Didier Ottinger, *Surréalisme et mythologie moderne: les voies du labyrinthe*, d'Ariane a Fantomas (Paris: Gallimard, 2002).
14. Havelock Ellis, 'The Conception of Narcissism' (1927), in *Studies in the Psychology of Sex, vol. 7: Eonism and Other Supplementary Studies* (Philadelphia, F.A. Davis Co., 1928), pp.347–375.
15. Bram Dijkstra, *Idols of Perversity: Fantasies of Feminine Evil in Fin-de-Siècle Culture* (Oxford: Oxford University Press, 1986).
16. The first use of the word 'narcissism' in English is in 1905. This term was taken from the German 'Narzissismus', which was first used by Paul Näcke in 1899 in 'Die sexuellen Perversitäten', following an article written in 1898 by Havelock Ellis. The first record of the use of the term 'narcissistic' is from 1916 and 'narcissist' is from 1930.
17. Sigmund Freud, 'On Narcissism: An Introduction', *Pelican Freud Library*, vol. 11, trans. James Strachey (Harmondsworth: Pelican Books, 1985), p.69.
18. For a useful introduction to the complex and contradictory status of narcissism in Freudian theory, see *Freud's 'On Narcissism: An Introduction'*, eds Peter Fonagy, Ethel Spector Person, Joseph Sandler (New Haven and London: Yale University Press, 1991).
19. See Michael Warner, 'Homo-Narcissism; or, Heterosexuality,' in *Engendering Men: The Question of Male Feminist Criticism*, eds Joseph Boone and Michael Cadden (New York and London: Routledge, 1990), pp.190–206.

20. Sigmund Freud, 'Leonardo da Vinci and a Memory of His Childhood', *Pelican Freud Library*, vol. 14, trans. James Strachey (Harmondsworth: Pelican Books, 1985), pp.191–192.
21. Jacques Lacan, *The Seminar of Jacques Lacan, Book I Freud's Papers on Technique 1953–1954*, ed. Jacques-Alain Miller (Cambridge: Cambridge University Press, 1988), p.221.
22. Freud, 'On Narcissism,' p.81.
23. Ibid., p.82.
24. Lacan, for his part, opines: 'That's what love is. It's one's own ego that one loves in love, one's own ego made real on the imaginary plane.'
25. Herbert Marcuse, *Eros and Civilization: A Philosophical Inquiry into Freud* (1955), (Boston: Beacon Press, 1966), chapter 8: 'The Images of Orpheus and Narcissus'.
26. Ibid., p.136.
27. It 'engulfs the "environment", integrating the narcissistic ego with the objective world.' Ibid., p.137.
28. Sigmund Freud, 'The Libido Theory and Narcissism,' *Introductory Lectures on Psycho-Analysis, Pelican Freud Library*, vol. 1, trans. James Strachey (Harmondsworth: Pelican Books, 1973), p.466.

Philippe Halsman *Salvador Dalí*, 1954

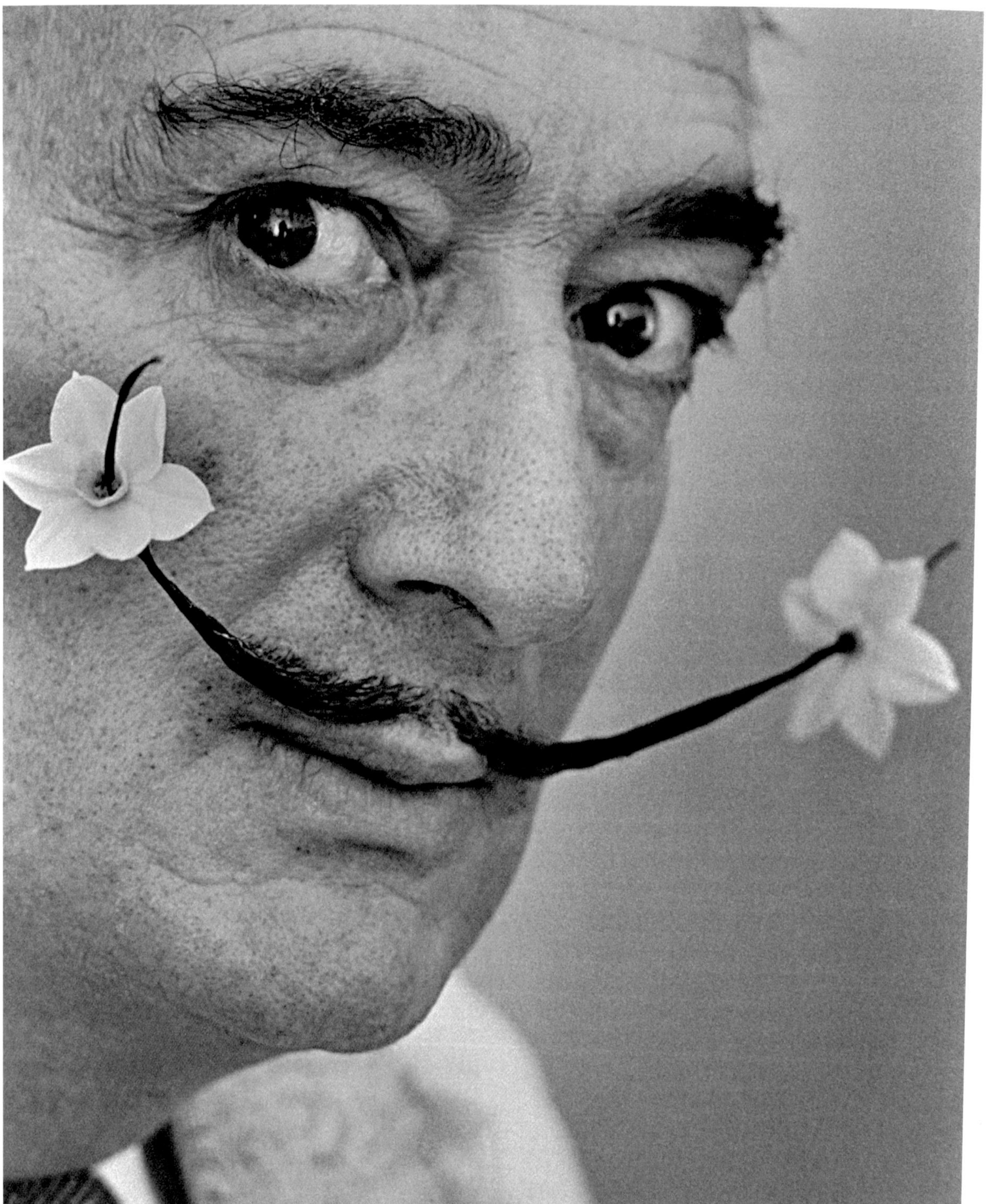

CHAPTER ONE
METAMORPHOSES OF NARCISSUS

The theme of Narcissus which I chose is a sort of poetic autobiography,
which calls for a few little explanations and clues.
Paul Valéry[1]

When Salvador Dalí's (1904–89) wish to meet Sigmund Freud, the founder of psychoanalysis, was at last realised in 1938, the picture he took with him on his pilgrimage was *Metamorphosis of Narcissus* (1937, pp.28–29). Edward James, owner of the work and midwife to its creation, accompanied Dalí on the visit that was arranged by the Austrian writer Stefan Zweig.[2] Freud had been forced into exile by the Nazi occupation of Vienna and was living in Hampstead in London. Immersed in Freud's writings, and familiar with his study of Leonardo da Vinci, which introduces the concept of narcissism, Dalí said that he had wanted to appear to Freud as 'a kind of dandy of "universal intellectualism"' but learned afterwards that the impression he had created was exactly the opposite.[3]

Freud was little more than a year away from death, but despite his illness, he seems to have been humored by his visitors that day and was thankful to Zweig for having introduced 'that young Spaniard with his candid fanatical eyes.'[4] As regards the painting he had brought with him, Freud acknowledged Dalí's technical mastery, although in other respects it seems they were destined not to see eye-to-eye. One supposes that Dalí had hopes of impressing the master with a picture that tackles a theme central to the psychoanalytic account of subjectivity. But therein lay a major point of contention. Freud looked to art and literature, as indeed he looked to myth, to provide innocent testimony to the secrets of human nature that could be unlocked by psychoanalysis. He supposedly said to Dalí that in classical art he looked for the operations of the unconscious, but in a surrealist painting only the conscious, a pronouncement that Dalí took as a death knell for surrealism.[5]

Dalí is the arch-narcissist. What he calls 'the Narcissus in me' is inseparable from the media-savvy performer that is Salvador Dalí, and it may have been a factor in Dalí's insouciant charm, Freud observed that 'the charm of a child lies to a great extent in his narcissism, his self-containment and inaccessibility.'[6]

This chapter explores Dalí's adoption of Narcissus as a personal myth. Dalí was the successor to a symbolist tradition that identified the artist or poet with Narcissus, but in his case this was compounded by his profound knowledge of psychoanalysis. The *Metamorphosis of Narcissus* – picture and poem – was an exercise in Dalí's self-analysis. In this work, the principal trajectories of the Narcissus myth from the 1890s onwards come together in the most stunning artistic and literary treatment of the theme in twentieth-century culture.

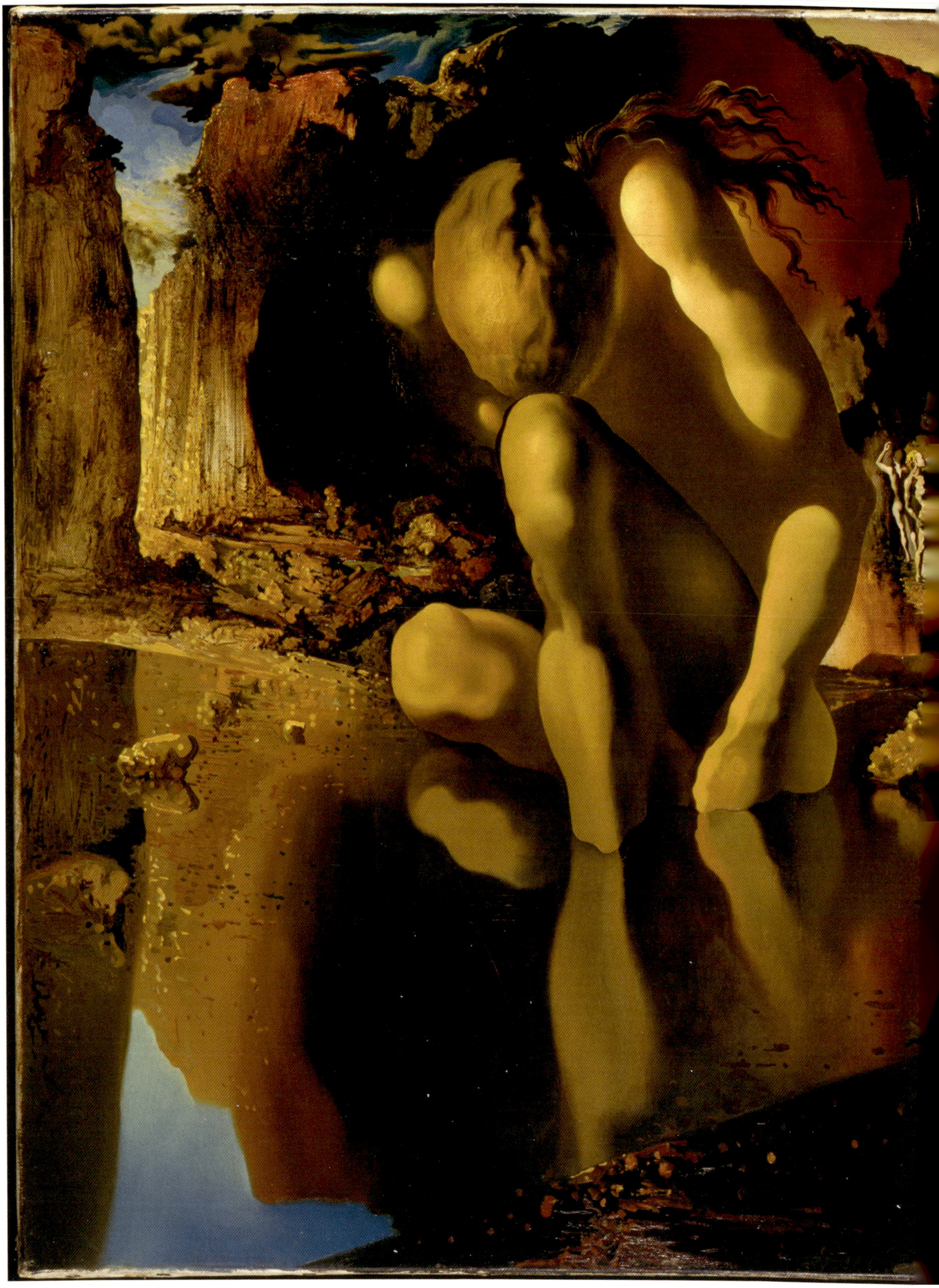

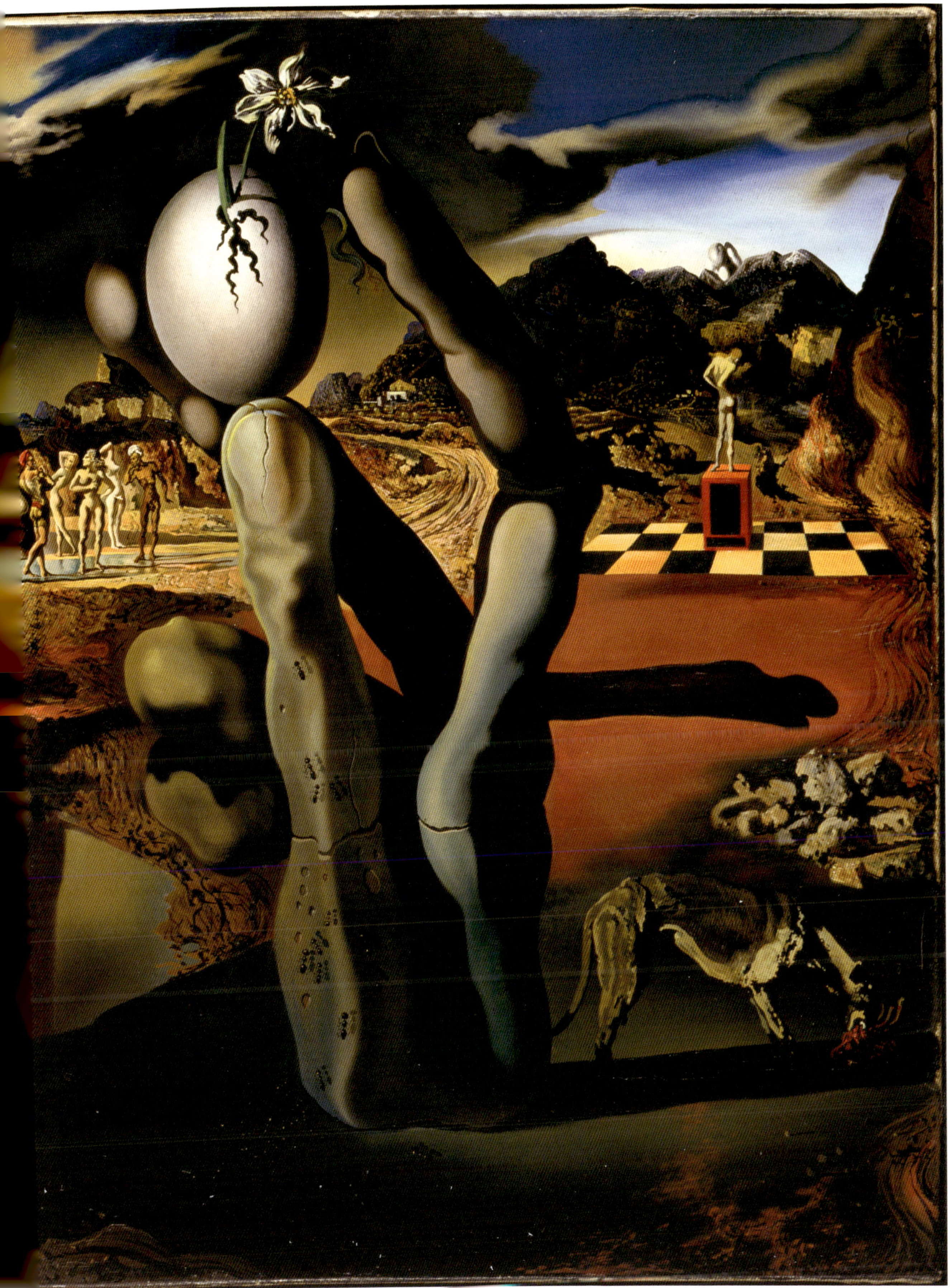

THE NARCISSUS POEM

Owing perhaps to the protocols of viewing art in the gallery or museum, few of the millions of visitors to Tate Modern who annually see *Metamorphosis of Narcissus* would realise that Dalí had intended his picture to be viewed in conjunction with a poem that he wrote simultaneously and published in the form of an illustrated pamphlet; the full text of the poem is reproduced on pages 160–67 of this book. The poem offers a commentary on the picture, with the net effect of a sort of mirroring of image and text. Crucially, in the poem Dalí also introduces some new material and seeks to guide the viewer's interpretation of the picture.

PROLOGUE

The poem itself is preceded by several pages of text, a preamble that serves a number of functions. Firstly, the prologue hints at an autobiographical interpretation of the picture, which is reconfirmed in the last stanza of the poem. It does so by means of a reported conversation between two Catalan fishermen who speak about a particular youth who spends his time self-absorbed, gazing at his reflection. They decide that he must suffer from 'a bulb in the head' – a Catalan expression, Dalí explains, that corresponds with the psychoanalytic notion of a 'complex' and he leaves one in little doubt about the identity of the youth to whom it refers. It is the poem, as a textual supplement to the visual image, which is burdened with the task of asserting Narcissus as a self-referential guise; the painting, by contrast, is devoid of any such explicit self-reference.

Secondly, the prologue provides a justification for Dalí's poetic activity. Though he had previously written a poem that bore the same title as a picture (*The Great Masturbator* of 1929), he had never before written a poem about one of his paintings. This was his first foray into the ekphrastic genre and it represents, he claims, a new triumph for the 'paranoiac-critical method' – Dalí's system for the deliberate misinterpretation of visual clues, his ability to 'see' things that are not really there which eventually resulted in the proliferation of double imagery in his work. (Dalí being Dalí he cannot resist crowing about his accomplishments.)

Thirdly, the prologue issues precise instructions for viewing the picture, which is reproduced alongside the poem in colour. The increasing complexity of Dalí's double and multiple images in the later 1930s, works that André Breton derisively branded 'picture puzzles', may have rendered such explanation and guidance necessary. It also seems possible, or indeed probable, that Dalí was motivated at this time by an interest in the potential of stereoscopy. The typical format of a stereo photo is that two views of an object are presented side-by-side. With the aid of lenses, or simply by diverging or crossing both eyes, the images can be made to fuse, thus simulating binocular vision. In his instructions, Dalí recommends that the picture be gazed at in a state of 'distant fixedness' whereupon the blurred figure of Narcissus gradually disappears. This suggests that the two components of the double image are meant to undergo optical fusion, but because they are not identical it is not possible for the eye to perceive both images simultaneously. The more sharply-defined image of the hand with the egg and Narcissus flower naturally tends to predominate and the metamorphosis takes place. Artists have traditionally shown Narcissus dying with flowers already sprouting beside him, in effect telescoping two separate moments in time. Dalí had found an ingenious and wholly novel solution to this age-old dilemma. In 1946, Dalí produced a stereoscopic snow-scene for the cover of the Christmas edition of *Vogue* magazine that was to be viewed with the naked eye. The same principle would appear to be at work with the paired images in *A Couple with Their Heads Full of Clouds* (1936), in which two cloth-covered tables in the foreground seem to be the same table viewed from a slightly different angle.

Stereoscopy replicates the structure and physiology of binocular vision in that separate images on each retina are combined to create a purely virtual image in the visual cortex. Small wonder that one

pp.28–29: **Salvador Dalí** *Metamorphosis of Narcissus*, 1937
oil on canvas
below: **Salvador Dalí** *A Couple with Their Heads Full of Clouds*,
1936, oil on panel

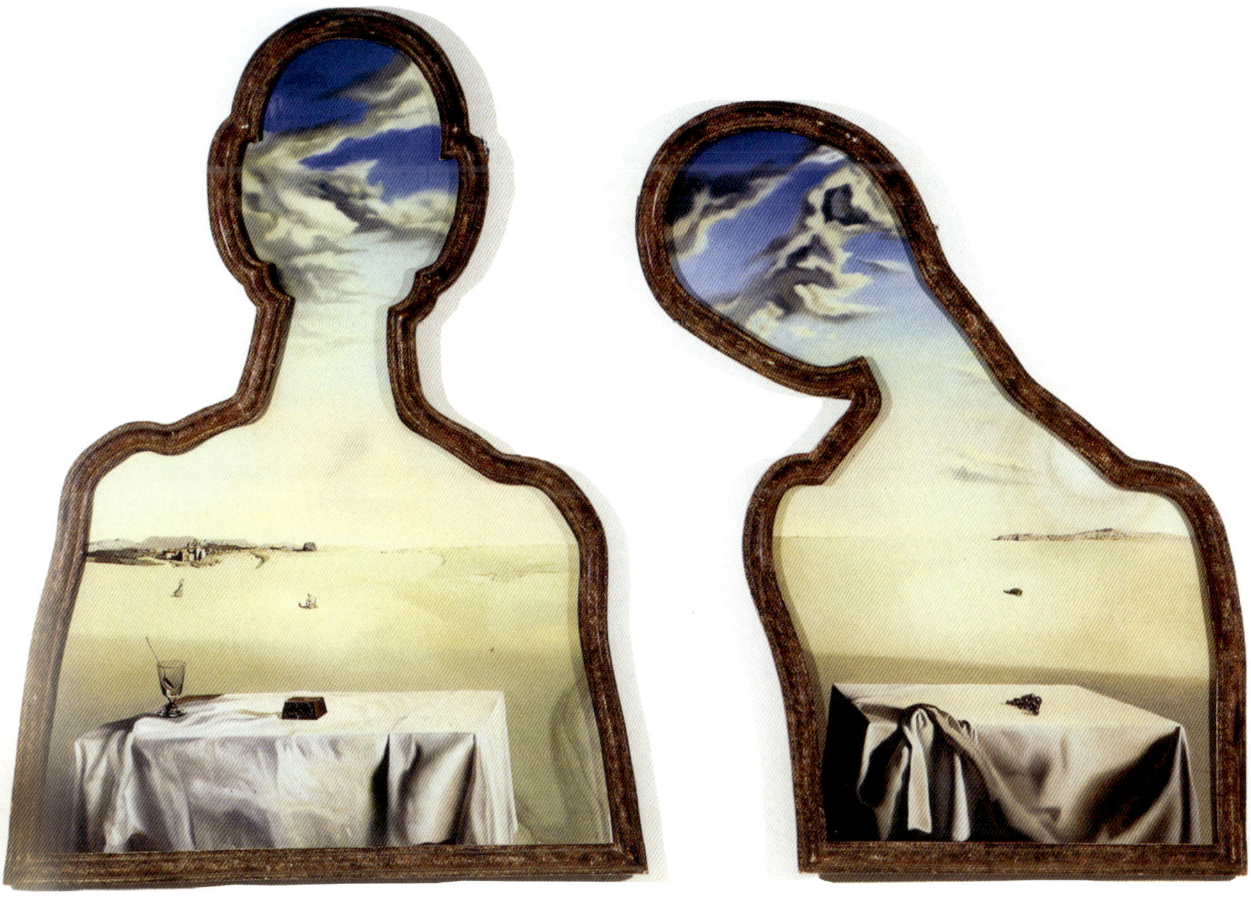

of the first makers of stereoscopic photographs should have seen fit to take Narcissus as a subject. Stereoscopy, like the Narcissus myth, testifies to the power of illusion and, it seems, our willingness as human subjects to be deceived. In the case of Dalí, it augmented his already formidable mastery of *trompe l'oeil* effects. Is there not a deliberate analogy between the kind of intent scrutiny Dalí demanded of the viewer and that engaged in by the 'hypnotically immobile' Narcissus absorbed in the contemplation of his reflection? Over and beyond simply illustrating the Narcissus myth, Dalí's purpose was to interpolate the beholder into a structure of viewing that is intrinsically narcissistic. This even extends to a kind of symmetry of the viewer and the work if one imagines staring at the two globular forms, like eyeballs, comprised by the head of Narcissus and the egg. We stare at the picture and it stares back at us.

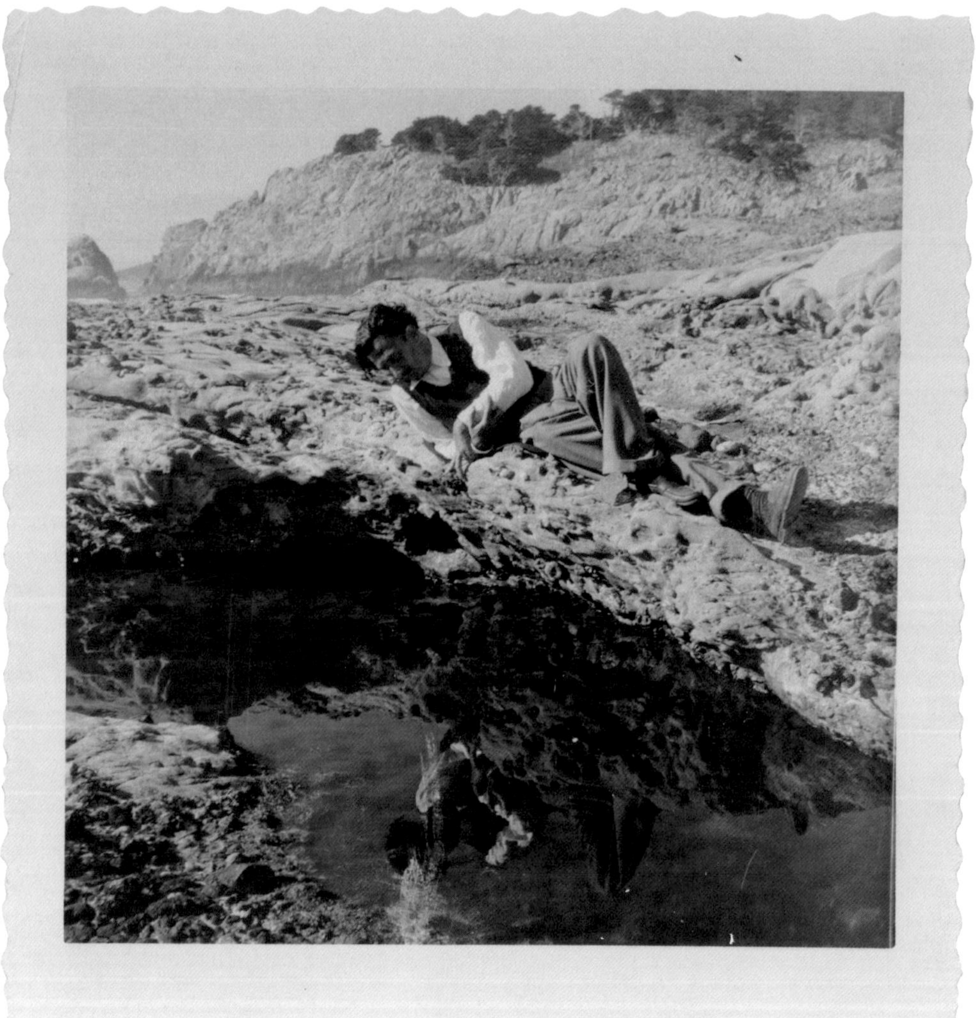

THE SETTING

Dalí's poem proper begins with a description of the landscape that forms a spectacular backdrop to the figure of Narcissus in the foreground of the painting. Dalí was staying at Zürs in the Austrian Alps in the spring of 1937 when the work was begun and the surrounding mountains with narcissi in bloom provided an immediate source of inspiration. Only a single, fairly rudimentary compositional drawing exists that may have been a view from a window across a lake. Dalí seems to have combined this Alpine scenery with the landscape most familiar to him. The setting is strikingly reminiscent of the view in north-east Catalonia looking back from the beach near Cap de Creus toward the mountainous Pyrenees, which on their lower slopes are lined with olive groves. This stretch of coastline was the setting of all the decisive moments of Dalí's personal history, from infancy through adolescence to adulthood. *Swans Reflecting Elephants* (1937, p.34), which has in common the preoccupation with reflections and doubling and may be considered a pendant image to *Metamorphosis of Narcissus*, has a very similar body of water in the foreground. Intriguingly, it also includes a portrait of Marcel Duchamp – one of the few artists to have shared Dalí's interests in optics, and in particular stereoscopy, at this time.

The section of the poem given over to evoking the setting is a kind of pre-figuration in which the melting snow and germinating narcissi rehearse the eventual disappearance of Narcissus – his melting away and ensuing metamorphosis. At the top right, one can just catch a glimpse of the 'god of snow', a third, miniaturised iteration, or morphological echo, of Narcissus perched at the water's edge. Dalí had employed this device frequently in the previous couple of years and it is a fairly small step from the idea of a morphological 'echo' to Narcissus. Narcissus's psychological drama is writ large in the landscape behind him. In the poem the stems of the narcissi rise up 'erect, tender, and hard', a virile force of new life, while the snow god melts away 'annihilating himself loudly among the excremental cries of minerals.' There is a fairly self-evident anthropomorphism behind this contrasting set of images that represents as a natural event, a cycle of the seasons, the conflict of Eros and death.

below: Page from Salvador Dalí's notebook showing a compositional sketch for *Metamorphosis of Narcissus*, c.1936–37
opposite: Salvador Dalí at Punta dels Tres Frares, Catalonia, 1930s

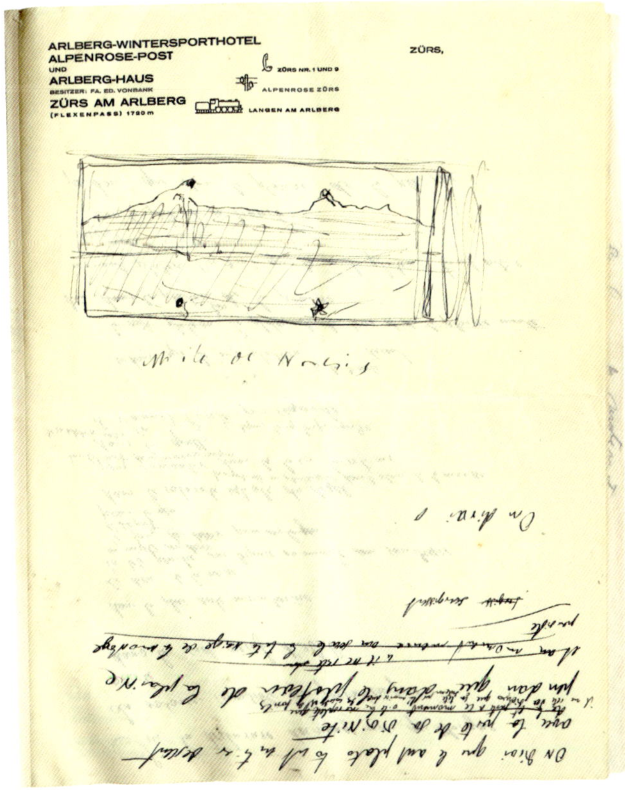

below: **Salvador Dalí** *Swans Reflecting Elephants*, 1937, oil on canvas
opposite: Roman bronze known as *Spinario*, c.1st century BC

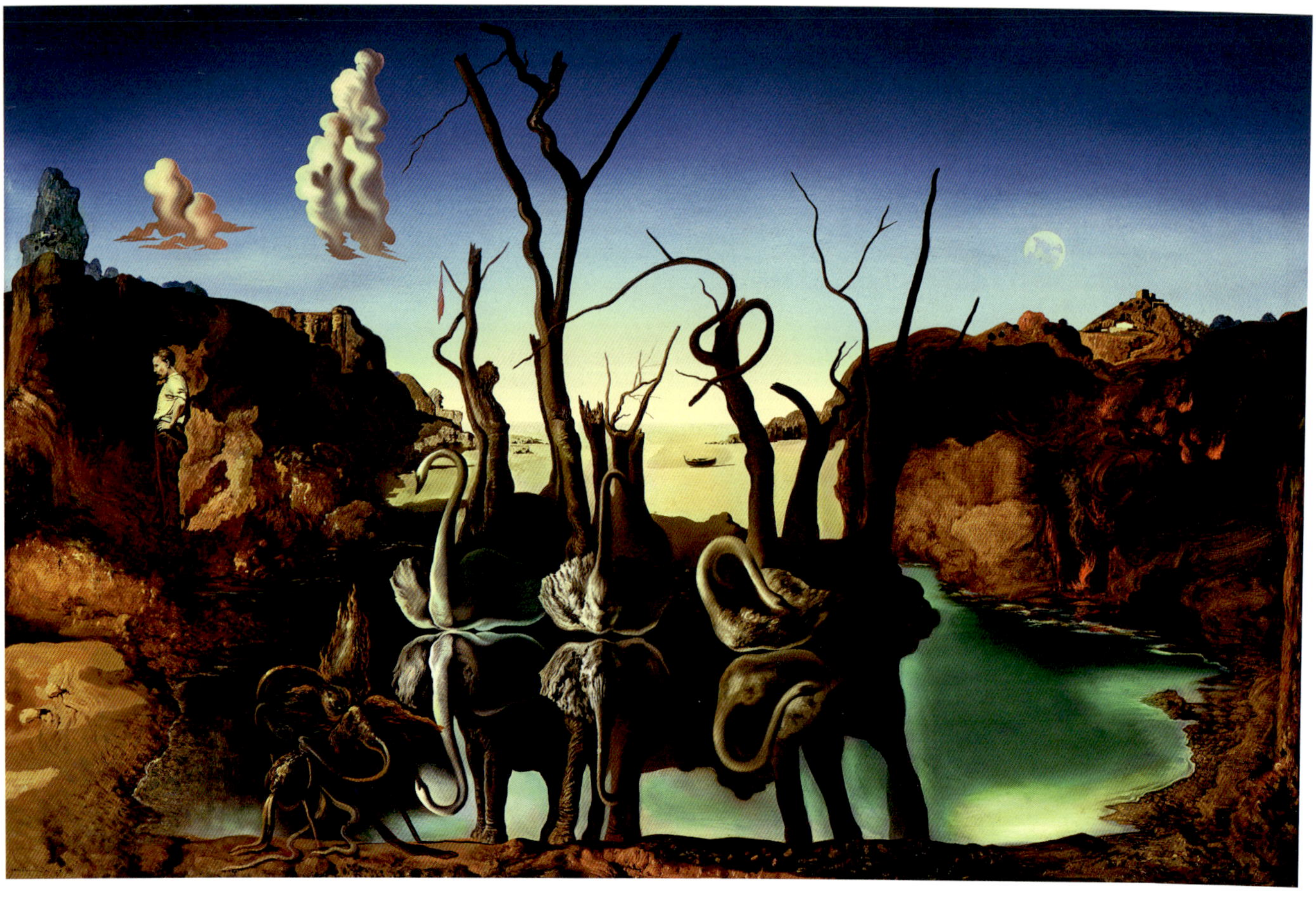

THE HETEROSEXUAL GROUP

The poem proceeds from a description of the landscape to what is termed the 'heterosexual group' in the middle distance of the painting. Clearly, they are meant as a foil to Narcissus whose isolation from them is stressed, though beyond that their significance is more than a little obscure. In the poem, Dalí takes the trouble to specify each individual as a distinct ethnic or national type – they comprise a veritable League of Nations, and given the ominous situation in Europe in April 1937, it may be that they are supposed to allegorize these background political events. More plausible, in my view, is the suggestion that they depict the assorted suitors, male and female, whose amorous designs Narcissus obstinately resisted. Ovid avers that 'Many lads and girls fell in love with him, but his soft young body housed a pride so unyielding that none of those boys or girls dared to touch him.'[7] Most famous of these unlucky admirers was the nymph Echo who pined away in despair until her voice was all that remained of her. However, Conon tells of a young man named Ameinias who was smitten with love for Narcissus but was also spurned, killing himself with a sword that Narcissus had cynically presented him with. Julia Kristeva evokes his solipsistic withdrawal in terms that are peculiarly resonant for Dalí, remarking that Narcissus is 'indifferent to love, withdrawn in the pleasure that a provisionally reassuring diving-suit gives him.'[8] Dalí reports in his mock-confessional 'autobiography', *The Secret Life of Salvador Dalí* (1942) that as an adolescent he craved only the 'imperialist sentiment of utter solitude' and the chapters of the book that precede his meeting with his wife Gala are littered with frustrated admirers whose torments are a source of vicarious pleasure for him.[9]

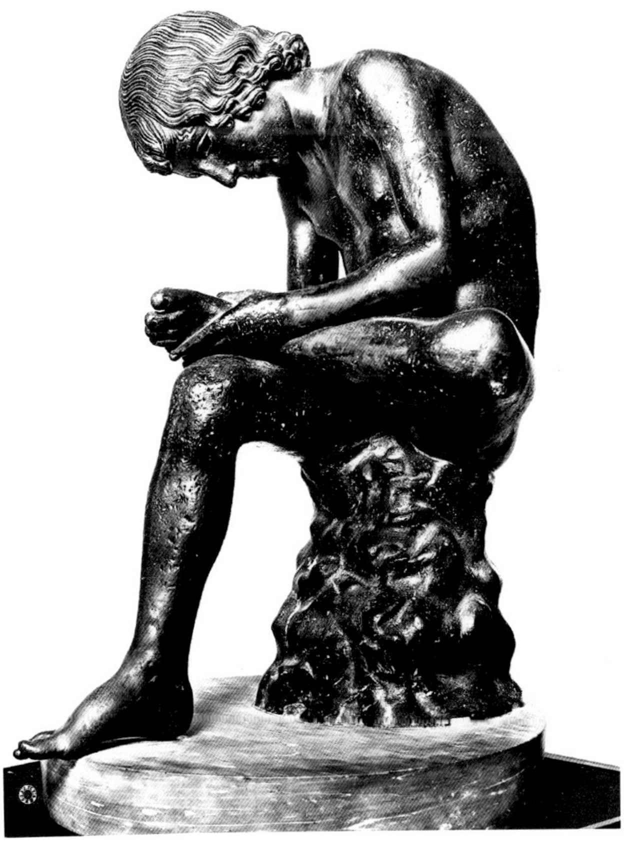

An exaggerated discrepancy in scale reinforces the oppositional contrast between the so-called heterosexual group and the action that transpires in the foreground. Whether or not any of these tiny figures are identifiable people from Dalí's past or present we can only conjecture. What is indisputable is that they are a club from which Dalí/Narcissus is firmly excluded. That Dalí himself is implicated in a narcissistic, and by inference *homo*-sexual, scenario in the foreground is a hypothesis with implications for a reading of *Metamorphosis of Narcissus* I shall come back to.

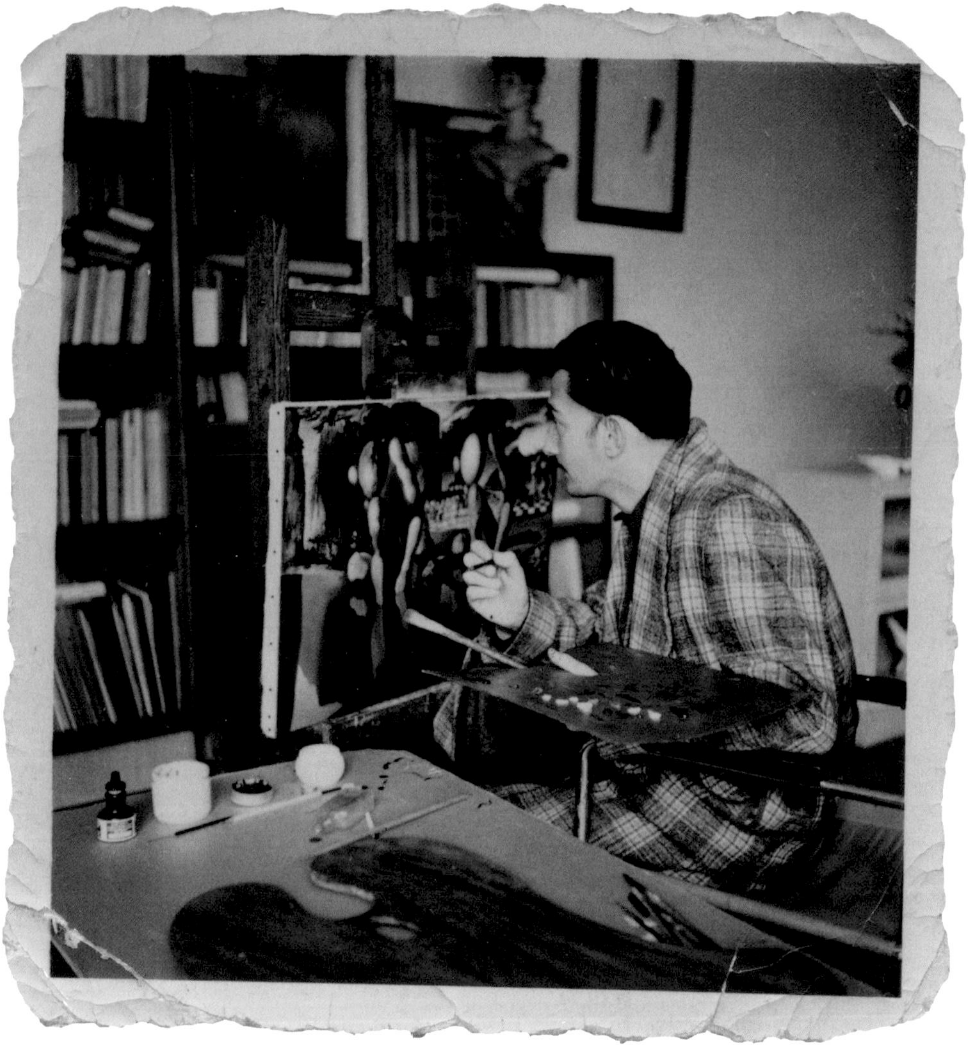

above: Salvador Dalí painting *Metamorphosis of Narcissus*, c.1936–37
opposite: Page from Salvador Dalí's notebook showing
a preparatory sketch for *Metamorphosis of Narcissus*, c.1936–37

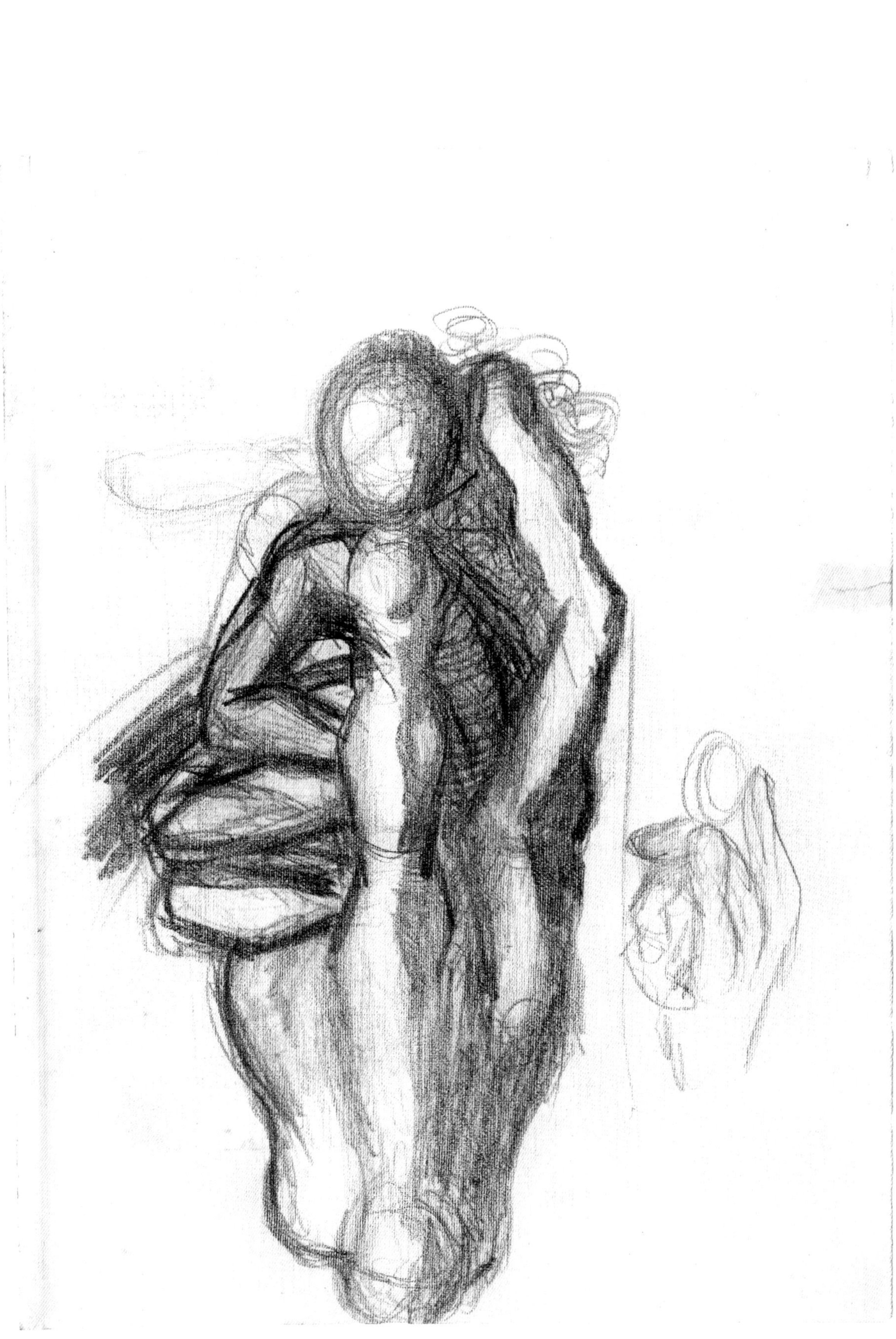

THE NARCISSUS-HAND

Bound into the original manuscript of the poem is a suite of drawings revealing the genesis of the Narcissus-hand configuration (p.37). It is notable that all the extant studies for the picture depict only a single reversing image, while in the final work the two elements of the 'double image' have been splayed apart.[10] It is likely that Dalí used a tracing to exactly replicate the shape on the canvas. Once settled upon, the separation permitted the two components – Narcissus and the hand holding an egg – to be differentiated to a greater extent than would have been possible otherwise, while also retaining evidence of their common origin.

In an essay from the winter of 1934–35, Dalí came extremely close to visualizing the naked figure of Narcissus hunched over his reflection on the left hand side of the composition. He writes of the *Spinario* (p.35) from around the first century BC, a Roman bronze statue now in the Capitoline Museum in Rome that depicts a seated youth extracting a thorn from his foot: 'Observe him, bent over his thorn, with the same fossil immobility of Narcissus, he, too, bent over the silvery comedo of his own death.'[11] In *L'Amour et la mémoire* (Love and Memory, 1931), a text that adumbrates several of the themes in *Metamorphosis of Narcissus*, Dalí had insisted that self-annihilation is one of our most violent and tumultuous desires. Poised above the abyss of his own reflection, Narcissus is half in love with easeful death, only too ready to answer its hypnotic siren call. A sequence of images in the poem narrate the step-by-step dissolution of Narcissus as a bounded and unified self until he attains, at the end, a pleasantly narcotised state of oblivion: 'incurable sleep, vegetal, atavistic, slow.' 'Narcissus, you are so immobile / one would think you were asleep', Dalí remonstrates with an unresponsive *alter ego*. The inexorable drag of the death drive manifests as a draining away of life force and a regression to a state of primary narcissism. Dalí had surely read in Freud's *Introductory Lectures on Psychoanalysis* that:

> Sleep is a state in which all object-cathexes, libidinal as well as egoistic, are given up and withdrawn into the ego … The picture of the blissful isolation of intra-uterine life which a sleeper conjures up once more before us every night is in this way completed on its psychical side as well. In a sleeper the primal state of distribution of the libido is restored – total narcissism, in which libido and ego-interest, still united and indistinguishable, dwell in the self-sufficing ego.[12]

In Dalí's painting Narcissus yearns to recreate the blissful solitude of life *in utero*. Crouching down in what can best be described as a foetal position he is bathed in a warm ethereal glow. When Dalí came to write about his improbably vivid memories of prenatal life in *The Secret Life of Salvador Dalí*, it is something very similar to this that he purports to recall: 'The intra-uterine paradise was the colour of hell, that is to say, red, orange, yellow and bluish, the color of flames, of fire; above all, it was soft, immobile, warm, symmetrical, double, gluey.'[13] In another of Dalí's paintings *Birth of Liquid Desires* (1931–32), the father and mother are fused while on the left of the composition the son, plainly another Narcissus, immerses his hand in a fountain that is inside a cavernous, overtly uterine space. This motif, with its meaning of a wished-for return to the mother's womb, carries over to one of the worked-up studies for *Metamorphosis of Narcissus*. In the painting, the grotto-like space that envelops Narcissus basically recapitulates the shape of his head, which the poem describes as like a chrysalis; it is a tomb in which he dies and becomes invisible, but also a womb-like place where he is preserved in order to be reborn.

The hand holding an egg from which a narcissus flower sprouts is one of the most startling and instantly recognizable products of Dalí's feverish imagination. Like certain other irrational-seeming motifs in Dalí's work, this one may have originated in a figure of speech. In Dalí's poem's prologue, the reference to 'a bulb in the head', a colloquial expression peculiar to Catalan speakers, is followed up with the irrefutable observation: 'If a man has a bulb in his head, it might break into flower at any moment, Narcissus!' Another rationale for this outreaching hand comes from Ovid who conveys remarkable poignancy in his description of the reciprocal exchange of glances and gestures as Narcissus moves in unison with a partner who mimics his every move: 'when I stretch my arms to you, you stretch yours to me in return.'[14] But the way that Dalí visualises the gesture is devoid of the gentle lyricism that suffuses the Ovidian verse. Such exquisite details as a crack running from the base of the egg down the length of the thumbnail, over which Dalí has laboured with perverse delight, cause us to recoil in horror.

While in general terms this configuration is reminiscent of the oversized hand holding a walnut in Max Ernst's dream-like *Oedipus Rex* (1922), and similar also in its explicit address to a Freudian subject, the emotional tenor plainly is not. Within Dalí's work, this detail harks back to the scene of a severed hand swarming with ants in the film that Dalí made with Luis Buñuel in 1929, *Un Chien andalou* (An Andalusian Dog). The monumental scale also brings to mind the famous colossal pointing hand, a fragment from the third century statue of Constantine the Great that now stands in the courtyard of the Capitoline Museum in Rome. Might Dalí also have known Henry Fuseli's drawing of *The Artist in Despair before the Magnitude of Antique Fragments* (1778–80), which shows a figure bent over pondering these bodily part objects? One of the studies for *Metamorphosis of Narcissus* shows Dalí as a small child dressed in a sailor suit and holding a hoop contemplating a gigantic hand in the form of a statue towering over him, a formula repeated from *The Spectre of Sex Appeal* of 1934. Inspiration for what the poem calls 'the limestone hand, the fossil hand' may have come partly from Ovid who deploys a metaphor of the petrified and statuesque to describe Narcissus, spellbound by his reflection, as 'like a statue carved from Parian marble.'[15] Transforming living flesh into a limestone cast, Dalí makes palpable the work of the death drive, a conservative instinct seeking to return the living organism to an inorganic state.

In the *Metamorphosis of Narcissus* poem, Dalí again returns to this image describing a lugubrious vision of an insensate, terrible, coprophagic and mortal hand. Related to this, in *The Secret Life of Salvador Dalí*, Dalí recounts an incident that must have occurred only a matter of a few months before he wrote the Narcissus poem while staying at Cortina d'Ampezzo in the Dolomites, on a second trip to Italy.[16] Over several days he had noticed with growing fascination what he thought was a glob of mucus adhering to the lavatory wall. When curiosity finally got the better of him and he tried to peel it off, it became lodged under a fingernail of his right hand. An infection set in soon afterwards causing the hand to become swollen and enlarged. As Dalí lay alone on his hotel bed, Gala having departed temporarily for Paris, the diseased part appeared to detach from the rest of his body and confronted him in the shape of an offensive, oversized *memento mori*: 'I imagined my hand already separated from my arm, a prey to the livid first symptoms of decomposition.'[17] This cadaveric hand was a chilling reminder of the death (drive) that infects life. Once it had dawned upon him that what he fearfully imagined to be mucus was only some dried glue left behind by painters, Dalí regained his composure and set about removing the offending sliver from beneath his nail. He reports that he did so 'with that strange attention and voluptuous vertigo that had been masterfully immortalised in the piece of sculpture of *The Boy Extracting [a] Thorn from His Foot [Spinario]* (p.35).' This passage harks back to his previous evocation of the *Spinario* in which Dalí associated the sculpture with the figure of Narcissus, showing he continued to picture himself as the hypnotically self-absorbed youth. After realising his error, Dalí persists in referring to the 'false mucus' that was the original cause of his obsession. An abiding preoccupation with the fake, or what he terms the simulacral, is another index of Dalí's deep solidarity with the figure of Narcissus.[18]

As it does elsewhere in his work, the enlarged hand in *Metamorphosis of Narcissus* may refer to the act of masturbation. Such a reading is supported by the onanistic repetition in this section of the poem as it rises toward its awful crescendo, in conjunction with which the line 'The seed of your head has just fallen into the water' (set off on a separate page) might refer to ejaculation. One of Dalí's many erotic drawings from the early 1930s shows a reclining youthful male figure with an enormous erection. Burying his head in shame, he turns away from the two women behind him who strike wantonly lubricious poses. The scenario, suggestive of masturbatory fantasies and associated feelings of guilt – the sinister proximity of a pair of scissors to the tumescent organ leaves no room for doubt about the theme of castration anxiety – is not dissimilar to Dalí's later treatment of the Narcissus subject.[19] In the painting a pronounced sexual threat emanates from the heterosexual group who strut about aggressively flaunting their sexual attributes like lethal weapons. Using a phrase Dalí coined to describe the female praying mantis about to devour its mate during the act of coitus, they adopt the 'famous poses of preliminary expectation.'

In *The Lugubrious Game* (1929) and *The Hand* (*The Remorse of Conscience*) (1930), pictures that allude to masturbation, together again with reactions of guilt and shame, the oversized hand that looms like a hallucination has the same, almost cadaveric, stony coldness as that in *Metamorphosis of Narcissus*. More or less exactly the same hand recurs in a drawing from 1937 known as *Narcisse fossile* where it is detached from and positioned above the reclining youth, a stand-in for Dalí, supporting a derivation of the Narcissus-hand from these earlier pictures. Dalí's insistent description of the draining away of Narcissus's physical body and life force in the poem curiously brings to mind the language of Victorian hygienists and physicians who issued dire warnings about the dangers of masturbation, which was believed to result in a depletion of virile masculinity, a state of enervation that some commentators thought would dispose one to homosexuality.[20] The evocation of a solitary, sterile pleasure, disengaged from the external world and directed narcissistically toward the subject's own body, becomes more obviously relevant later on as an unexpected twist occurs in the final stanza of Dalí's poem.

THE METAMORPHOSIS

'Now the great mystery draws near, the great metamorphosis is about to take place': in terms that are perhaps meant to recall the mystical doctrine of transubstantiation, we are told that the metamorphosis of Narcissus is imminent. The next stanza recounts the complete disappearance of his corporeal body, to be resurrected as the flower that springs from his blood, the annual rebirth of which assures his immortality. In the final lines, Dalí supplies the reader with an updated, psychologised form of this myth, namely the creation of a narcissistic double of himself in Gala. He christens his wife 'the new Narcissus.' Just as the poem reaches its terrible finale, the death foretold by the Ovidian myth, which we now expectantly await, is miraculously averted. In what appears almost a sleight of hand Eros – life, immortality – snatches Dalí back from the clutches of death. The introduction of the figure of Gala, whose presence is nowhere to be inferred from the painting, could be seen as a strategy for defusing the homoerotic elements of the theme. It also reconfirms the autobiographical nature of the poem and the painting insinuated in the prologue.

Salvador Dalí *Narcisse fossile*, 1937, pen and ink drawing

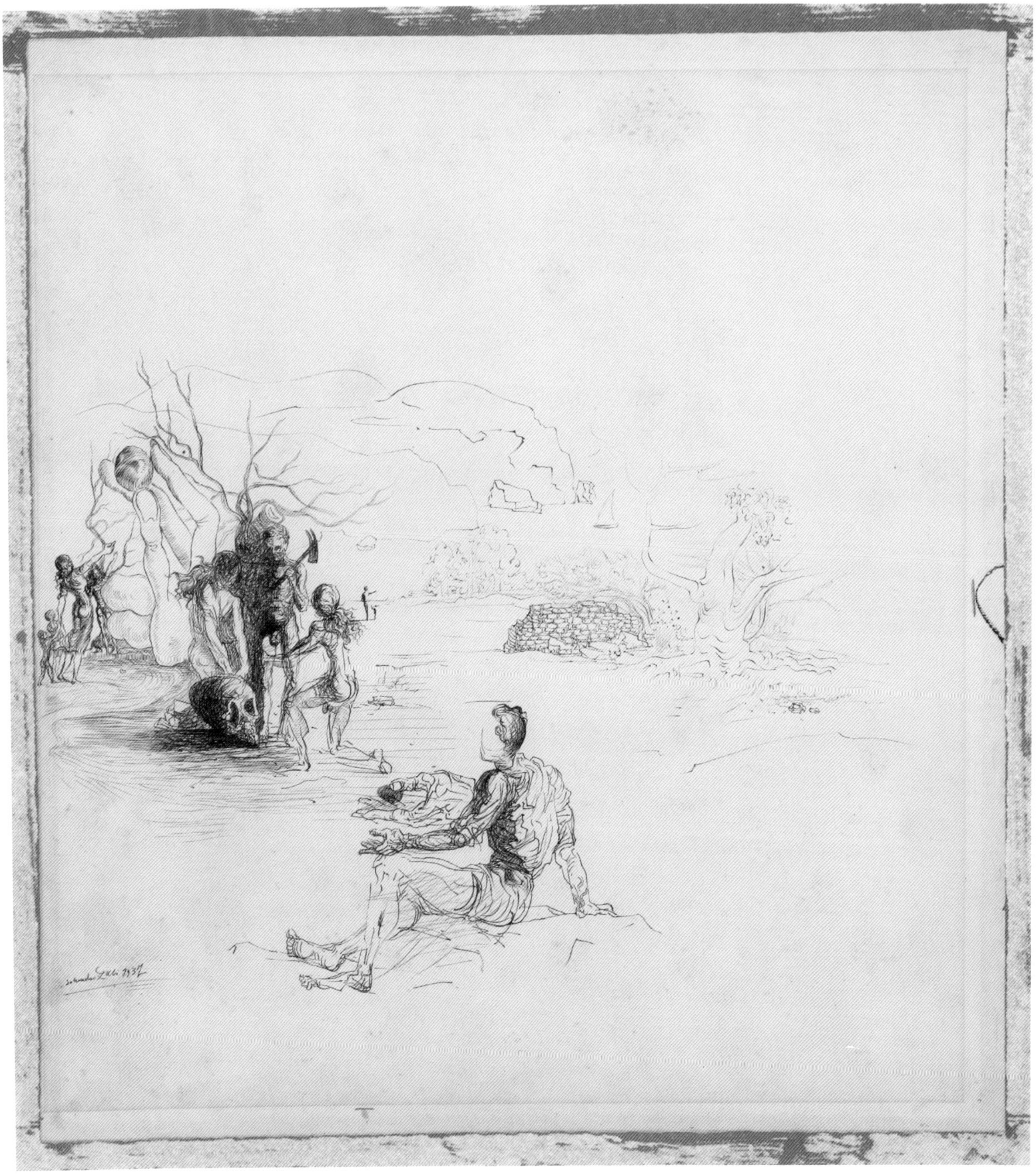

René Magritte *La reproduction interdite* (Not to be Reproduced)
1937, oil on canvas

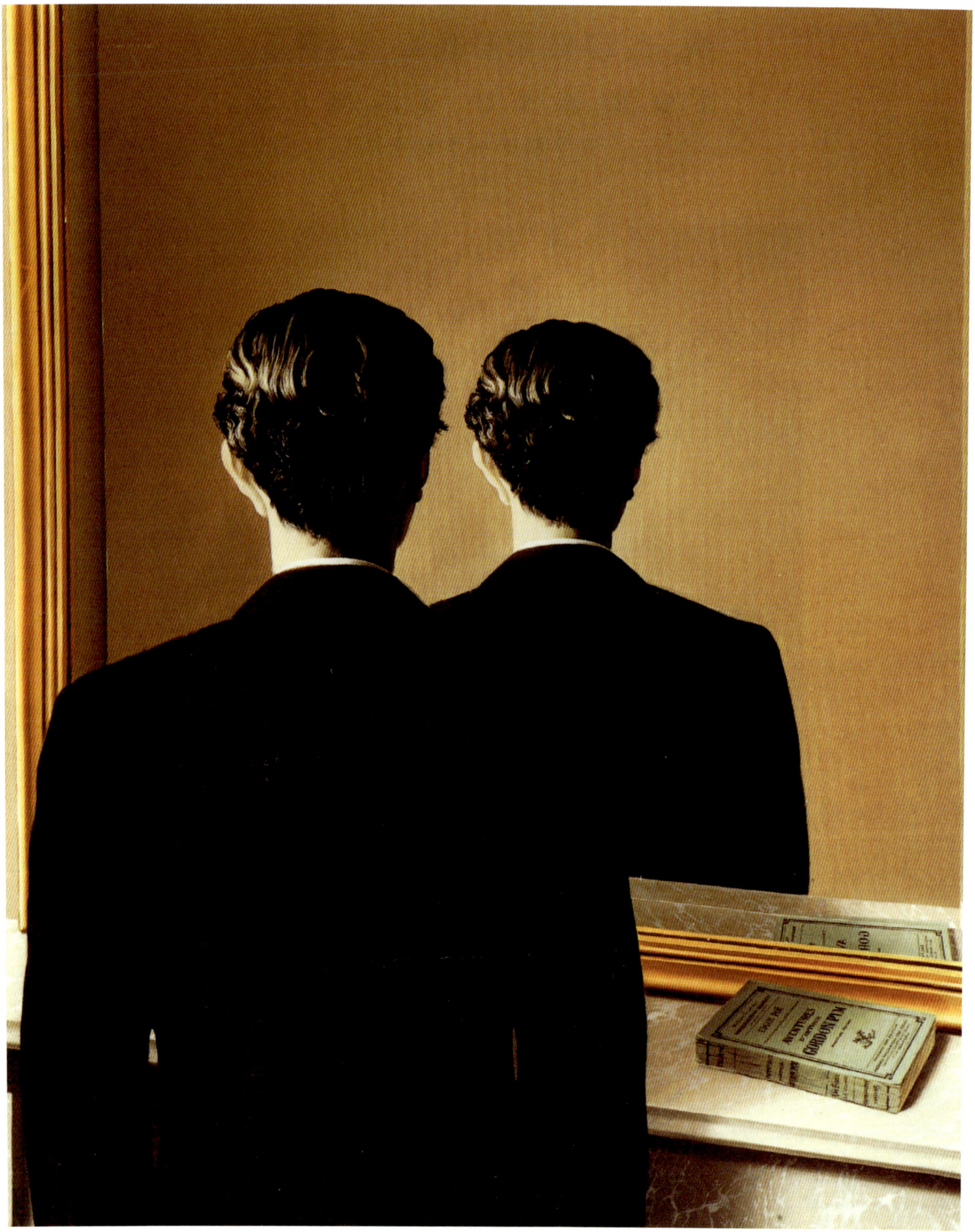

DOUBLE TROUBLE

Otto Rank, in his 1914 study of *Der Doppelgänger* (The Double) (which was influential on Freud's 1919 essay the 'Uncanny'), traces the origin of the idea of the soul to the shadow as the first double or replica.[21] From the shadow stems the archaic belief in shades and ghosts (phantoms) and superstitious fears about mirror images and other reproductions as having the diabolical power to steal away the person's soul – as illustrated, for example, in the myth of Narcissus. It is clear that such conceptions of an uncanny double are applicable to *Metamorphosis of Narcissus* and its introduction of a new variation on the established Dalínian motif of the double or reversible image. René Magritte's *La reproduction interdite* (Not to be Reproduced) of the same year affords an intriguing conceptual, if not precise pictorial parallel for this configuration. In his portrait of Dalí's patron Edward James gazing (narcissistically) at himself in a mirror, Magritte has the reflection turn its back on the subject, and in doing so it takes on an independent vitality all of its own. Who is the model and who the copy here? Written on the canvas stretcher is another title, *l'image fidèle* (the faithful image), which has been scored across and deleted. This is not the 'good likeness' of Plato, a faithful image or reflection, but a diabolical simulacrum that saps the lifeblood and authority of the original.[22] In Magritte's work, duplication attains an extreme degree, resulting in the murder of the real by its representation. As the book on the mantlepiece reveals, Magritte was steeped in Edgar Alan Poe and the nineteenth-century literary interest in uncanny doubles, and the choice of title, *La reproduction interdite*, hints at vestigial fears and taboos still attached to the making of illicit copies. Magritte's picture was based on a photograph of James, to whom he wrote when it was finished: 'I think that you will be very pleased by your portrait which is called "Not to be reproduced" and I am impatient to know how it strikes you, and Dalí as well. (I suppose he is staying in London for some time?)'[23]

As others have noted, there is considerable common ground between Dalí's interest in doubles and doubling and Lacan's notion of a paranoiac style as discussed in the first issue of the surrealist magazine *Minotaure* in May 1933. 'We have characterised,' writes Lacan:

> A fundamental tendency … designated by the term 'iterative identification of the object': the delirium reveals itself in effect extremely fecund in phantasms of cyclic repetition, of ubiquitous multiplication, of periodic recurrence without end of the same events, in doubles and triplets of the same persons, sometimes in hallucinations of doubling ('dédoublement') of the personality of the subject.[24]

The next issue of *Minotaure* contained another contribution by Lacan on the subject of paranoia, this time concerning the Papin sisters, two maids in a bourgeois household who inexplicably attacked and killed their employer and her daughter.[25] Lacan imagines the two sisters, both of whom displayed symptoms of a *folie à deux* – a shared paranoiac psychosis – together with their hapless victims as forming an 'atrocious quadrille' with a gruesome symmetry that bore out his thesis in a sensational manner. True Siamese twins is how Lacan describes them, and he cites the examining psychiatrist Dr Logre, who testified that to read their depositions after the crime 'one could believe one was reading double.'[26] The surrealists championed the cause of the Papin sisters whose 'before' and 'after' photographs reproduced on the back cover of *Le Surréalisme au service de la révolution* in May 1933 convey a powerful impression of 'dédoublement'.

This identification of doubling with a sibling relationship points to an alternative reading of Magritte's portrait of James as a man marching in the footsteps of a fraternal clone. Again this relates to Dalí's personal history as he revealed himself to be afflicted by a paralysing sense of belatedness in relation to an elder brother, also named Salvador, who died just over nine months before he was born. Dalí exploits this tragedy in *The Secret Life of Salvador Dalí* in order to portray himself as a simulacral replica of a non-existent original. He and his brother were, he says, indistinguishable, like two drops of water.[27] Dalí references this story explicitly in the title of his painting, *Portrait of My Dead Brother* (1963), which features a blow-up of the one extant photograph of the disappeared elder brother and multi-layered allusions to processes of replication, including a depiction of the molecular structure of DNA. Ian Gibson, in *The Shameful Life of Salvador Dalí*, scoffs at this, but in his dogged biographer's quest for the real Dalí I think that Gibson misses the point. More in sympathy with Dalí's thinking, the cultural historian Hillel Schwartz, in his book *The Culture of the Copy: Striking Likenesses, Unreasonable Facsimiles* (1996), presents an amazing compilation chronicling the myriad ways in which living in a culture of the copy redefines our sense of ourselves. Schwartz asks a question that is extremely pertinent to Dalí: 'Are we little else but futile re-enactments, or is re-enactment the little enough that we can truly be about?'[28]

The theme of twinning is one that is also found in the photography of Cecil Beaton. Dalí and Gala were introduced to Beaton by James and he photographed them as a glamorous couple (p.51) – an image from this series of photographs featuring Gala alone was used for the cover of the published version of Dalí's poem (p.160). Beaton's many portraits of the rich and famous abound with mirror reflections, doubles and such like. One of the most striking visual formulae employed by Beaton is when the photographic subject is pressed up against a mirror so that they and their reflection are fused like conjoined twins (p.69). It is notable that Dalí's Narcissus-hand exhibits a similar fusion of the self with its watery reflection, and, as sometimes happens with conjoined twins, the reflected double thrives at Narcissus's expense:

> The body of Narcissus flows out and loses itself
> in the abyss of his reflection,
> like the sand glass that will not be turned again.[29]

The resultant collapse of the distance and distinction between the ostensibly real subject and their merely virtual image is pregnant with meaning. In 1962, the American social commentator Daniel Boorstin coined the term 'pseudo-event' for what he understood as the dominance of images over reality in contemporary American life.[30] Boorstin attributes this transformation to the advent of the Graphic Revolution, for example the mass media. Contrasting celebrity with an older notion of heroism, the latter hard-earned and based on real achievements, Boorstin asserts that celebrity is a species of tautology: one is famed for being famous. It is a fabricated and factitious product. Already, in the 1930s, Dalí had started to become a publicly recognisable image and brand name. His appearance on the cover of *Time* magazine in 1936 was an index of his steadily growing fame. From the mid-1930s Dalí was also surrounded by celebrity in Hollywood working on movies with Walt Disney and Alfred Hitchcock. It may be no accident that while undergoing the makeover into 'Divine Dalí' he should also have been preoccupied by the fate of Narcissus (p.26).

The convergence between Dalí and Lacan over the issue of narcissism is tantalising. It raises the question, which a number of commentators have addressed, of how far *Metamorphosis of Narcissus* may or may not have been indebted to Lacan's 'mirror stage'. The pair met in 1933; Dalí reports that they did so at Lacan's behest after he read Dalí's article on the subject of paranoia in the journal *Minotaure*. Lacan's mirror stage hypothesis was an attempt to elucidate an obscure yet crucial passage in Freud's essay on narcissism which describes the emergence of a unified subject: 'We are bound to suppose that a unity comparable to the ego cannot exist from the start,' Freud writes, 'the ego has to be developed.'[31] Freud posits 'a new psychical action' as bringing about the transformation from infantile autoeroticism to a state of secondary narcissism. For Lacan, it is the infant's anticipatory recognition of itself in the form of an externalised image that is crucial to this process.[32] Comparative biology has shown that only

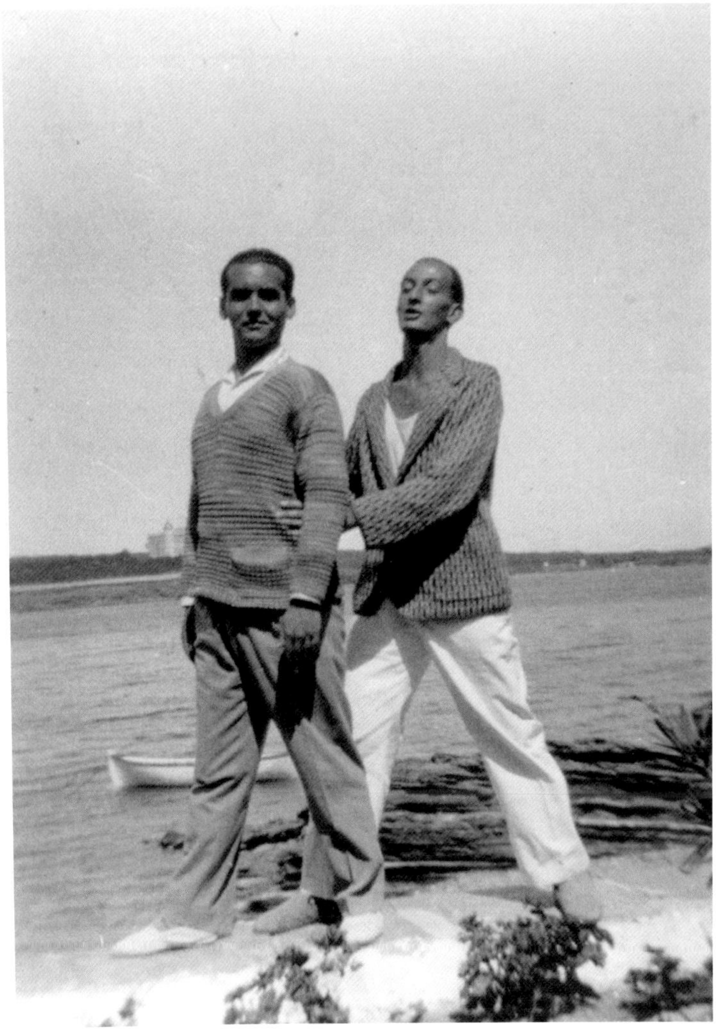

Salvador Dalí and Federico García Lorca at Cadaqués, 1927

relatively few animal species are capable of recognising themselves in a mirror. A dog will bark and growl at its reflection as if it were another dog. The human infant, likewise, is unable to recognise itself in a mirror before approximately eighteen months of age. There appears to be a connection between this ability and brain size and maturation, and perhaps also the capacity for self-consciousness.[33] Initially failing to recognise his own reflection, the Narcissus of Ovidian myth replicates a pattern that every human follows in the course of normal maturation. Only later does he realise that the reflection is himself and that he can never attain the object of his desire. With Lacan's mirror stage, also, the dialectic of subjecthood is never completed. Lacan's theory, which most certainly would have been of intense interest to Dalí, was presented at a conference in Marienbad in 1935, but the published version did not appear until much later. Hence, it is doubtful whether Dalí could have known about it in any detail when he embarked upon *Metamorphosis of Narcissus.*

A MYTH SHARED

Interpreters of *Metamorphosis of Narcissus* who have broached the issue of homoeroticism have tended to point the finger of suspicion at Dalí's intense friendship with the poet Federico García Lorca, which reached a high point when they holidayed together at Cadaqués in 1925 and again in the summer of 1927. However, Dalí's retrospective accounts portray Lorca as like Ameinias in the myth, his amorous designs on the artist teasingly rebuffed. Yet these same accounts intimate that Lorca's persistent efforts at seduction may have come nearer to achieving their goal.[34] Dalí's last contact with Lorca was in 1935, a year before he was murdered during the first months of the Spanish Civil War. The poem *Metamorphosis of Narcissus* contains a direct homage to Lorca in the form of a footnoted quotation. Ian Gibson locates its source in a poem that remained unpublished until four years after the poet's death, which Lorca must have personally given to Dalí, and discerns an 'indication of how much Lorca, a year after his assassination, was haunting Dalí.'[35] Another possible model for a suicidal Narcissus in the grip of the death drive is the writer René Crevel (p.54), who stayed with Dalí and Gala at Port Lligat several times in the early 1930s and was his most loyal supporter in the surrealist camp. Crevel's tragic death by suicide in 1935, in the same circumstances as the death of the homosexual protagonist of his 1926 novel *La Mort difficile* (Difficult Death), is said to have deeply distressed Dalí, though he later tried to make light of it.

It is probable that Dalí was still grappling with his ambivalent feelings towards these lost friends in 1937 when he painted the picture. In the 1917 essay 'Mourning and Melancholia,' Freud proposes that in mourning 'a narcissistic identification with the object' occurs. Paralleling the argument of the Leonardo da Vinci case, he claims that a strong fixation on the object leads to an identification with the loved, and now lost, object. 'Thus the shadow of the object [falls] upon the ego,' Freud writes.[36] It is possible that Dalí subconsciously echoes this famous phrase when he states rather similarly in *The Secret Life of Salvador Dalí* that for the duration of an eclipse the 'shadow' of Lorca darkened the virginal originality of his spirit and of his flesh.[37] That Narcissus may be infused with Dalí's memories of Crevel and Lorca does not rule out it also having a self-referential aspect.

The evidence that Dalí and his patron were in constant contact throughout this period raises questions as to whether James might also have exerted some influence over Dalí's choice of the Narcissus subject and his decision to accompany the picture with a poem. James was at this point Dalí's exclusive patron, having signed a contract in 1936 to purchase his entire output. He was staying with Dalí in April 1937 when work on *Metamorphosis of Narcissus* began and the following year it was James who accompanied Dalí when he took the picture on his visit to Freud. James has been linked with a group of English poets known as Uranians, the majority of whom were educated in classics at Oxford or Cambridge. It was while studying at Oxford that James's love of art and poetry was cultivated. It has been argued that the poetry of this small and fairly clandestine clique (it lasted from 1858 through to 1930) was important for the development of a homosexual consciousness that defied the opprobrium of mainstream English society. The Uranian poets extolled a Hellenic ideal of pederastic love and Narcissus was one of a number of stock subjects they thought amenable to the expression of a homoerotic sensibility. The author Timothy d'Arch Smith cites an anonymous article in the *Artist and Journal of Home Culture* for 1889 identifying classical myths suitable to be painted, among them Narcissus with 'the pale, sweet face, the sleepy, liquid eyes, the dark, night-sheltering hair.'[38] James married an Austrian dancer Tilly Losch in 1931, but by the time of his divorce in 1934, in which his wife alleged homosexuality in her suit, aspersions had also been cast on his poetry. James's privately published *Carmina Amico* (1932), a collection of sonnets addressed to a young man, contained a reference to 'the love that dare not speak its name', a well-known phrase from a poem by Wilde's lover Lord Alfred Douglas (Bosie), which was mentioned as part of the trials in 1895, and was seized upon in James's divorce proceedings as an admission of its author's homosexual proclivities. By 1937, James was collaborating with Pavel Tchelitchew, which Dalí may have surmised was based on an amorous inclination; Beaton was another member of this homophile circle of James's acquaintances.

I have reason, therefore, to think of Narcissus as a myth shared.[39] In a letter of 15 June 1937, proudly announcing the completion of the picture, Dalí

Cecil Beaton *Edward James*, 1931

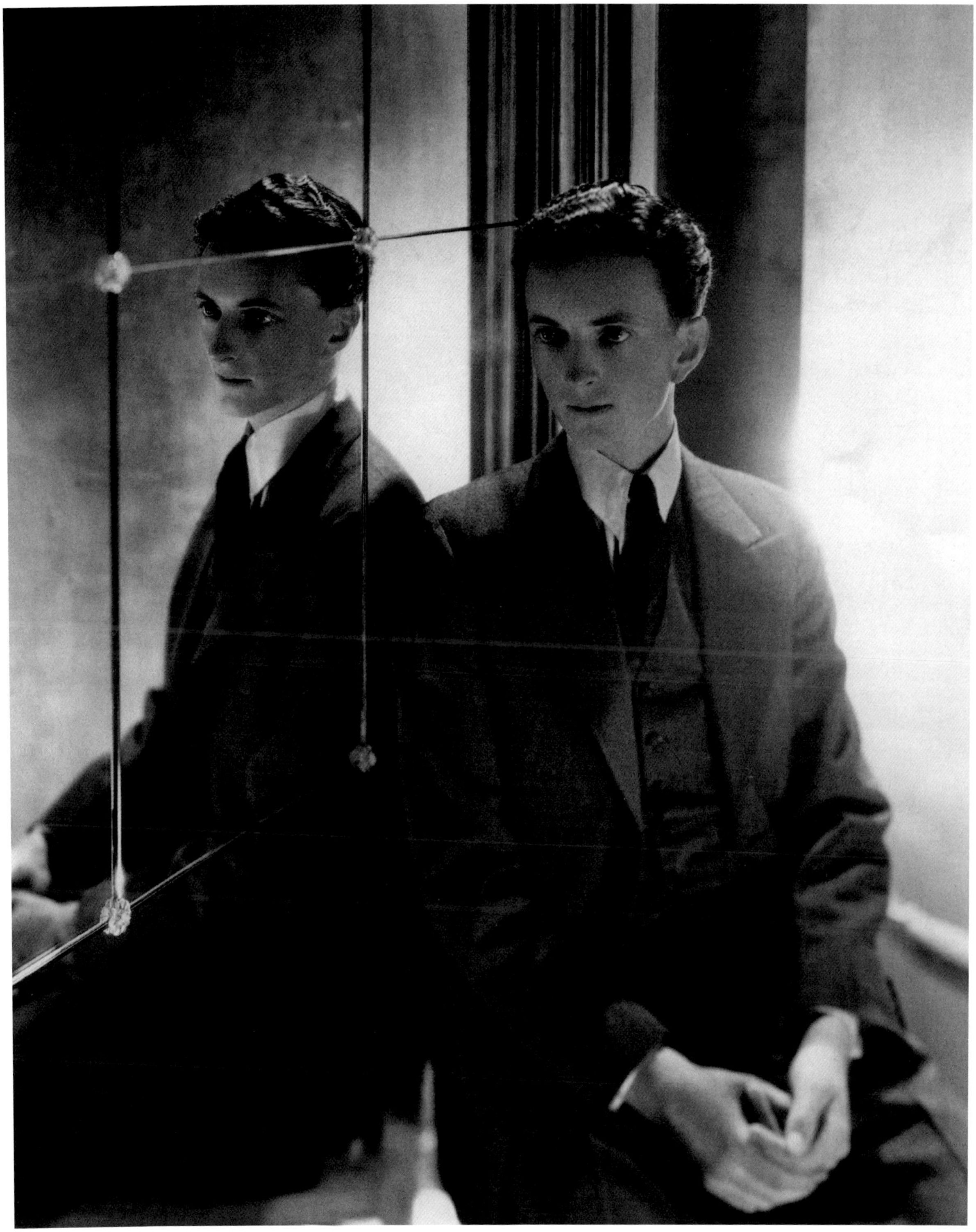

Salvador Dalí *Study for Narcissus*, 1937,
published in *Vrille* magazine, 1945

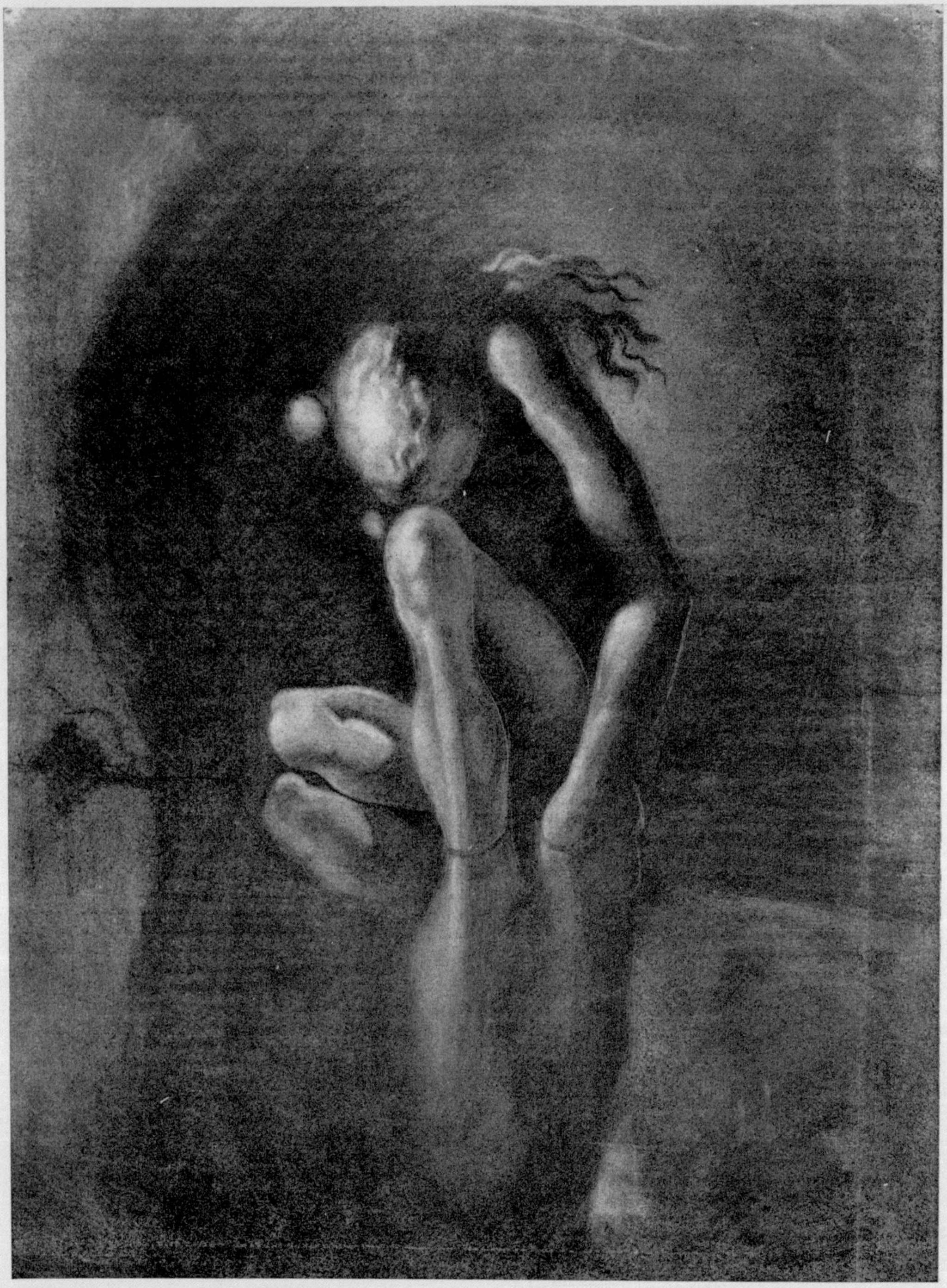

S. DALI : Étude pour Narcisse. Collection G. Hugnet.

imputes a narcissistic inclination to James, inviting him to explore the 'geological recesses' of his latest acquisition, but warning him not to be too easily seduced. 'Don't tire yourself too much', he writes to James, who was taking a rest cure, 'and don't fall into the water like him.'[40] Further along, he pictures James convalescing at his clinic, 'sitting on the banks of Narcissus's lake.' The figure of Narcissus is not dissimilar in its function to that of Saint Sebastian, under whose banner Dalí and Lorca had honed their aesthetic stances inasfar as they are both popular gay icons.[41] Gide's *Treatise on Narcissus* (1892) would have afforded a precedent for the use of Narcissus in order to signal an aesthetic ideology, as well as being a rallying point for the expression of sexual dissidence.[42]

It ought to be recalled that *Metamorphosis of Narcissus* coincides with Dalí's deepening engagement with the Italian Renaissance and with works by Cellini and Caravaggio that revel unashamedly in the homoerotic delectation that the Narcissus subject invites. A study for the figure of Narcissus that was reproduced in *Vrille* magazine in France in 1945 that is strongly reminiscent of Caravaggio's *Narcissus* (c.1597–99, p.99) in its self-enclosure of a figure isolated by utter darkness, alone with its reflection. Had Dalí availed himself of the chance to see this work at firsthand on his trip to Italy in 1935, he would surely have noticed a double image worthy of himself, with its curiously inept depiction of the subject's right knee, which art historian Stephen Bann describes as phallic but is perhaps more like a buttock. Dalí goes one better, twinning the flexed knee with its reflection so that both 'buttocks' are visible together. The same analogy of knees and buttocks occurs in a passage from *The Secret Life of Salvador Dalí* in which Dalí recounts his homoerotic infatuation with a schoolboy nicknamed Buchaques, and it is revealing that Dalí chose to discuss this in a lecture he gave at the Sorbonne in 1955.[43] One may regard it as symptomatic that in the *Metamorphosis of Narcissus* poem Dalí seeks to disguise the true nature of the phantasy by displacing it onto a male figure in the heterosexual group, a blond German with 'brown mists of mathematics in the dimples of his cloudy knees.' In the painting Dalí did not neglect the golden hair of Caravaggio's *Narcissus*, but he generalizes the colour as a radiance that suffuses the figure as a whole, a pictorial counterpart to a libidinal cathexis. It seems that Dalí added the figure at the extreme right after the rest of the picture was painted: a male nude on a sculptural plinth with his back to the viewer who swivels round as if to admire his own pert buttocks – a paraphrase of Philostratus's ekphrasis perhaps?[44]

MAD LOVE

Ovid accomplishes the heterosexualisation of the Narcissus myth by introducing Echo. Dalí does likewise in his Narcissus poem, but in a manner that departs from the original story. James, who made a translation of the poem (not the one used in the published version), clearly had misgivings about the ending which he thought was rather unsatisfactorily tacked on, remarking that: 'Dalí ends by turning the poem with his last lines into a tribute to his wife; but, graceful though this is, it seems to me out of place in the context and dragged in "*par quatre épingles*".'[45] Given the nature of James's investment in the Narcissus subject, one can readily understand his disappointment at the trite conventionality of this ending.

So love triumphs in the end. Dalí recounts a similar tale in *The Secret Life of Salvador Dalí*, portraying Gala as the intercessor whose love enables him to conquer a quite alarming miscellany of neurotic tics and obsessions that caused serious consternation among his newfound friends.[46] Dalí met his wife when she and her then husband Paul Éluard, along with the dealer Camille Goemans, Luis Buñuel, René Magritte and his wife Georgette, descended on Cadaqués to holiday with Dalí in August of 1929. It is only appropriate that the flames of a love that would eventually attain the stature of a myth on a par with that of Narcissus were kindled in the very setting of *Metamorphosis of Narcissus*.

In terms of the poetic narrative, the blossoming of Dalí's love for Gala functions to domesticate his wayward desires by channeling them in the direction of a normative heterosexuality. A mistaken desire for some shadowy will-o'-the-wisp illusion is now redirected towards a real flesh-and-blood woman. Narcissism is thus safely inscribed as a transitional phase in a developmental schema that reaches its socially-accepted terminus in the love for Gala. The justification for this scenario lies in Freud's later theory of narcissism as a *stage* in sexual development interposed between autoeroticism and object-love. Change and development are implicit in the notion of metamorphosis, contrasting with the imagery of frozen stasis in the earlier description of Narcissus (that we might furthermore relate to Freud's conception of homosexuality as an 'arrested' development at the narcissistic stage.) Without the textual supplement to the painted image, it would not have been evident that the metamorphosis of Narcissus concludes in this normative outcome. After the initial concerns voiced by the fishermen of Port Lligat about the self-absorbed youth in their midst, one is prepared to believe that this denouement coincides happily with Dalí's cure.[47]

Dalí often used the nickname 'Gradiva' for Gala. The name is taken from the title of a short story written by Wilhelm Jensen in 1903 and later analysed by Freud who investigated the way Gradiva, the heroine, brings about the protagonist's psychological healing. *The Secret Life of Salvador Dali* is dedicated to Gala-Gradiva, with the inscription, 'She was destined to be my Gradiva, the one who moves forward, my victory, my wife'. *Metamorphosis of Narcissus* is also dedicated, implicitly, to his wife. It is signed at the bottom right 'Gala Salvador Dalí' in recognition of Gala's Gradiva-like role as Dalí's saviour and inspirational muse. The poem and painting thus establish a formula that is repeated by the autobiography.

Jensen's Gradiva, and the study by Freud that brought it to the attention of the surrealists, were published together in French in 1931.[48] It is the story of a young archaeologist, Norbert Hanold, who succumbs to a delusional phantasy about a girl portrayed on a Roman relief named Gradiva. He believes she is real and after dreaming that she was buried in the eruption of Vesuvius sets off to Pompeii in search of her. It transpires that the source of his delusion is the repressed memory of a childhood sweetheart, Zoe Bertgang, whom he encounters as if by chance while wandering the streets of Pompeii. Recognising the nature of his illness, Zoe initially acquiesces in the delusion by pretending to be Gradiva. By transferring his love from the phantasied object back onto herself, she ingeniously brings about his cure. Freud marvels at her skill in a role that he compares with that of the psychoanalyst; the theme of archaeology, of the burial and retrieval of the past, also supplies him with a potent metaphor for the psychoanalytic enterprise. The surrealists for their part were enchanted by this touching vignette because of the redemptive power of love revealed by it. Had Dalí's intention been to place *Metamorphosis of Narcissus* under a surrealist banner, he could not have done so more unequivocally than by endorsing this article of the surrealist faith.[49] It cannot be coincidental that Breton had opened the Galerie Gradiva in Paris in the same year as Dalí completed his painting.

With surreal irony, Éluard, who was married to Gala when she fell in love with Dalí, may have supplied Dalí with Jensen's book and the means by which Dalí would mythologise his relationship with her. Some time after Gala had left him, Éluard wrote to her 'J'espère que tu as bien reçu Gradiva' (I hope you have received Gradiva), indicating that Dalí probably acquired his copy of the book from Éluard.[50] Éluard kept up an affectionate correspondence with Gala for many years despite being the cuckolded

Cecil Beaton *Salvador Dalí and Gala with* A Couple with Their Heads Full of Clouds, 1937

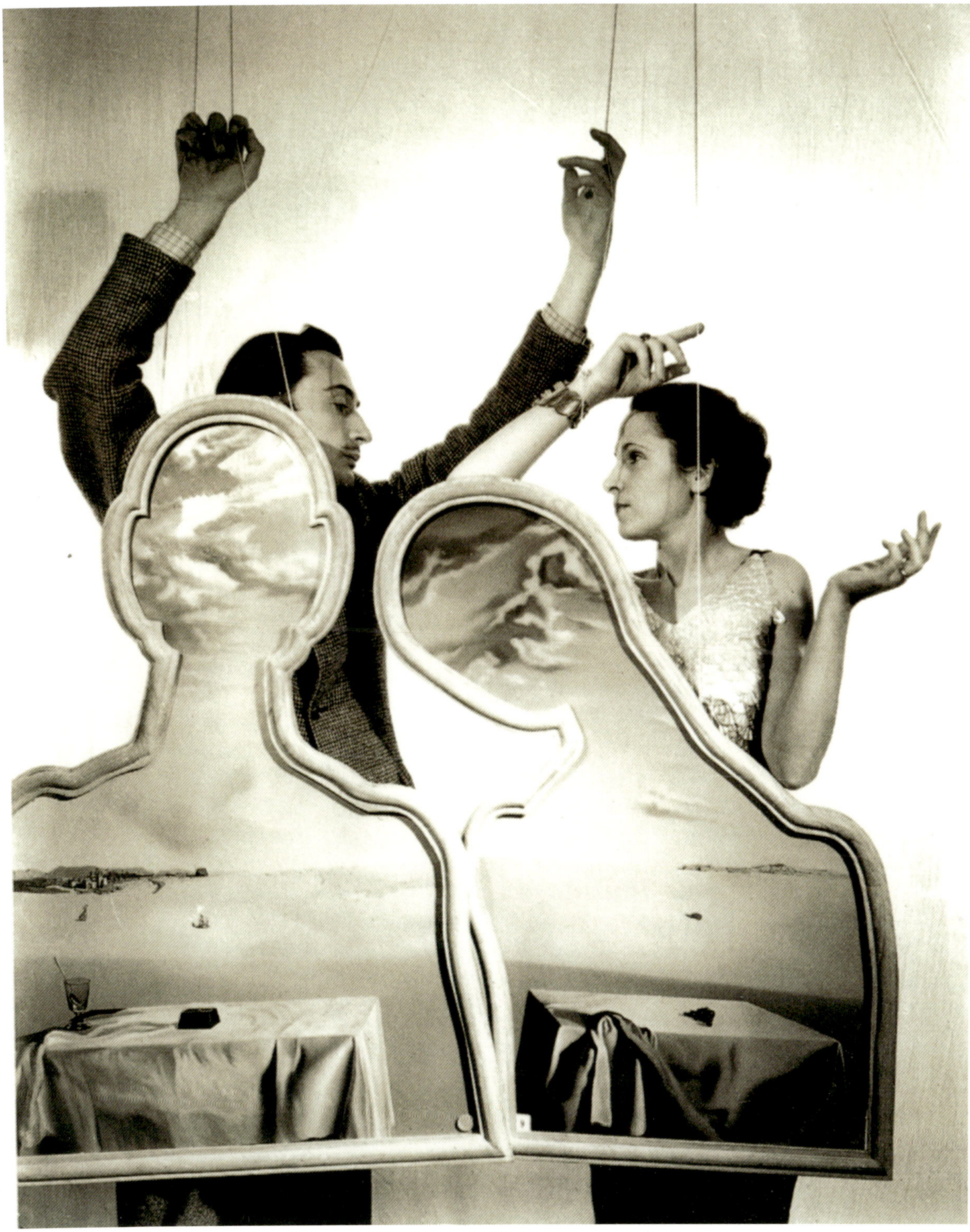

husband, proof of a sort that the surrealists' belief in the capacity of love to transcend strife was not wholly misplaced. Given his magnanimity under circumstances that must have been a severe test for his masculine amour-propre. Dalí's dedication of the *Metamorphosis of Narcissus* poem to the former husband strikes one as a belated, and grossly insufficient, payback.

And yet, another look shows that the reform of Narcissus is less certain than I at first too hastily supposed: as 'my Narcissus' Dalí enlists Gala into the class of narcissistic love objects. From the extreme idealisation of her, we infer that she is an externalised portion of Dalí's ego – an ego ideal, in which capacity she affords a roundabout way of satisfying his narcissism. I conclude, with Freud, that: 'What he projects before him as his ideal is the substitute for the lost narcissism of his childhood in which he was his own ideal.'[51] Dalí is fully aware that it is really only himself whom he loves in the guise of an other – 'Narcissus knows one cannot go beyond narcissism' writes Kristeva.[52] Exceeding the parameters of a transient affliction from which Dalí could hope or expect to be cured, maybe the picture and accompanying poem ought to be retitled the *persistence* of narcissism? It may very well be the most radical accomplishment of *Metamorphosis of Narcissus* to lay bare the narcissistic basis of surrealist *amour fou* – to have shown that the 'madness' of Narcissus is in essence no different from mad love.

NOTES

1. Paul Valéry, *Oeuvres* (Paris: Gallimard, 1957), vol. 1, p.1557.
2. A letter from Stefan Zweig to Dalí dated 11 January 1932 (Fundació Gala-Salvador Dalí) testifies to his liking for Dalí's work already at that early stage. Zweig, who was residing in Paris at the time, was deliberating about whether or not he could afford to buy one of Dalí's pictures.
3. Salvador Dalí, *The Secret Life of Salvador Dalí* (1942), trans. Haakon M. Chevalier (London: Vision Press, 1968), p.24.
4. Sigmund Freud, *Letters of Sigmund Freud, 1873–1939*, ed. Ernst Freud, trans. Tanya and James Stern (London: Hogarth Press, 1961), p.444.
5. Dalí, *The Secret Life of Salvador Dalí*, p.397.
6. Sigmund Freud, 'On Narcissism: An Introduction' (1914), *Pelican Freud Library*, vol. 11, pp.82–83.
7. Ovid, *Metamorphoses*, trans. Mary M. Innes (Harmondsworth: Penguin, 1955), book III.
8. Julia Kristeva, *Tales of Love*, trans. Leon S. Roudiez (New York: Columbia University Press, 1987), p.35.
9. Dalí, *The Secret Life of Salvador Dalí*, p.70. Dalí emerges from the pages describing his adolescence as a self-styled Narcissus, but one who would avoid succumbing to the fate of his mythical predecessor.
10. The manuscript, now held at the Fundació Gala-Salvador Dalí, includes two crayon drawings that must be the initial experimental workings out of this idea. If, as seems most probable, Dalí was drawing his own hand then it must have been with the aid of a mirror – Dalí was right-handed and it is a right hand that he draws.
11. Salvador Dalí, *The Collected Writings of Salvador Dalí*, ed. Haim Finkelstein (Cambridge: Cambridge University Press, 1998), p.210.
12. Sigmund Freud, 'The Libido Theory and Narcissism,' *Introductory Lectures on Psycho-Analysis, Pelican Freud Library*, vol. 1, trans. James Strachey (Harmondsworth: Pelican Books, 1973), p.466.
13. Dalí, *The Secret Life of Salvador Dalí*, p.27. Dalí acknowledges Otto Rank's *The Trauma of Birth* (1929) as the source for his speculations on prenatal existence.
14. Ovid, *Metamorphoses*, book III.
15. Ibid. Similarly, Echo's bones are transformed to rock as her incarnate self withers away until only her voice remains.
16. The approximate date of this incident is September or early October 1936.
17. Dalí, *The Secret Life of Salvador Dalí*, p.367.
18. Kristeva, *Tales of Love*, p.126, notes 'the concomitance of *narcissism* and the *fake*.' Dalí consistently prefers the 'false' to the 'true': in *The Secret Life of Salvador Dalí* (p.38) he affirms that, as with jewels, false memories are always more brilliant, more real than true ones.
19. This drawing, not reproduced in the catalogue, was titled *Narcissus* in the 2004 Dalí retrospective at Palazzo Grassi, Venice.
20. See Tomas Laqueur, *Solitary Sex: A Cultural History of Masturbation* (New York: Zone Books, 2004).
21. Otto Rank, *The Double. A Psychoanalytic Study*, trans. Harry Tucker (1914) (Chapel Hill: University of North Carolina Press, 1971). The 'double' is of course one of the main sources of the uncanny analysed by Freud.
22. The absence of distinction between model and copy in the double makes it the supreme form of the simulacrum.The

double is hence an impossible aporia for Platonic thought.

23. The letter is dated 18 May 1937. René Magritte, *Catalogue raisonné*, ed. David Sylvester, vol. 1 (London: Philip Wilson Publishers, 1992), p.244.
24. Jacques Lacan, 'Le problème du style et la conception psychiatrique des formes paranoiaques de l'expérience,' *Minotaure* no. 1 (1 June 1933), p.69.
25. Jacques Lacan, 'Motifs du crime paranoiaque,' *Minotaure* no. 3–4 (12 December 1933), pp.25–28.
26. Ibid., p.28.
27. Dalí, *The Secret Life of Salvador Dalí*, p.2. This remark echoes a passage from an essay by André Breton that was hugely important for Dalí, 'Introduction to the Discourse on the Paucity of Reality': '[W]hatever may be written to the contrary, two leaves of the same tree are exactly alike. They are even the same leaf. I insist that if two drops of water have such a resemblance, it is because there is but one drop.' André Breton, *What is Surrealism? Selected Writings*, ed. Franklin Rosemont (New York: Monad Press, 1978), p.23.
28. Hillel Schwartz, *The Culture of the Copy: Striking Likenesses, Unreasonable Facsimiles* (New York: Zone Books, 1996), p.377.
29. Dalí, 'Metamorphosis of Narcissus' (1937), *The Collected Writings of Salvador Dalí*, p.327, see also p.165 of this book.
30. Daniel J. Boorstin, *The Image: A Guide to Pseudo-Events in America* (1961), (New York: Atheneum, 1971).
31. Sigmund Freud, 'On Narcissism: An Introduction' (1914), *Pelican Freud Library*, vol. 11, trans. James Strachey (Harmondsworth: Pelican Books, 1984), p.69.
32. Jacques Lacan, 'The Mirror Stage as Formative of the Function of the I', *Écrits: A Selection*, trans. Alan Sheridan (London: Routledge, 1980), pp.6–7.
33. The literature on self-recognition in animals has grown exponentially since a study in chimpanzees using a mirror test was developed by G.G. Gallup in 1970. See G.G. Gallup, *Self-Recognition in Chimpanzees and Man: A Developmental and Comparative Perspective* (New York: Plenum, 1979).
34. Dalí comments on this incident in conversation with Alain Bosquet. The film *Little Ashes* (2008; dir. Paul Morrison) infers that panic provoked by it drove Dalí into the waiting arms of Gala.
35. Ian Gibson, *The Shameful Life of Salvador Dalí* (London: Faber and Faber, 1997), pp.373–374.
36. Freud, 'Mourning and Melancholia,' *Pelican Freud Library*, vol. 11, p.258.
37. Dalí, *The Secret Life of Salvador Dalí*, p.203.
38. Timothy d'Arch Smith, *Love in Earnest: Some Notes on the Lives and Writings of English 'Uranian' Poets from 1889 to 1930* (London: Routledge & Keegan Paul, 1970).
39. My notion of Narcissus as a myth shared comes from the example of André Gide and Paul Valéry. The latter wrote to Gide: 'My Narcissus is finished … the effort of writing it was not wasted because it sorted out my whole aesthetic, my morality and my philosophy.' *Correspondance d'André Gide et de Paul Valéry 1890–1942*, ed. Robert Mallet (1955), (Paris: Gallimard, 2009).
40. Salvador Dalí, letter to Edward James dated 15 June 1937. Edward James Foundation, West Dean. As previously noted, Magritte turned an act of looking by James into an active self-regard.
41. See *Sebastian's Arrows: Letters and Mementos of Salvador Dalí and Federico García Lorca*, edited and introduced by Christopher Maurer (Chicago: Swan Isle Press, 2004).
42. Dalí possessed a 1946 edition of Gide's symbolist *Traité de narcisse*, though it is probable that he knew it before this date.
43. Dalí, *The Secret Life of Salvador Dalí*, p.47.
44. Philostratus describes a standing Narcissus in a contrapposto pose that throws the figure's buttocks into relief. It has been argued that Philostratus's *Imagines* served to instruct in homoerotic codes of viewing – see chapter 3.
45. James, letter to Mr Kornfeld.
46. They anxiously quizzed him about coprophagic tendencies – concerns that the coprophagic hand pointedly recalls.
47. It sheds light on the dynamics of a psychoanalytic cure implicit in Dalí's portrayal of his romance with Gala to recall the conservatism of the French psychoanalytic establishment during this period with regard to homosexuality. When a homosexual had the misfortune to present on the analyst's couch, the treatment he received aimed to rid him of his unnatural inclinations often with disastrous results. The virulent homophobia of French psychoanalysis in the interwar period forms a telling parallel to the general intolerance that prevailed within the surrealist group.
48. Sigmund Freud, 'Delusions and Dreams in Jensen's "Gradiva"' (1907), *Pelican Freud Library*, vol. 14, pp.33–116.
49. The subject of Dalí and Gradiva is treated in incomparable fashion by Fiona Bradley in *Salvador Dalí: A Mythology* (London: Tate Publishing, 1999).
50. Paul Éluard, *Lettres à Gala 1924–1948*, ed. Pierre Dreyfus (Paris: Gallimard, 1984), p.248. Dalí corresponded with Éluard from Zürs in April 1937, sending him photographs of *Metamorphosis of Narcissus* and a version of the poem.
51. Freud, 'On Narcissism: An Introduction,' *Pelican Freud Library*, vol. 11, p.88.
52. Kristeva, *Tales of Love*, p.125.

George Platt Lynes *Portrait of René Crevel*, 1928

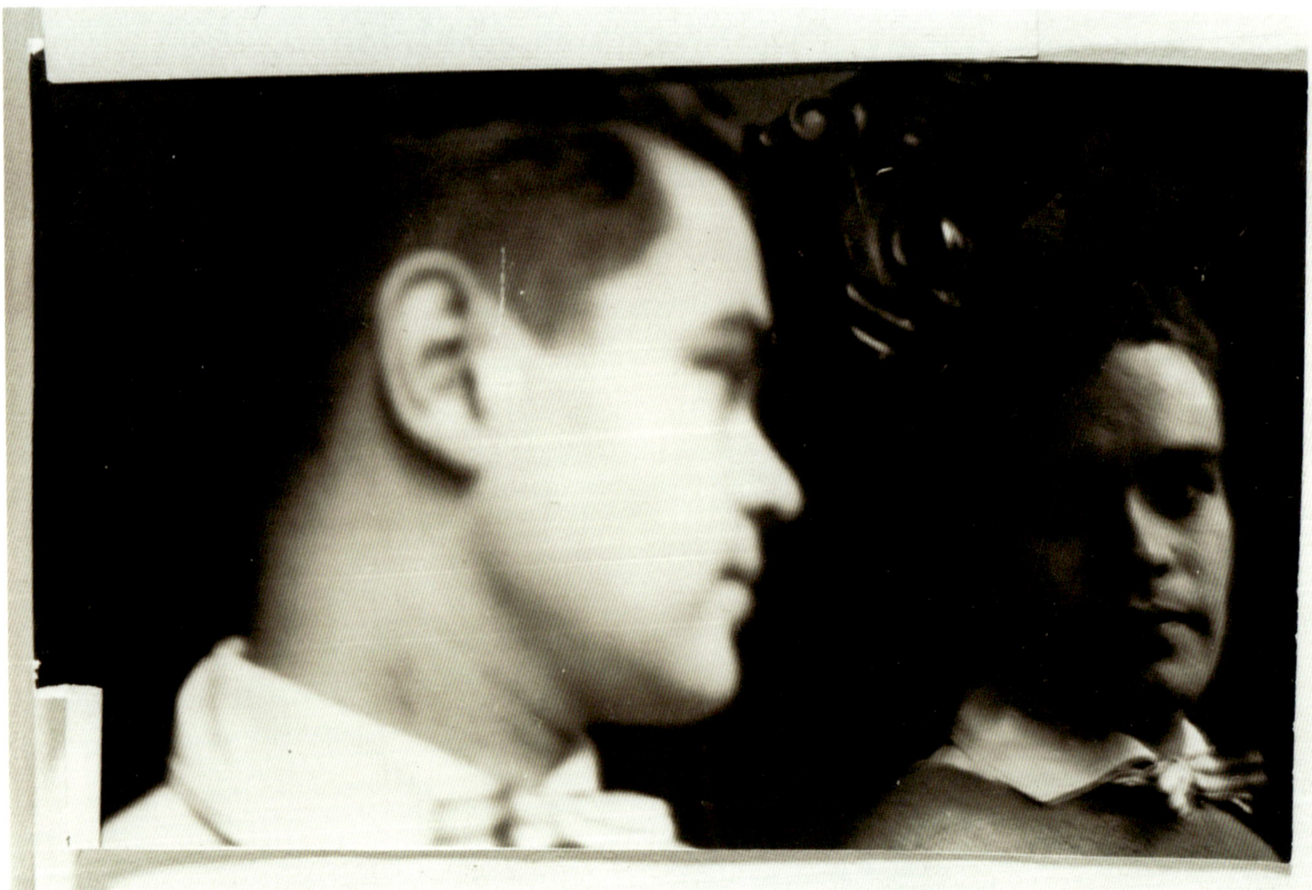

CHAPTER TWO
MYTH AND MASQUERADE

> Like Narcissus, I used to lean over my image; all the phrases that
> I wrote then remain on that account somewhat bent.
> André Gide[1]

This book contends that Narcissus imagery affords a means for tracking a current of dissident or non-normative desire within surrealism and its identifiable legacies. In this chapter, I explore issues of gender and sexuality in relation to Narcissus principally in the media of photography and film. My objectives are to begin to map what, in homage to Rosalind Krauss, I shall call the photographic conditions of (queer) surrealism. Krauss's seminal essay, 'The Photographic Conditions of Surrealism' (1981), laid out an agenda for what became the 1985 exhibition 'L'Amour fou: Photography and Surrealism'. 'What is at stake,' Krauss wrote, 'is the relocation of photography from its eccentric position relative to surrealism to one that is absolutely central – definitive, one might say.'[2] My task involves taking up her project of moving the marginal to centre stage. Of particular interest to me is the comparison with which Krauss's essay began: a self-portrait photograph by Florence Henri (p.66) and Man Ray's *Homage to D.A.F. de Sade*. This Man Ray photograph of a woman's behind, which was published in *Le Surréalisme au service de la révolution* in May 1933, alludes none-too-subtly to the act of sodomy. Reversing the neglect of queer sexuality by scholars of surrealism necessarily embraces both persons as well as practices, as represented by these two images opening a Pandora's box of the perverse desires at play within surrealism. The Marquis de Sade, incidentally, was one of only two people André Breton exempted from his notorious tirade against homosexuality, the other being the symbolist poet Jean Lorrain.

A photograph of André Breton, Salvador Dalí, René Crevel and Paul Éluard by Anna Riwkin (p.56), a Russian-born Swedish photographer who was not formally a part of the surrealist group, is revealing for the gestures and exchanged glances that seems to tell us something about the personalities and their interactions with each other. Assigned a date of 1935, the photograph cannot have been taken any later than 18 June, when Crevel, the only openly homosexual member of the French surrealist group, committed suicide. Without knowing the topic of their conversation, we must consider that his sexuality was an unspoken (or unspeakable) presence, an elephant in the room. Towering over the rest, Crevel is marooned awkwardly in the midst of the assembled company. Breton's body language is forceful, macho, and expostulatory. His posturing might have reminded the others of his intemperate outburst against homosexuality during the surrealist discussions on the topic, that were later published. Breton overcame his homophobia scarcely enough to tolerate the presence of Crevel and Claude Cahun in the French surrealist group.[3]

Crevel was a staunch supporter of Dalí whose surrealism of the 'polymorphously perverse'

Anna Riwkin *Members of the Surrealist Group*, 1935
left to right: André Breton, Salvador Dalí, René Crevel and Paul Éluard

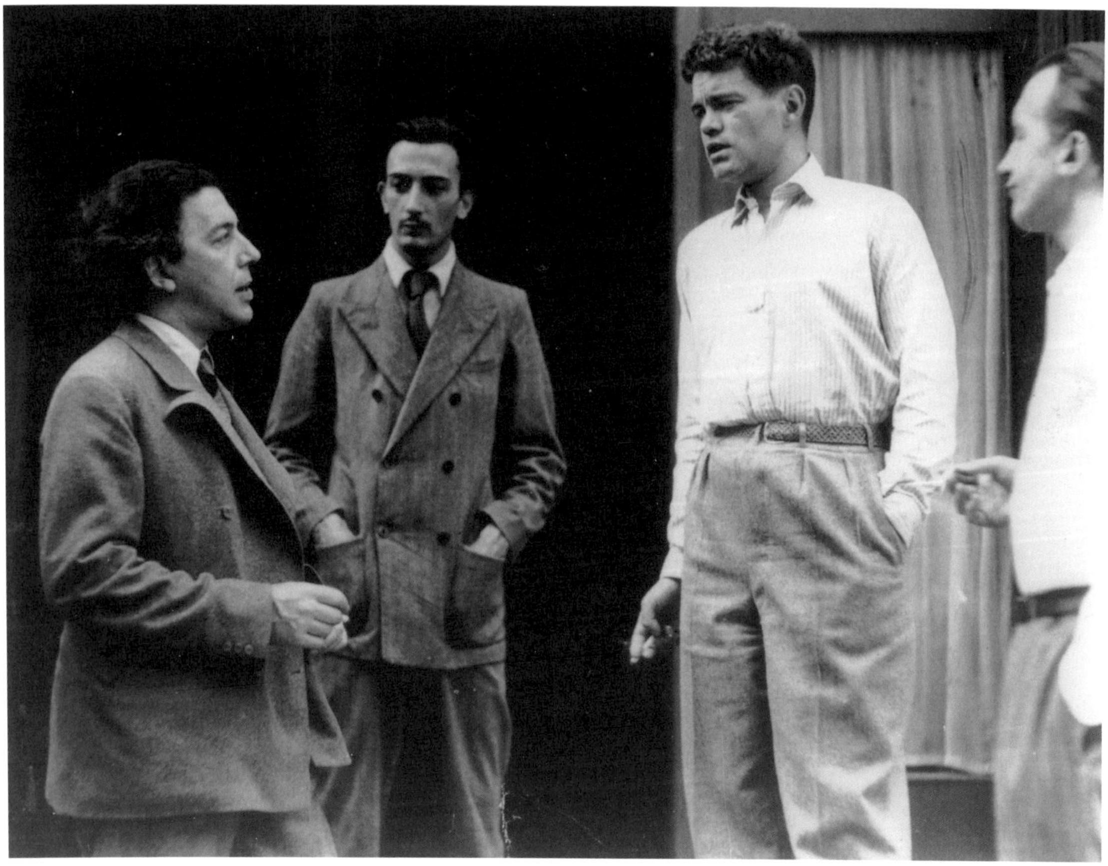

was a dissident alternative to Breton's orthodoxy, and a provocative challenge to its uncritical heterosexism. 'In love, I attach a special value to everything generally labelled perversion and vice', Dalí professed, asserting them as 'the most revolutionary forms of thought and activity.'[4] Though he denied he was homosexual, Dalí was aware of the contentious nature of the anal eroticism displayed by certain of his pictures, remarking that: 'I was authorised to represent sexual organs, but not anal fantasies. Any anus was taken in very bad part. They rather liked lesbians, but not pederasts.'[5] In 1934, Dalí was subjected to a show trial by the surrealist group, in an attempt to exclude him. Dalí, who was accused of painting subjects unacceptable to the surrealists, defended himself by saying that were he to dream of sodomising Breton he would feel compelled to paint it the next day. The point ostensibly was about his refusal to censor the unconscious but Dalí knowingly exploited Breton's prudishness to turn the situation to his advantage. The surrealist leader was livid with rage but the rest of the audience fell about in laughter and the united front against Dalí collapsed. In Riwkin's photo, Dalí hangs back, sullen, hands in pockets, his body language an exact counterpoint to Breton's.

It should be recognised that, in spite of Breton's intolerance, surrealism did attract a formidable array of queer artists, writers and photographers. This was particularly the case as it moved away from Breton's control in Paris, where the movement originated in the 1920s, to England, the USA, Australia and elsewhere. In these locations, surrealism offered a sympathetic haven amid a climate of oppression to individuals whose sexuality did not conform to a heterosexual norm. It provided a cultural space where their identities and desires could be acknowledged and affirmed and, crucially, it supplied a visual vocabulary that could be re-inflected – bent, shall we say – to their purposes. A major accomplishment of these photographers and film-makers was to reformulate the surrealist concept of avant-gardism by making their own sexuality central to its definition.

SURREALIST INVERSIONS

The Secret Life of Salvador Dalí recounts an incident from the artist's childhood that positively brims with allegorical psychosexual meanings.[6] Dalí, a seriously indulged child, had received a gift from an uncle of an ermine cape, a gold sceptre and a crown from which hung a long wig. In Dalí's recounting of the tale, looking back as it were from the other side of his 1930s meeting with Lacan, he described a classic mirror stage encounter in which he stood before a full-length mirror naked apart from these regal accoutrements: 'I, a solitary child, a King' he writes – the diminutive Dalí embodying His Majesty the Ego and enacting the narcissism for which he would later be renowned. But that is not all. Dalí also described how he felt impelled to squeeze his genitals between his thighs so that he might appear like a girl.

Recently the concept of a gender masquerade, of gender as performance, has been mobilised in the service of a postmodern critique of theories of gender essentialism.[7] These theories, originating in the 1920s, have been viewed as a counterpart to avant-garde strategies of cross-dressing and 'gender bending' seen within and outside the surrealist circle among artists and photographers like Marcel Duchamp, Man Ray and Cahun.[8] The psychoanalytic theorisation of femininity and homosexuality in the 1920s built upon Freud's study of hysterical phantasies. One such phantasy described by Freud concerned a hysterical woman who simultaneously occupied male and female positions in the phantasy. The evident lability of gender identifications in the condition supported his thesis of inherent bisexuality. This derivation from hysteria can be seen in Joan Riviere's 1929 article, 'Womanliness as Masquerade', a key reference point for contemporary notions of gender as performance.[9] Riviere is concerned with intermediate types within a spectrum from the hetero- to the homo-sexual, women who are predominantly heterosexual but display certain characteristics of the opposite sex. According to the British psychoanalyst Ernest Jones, who published a paper 'The Early Development of Female Sexuality' in 1927, this is one of the vicissitudes of female development as certain women, while retaining an interest in men, set their hearts on being accepted by men as equals. 'To this group,' he writes, 'belongs the familiar type of women who ceaselessly complain of the unfairness of women's lot and their unjust ill-treatment by men.'[10] Translated into psychoanalytic terminology, these harridans and proto-feminists of the 1920s are prey to biting phantasies, Jones tells us, that 'gratify both the desire to obtain a penis by force and also the impulse to revenge themselves on the man by castrating them' Riviere who, as an intellectual woman, might easily have been lumped in this category herself, states: 'I shall attempt to show that women who wish for masculinity may put on a mask of womanliness to avert anxiety and retribution feared from men.'[11] Riviere reported the case of a woman who, after proficiently giving a lecture, would compensate by flirting in an exaggeratedly feminine way with her male colleagues. From this woman's masquerade of femaleness, Riviere took the radical step of extrapolating to the nature of gender in general.

> Is insincerity such a terrible thing? I think not. It is merely a method by which we can multiply our personalities.[12]

Oscar Wilde's witticism here is relevant to the photographers to be discussed in this chapter: Claude Cahun, Florence Henri, Cecil Beaton, and Pierre Molinier. Ironically, Henri, one of whose mirror self-portraits introduced Krauss's essay on the photographic conditions of surrealism, was never a member of the surrealist group. Krauss did not claim Henri was a surrealist, but the fact that she best exemplifies the features of doubling, reflection and so forth that Krauss took to be definitional of surrealist photography gives one pause for thought. Perhaps there is no such thing as surrealist photography, only photographs taken by surrealists.

The features that Krauss considered as defining surrealist photography are, I shall argue in the case of these artists, indices of their peripheral sexuality. It will come as no surprise that I consider their work in terms of performance, in particular in the case of Cahun and Molinier. In looking at their works together, the ubiquity of the mirror as a prop for the performance of their subjectivity becomes clear, as does the prevalence of formal tropes of reversal, inversion, doubling and multiplication. I shall posit a link between version (*vertere*, to turn) as a formal operation, produced with the aid of a mirror or by reversing or inverting a photographic negative, and sexual inversion. In his contribution to the 1998 book *Sexology in Culture: Labelling Bodies and Desires*, Jay Prosser usefully demonstrates that the term 'sexual invert', when it was first coined, had a more capacious meaning that encompassed transgenderism as well as homosexuality.[13] Conventional histories of homosexuality, Jay argues, have erased the figure of the transgendered subject. This more inclusive definition of inversion is germane especially with regard to Molinier.[14]

CLAUDE CAHUN

Claude Cahun (1894–1954) is a notable exception to the general neglect of sexuality in surrealist studies.[15] At the time of the 'L'Amour fou' photography exhibition in 1985, very little was known about her. In fact, Cahun, who eschewed a conventional feminine appearance and adopted a gender ambiguous pseudonym in place of her given name Lucy Schwob, was thought to be a man. The retrieval of her life and work has mostly occurred since then. Her commitment as a politically-engaged artist to the cause of homosexual liberation was shown by her support for the magazine *Inversions* when its editors were tried for obscenity in 1925. She was the translator of a book by Havelock Ellis, the author of the first medical study of sexual inversion in English in 1897. Cahun's insistent focus upon her self-image allows us to see her oeuvre as the expression of a historical struggle for recognition, the 'enunciation of a queer subjectivity', as art critic Abigail Solomon-Godeau aptly puts it.[16]

Narcissus plays a significant, though ambivalent, role in that process. The relation to a mirror, as in *Self-portrait* (1928, p.60) where her face is pressed right up against one, is a not infrequent trope in her photography. In other photographs, Cahun combines two or more images of herself using techniques of double exposure or montage, while elsewhere she reverses and/or inverts a negative and combines it with its pair. A manipulated photograph such as *Que me veux-tu?* (What do you want from me?, 1929) differs from the earlier *Self-portrait* in a number of respects, one being that the two images of herself are no longer distinguishable as model and copy. In addition to the theme of doubling, Cahun's close-cropped hair conveys a strongly-marked androgyny that could also link these images to the subject of Narcissus. The checkerboard pattern of her coat sets up an intriguing inter-textual dialogue with Man Ray's famous photograph of Duchamp dressed as his fictional alter-ego, Rrose Sélavy. Cahun's gender crossing is in the opposite direction. In 1930, Cahun wrote *Aveux non avenus* (Disavowals), a textual iteration of the themes in her photographic self-presentation. A whole section of the book is devoted to a discussion of self-love. Viewed alongside the photographs, as a gloss or commentary on them, *Aveux non avenus* can be seen as belonging to the ekphrastic tradition that is so relevant to Dalí's *Metamorphisis of Narcissus.*

Claude Cahun *Que me veux-tu?* (What do you want from me?), 1929

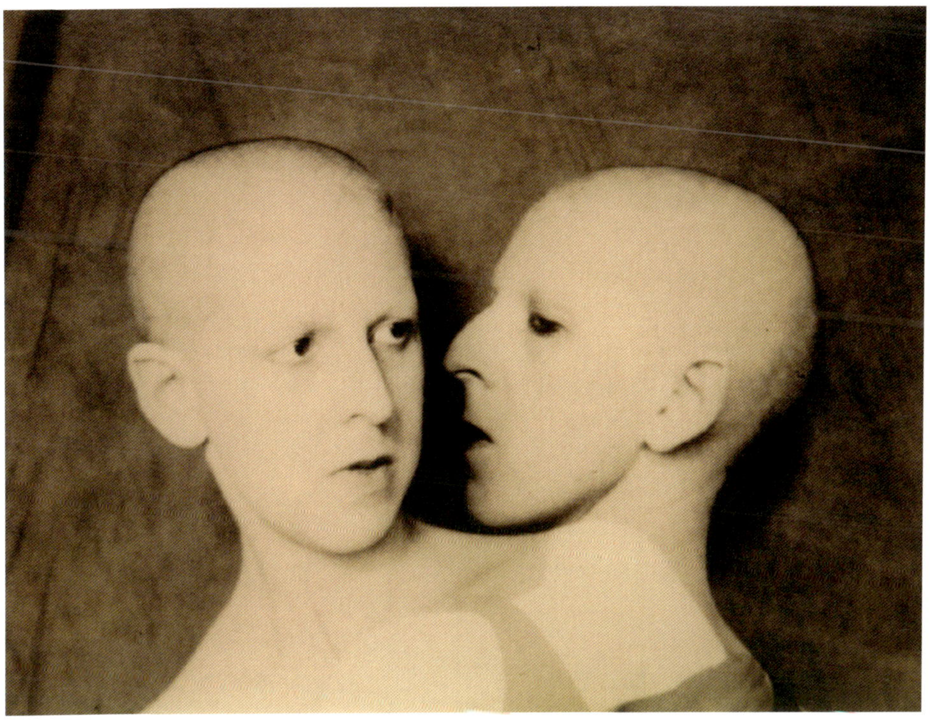

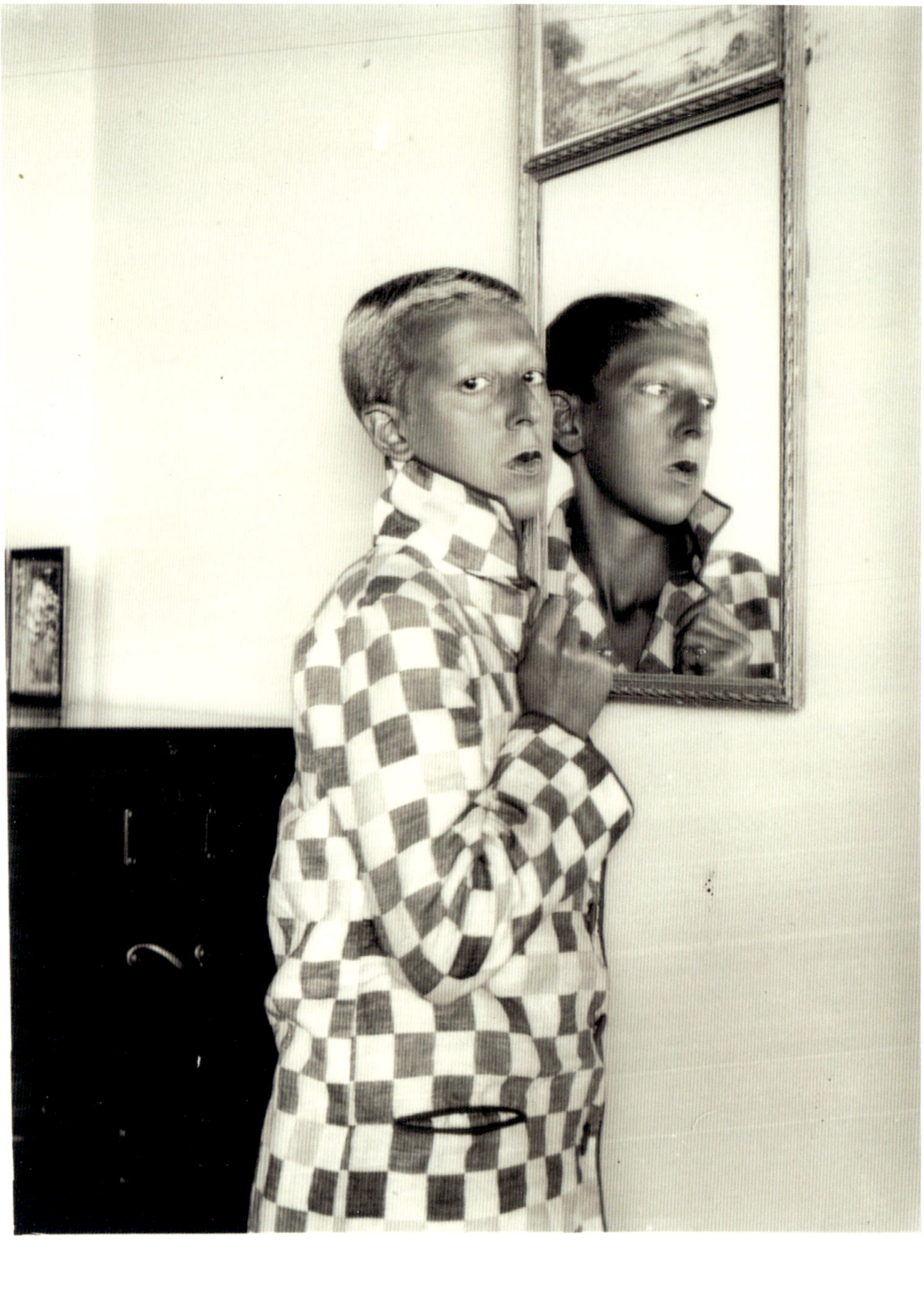

Claude Cahun *Self-portrait*, 1928

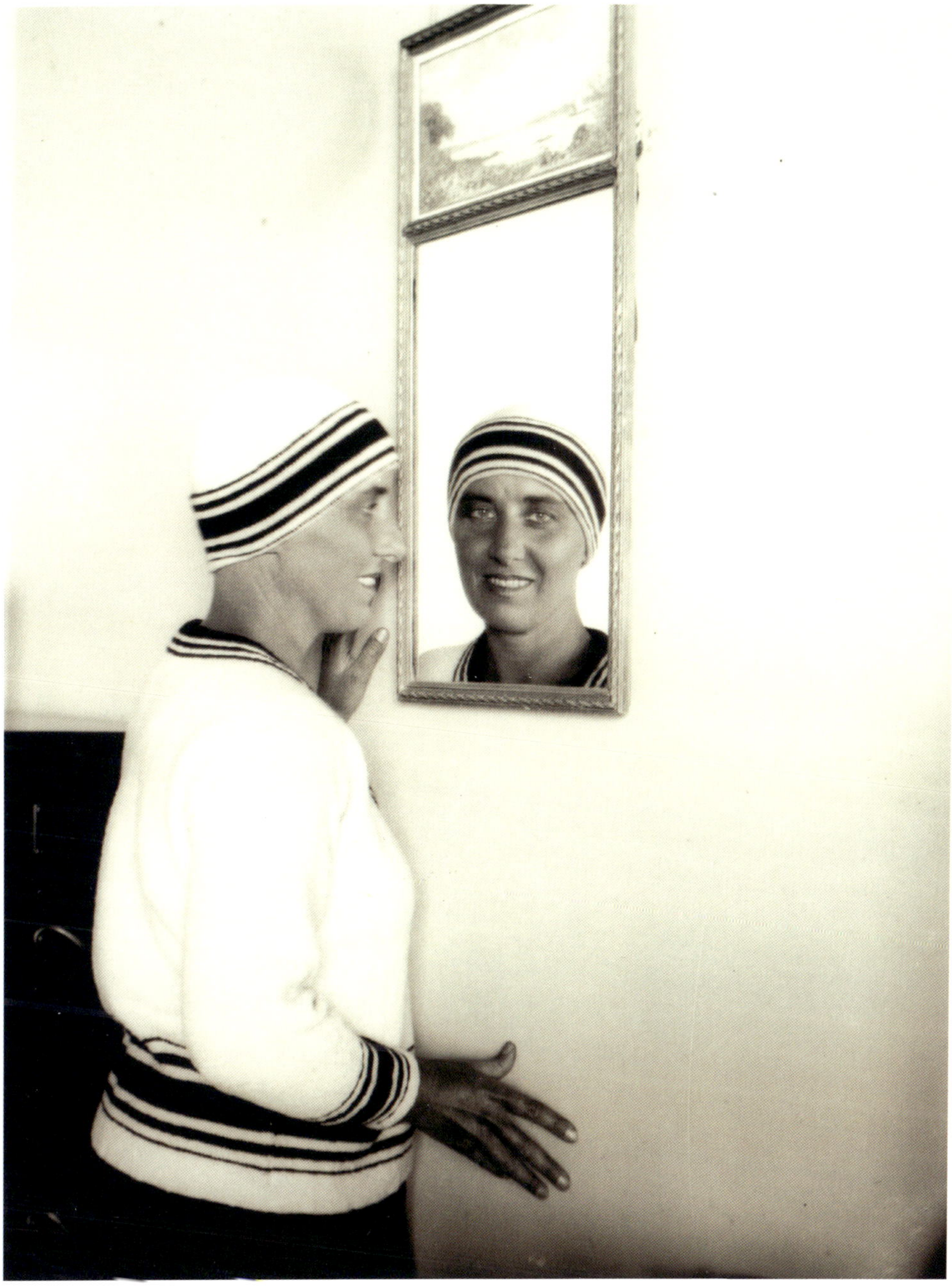

Claude Cahun *Suzanne Malherbe/Marcel Moore*, 1928

Cahun was steeped in symbolist literature. Her uncle was the eminent journalist and symbolist writer Marcel Schwob. Behind Cahun's musing on the Narcissus subject one can safely assume her knowledge of André Gide's *La Traité de Narcisse* (Treatise on Narcissus, 1891) and poems by a good many other *fin-de-siècle* authors. Craig Owens has argued that the mirror in surrealist photography is an index of self-reflexivity, which he compares with Gide's concept of the *en abyme*. Gide adopted the term from heraldry where it refers to the repetition in miniature of the whole form within one section of a heraldic shield.

Claude Cahun *Self-portrait*, c.1928

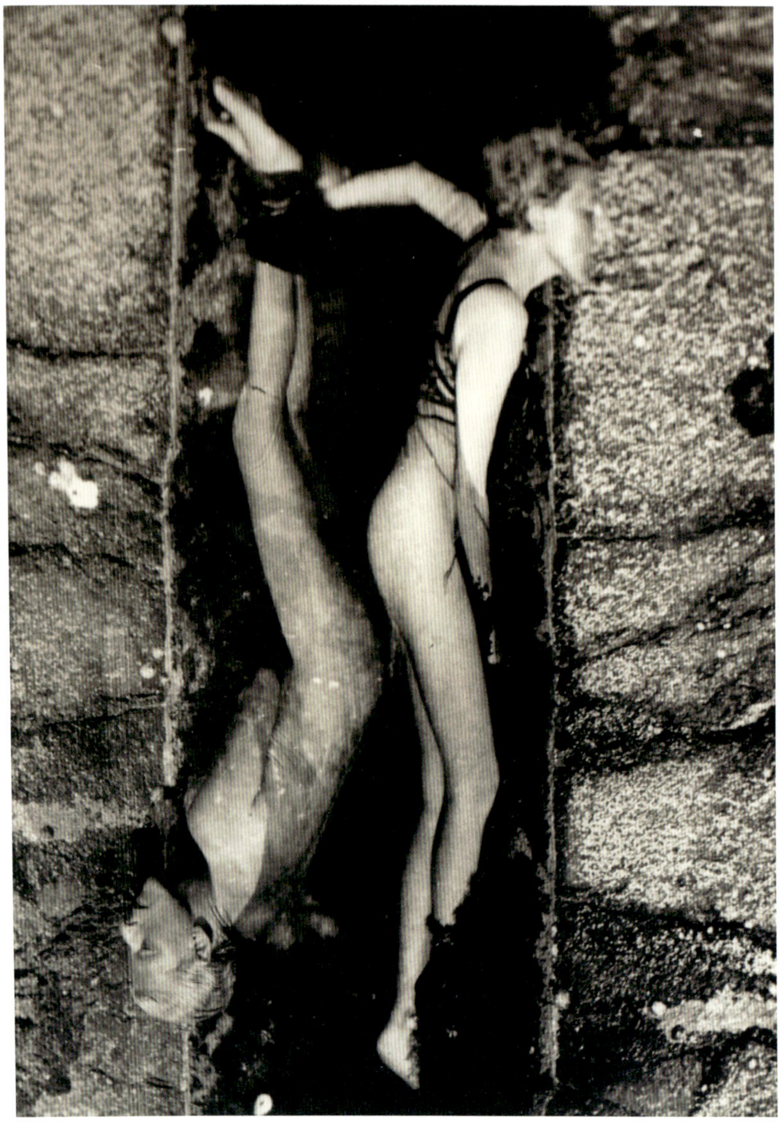

Owens states that: 'It [the mirror] tells us in a photograph what a photograph is – *en abyme*.'[17] Now, the *en abyme* is built into representations of the Narcissus myth. Philostratus, in the course of his ekphrasis, reflects that: 'The pool paints Narcissus and the painting represents both the pool and the whole story of Narcissus.' Owens cites a passage which reveals that Gide saw his own Narcissus treatise as exemplifying the device. In Cahun's case, it would surely be important to supplement this account, relevant for understanding the centrality of mirroring in her photography, with our recognition of sexuality as influencing any transaction with Gide's aesthetics.[18] In the wake of the championing of the myth by *fin-de-siècle* authors, namely Gide and Wilde, it seems that Narcissus became a rallying point for the articulation of a non-normative desire and sexuality.

That said, Cahun cannot but have been in two minds about Narcissus. Bram Dijkstra, in *Idols of Perversity* (1986), a study of the visual culture at the turn-of-the-century, documents a plethora of images of women gazing dreamily into mirrors or pools that reinforce a negative stereotype of femininity as 'imitative, circular, narcissistic'.[19] By actively turning her head away from the mirror, Cahun interrupts the 'uroboric circularity of self-love.' The psychoanalytic theorizing of homosexual desire, centred on Freud's study of Leonardo da Vinci which was made available to French readers in translation from 1927, would not have been especially congenial to her either. Freud claims that, owing to the circumstances of his early childhood, da Vinci had an excessively strong attachment to his mother which he was reluctant to give up. In adulthood he preserved the bond with his mother by identifying himself with her. 'He becomes a homosexual', Freud writes, since:

> the boys whom he now loves as he grows up are after all only substitutive figures and revivals of himself in childhood … He finds the objects of his love along the path of *narcissism*, as we say…[20]

It is an illusory modality of desire in which the desired other is actually oneself in the guise of another.[21] The homosexual, construed on the model of Narcissus, is thus deprived by psychoanalysis of an authentic love object. What is left for this tragic character to do but to kill himself? Kristeva writes: 'Narcissus kills himself because he realises that he loves a fake.'[22]

In *Aveux non avenus*, Cahun is careful to keep Narcissus, or at least the usual reading of the myth, at arm's length. She reproaches Narcissus, and his band of symbolist followers, for having been content with a merely virtual other:

> The death of Narcissus has always seemed totally incomprehensible to me. Only one explanation seems plausible: Narcissus did not love himself. He allowed himself to be deceived by an image. He didn't know how to go beyond appearances.

Art historians Tirza Latimer and Jennifer Shaw have each argued that Cahun escapes the 'narcissism of appearances' through her incorporation of an actual other, her partner Marcel Moore, into a structure of self-sameness.[23] These writers make the case that Moore participated as a collaborator in much of Cahun's work, and not just in the collages for *Aveux non avenus* in which her role is well-established. The term 'self-portrait' may be a misnomer for many of Cahun's pictures if this hypothesis turns out to be correct. Indeed, in the case of the self-portrait of Cahun in front of the mirror, if we imagine Moore standing behind the camera, perhaps even taking the shot, Cahun's forthright gaze in our direction becomes an exchange of looks with her partner and photographer.

Cahun's photographs attest to the mutability of her own appearance. In her hands, mirroring is a technique for multiplying the singular. She introduces a spacing within the subject through doubling – sometimes with the aid of a mirror, sometimes by double exposure – a spacing that opens onto an affirmative play with multiple, fictive selves. In her words, a play of masks behind masks repeated *ad infinitum*.[24] Turning back to Cahun's self-portrait with a mirror, let us consider it in terms of the modernist critic Michael Fried's polarity of 'absorption' versus 'theatricality'. Fried traces the dominance of an absorptive mode within a pictorial tradition that becomes modernist painting. Its correlate is the presence, or self-presence, of the modernist work of art, a state of reflexivity that is predicated on the suppression of theatre. With the eclipse of modernism, the features that Fried says must be rejected by authentic modernist art have become dominant once again. Ironically, that which Fried denounced under the umbrella term 'theatre' prophetically describes much of what has since become known as postmodern. Now, it is pretty evident that Cahun's performative art practice sides firmly with theatricality, a fact that adds to the contemporary relevance of her work. Her skewed glance in our direction breaches a modernist self-enclosure and simultaneously queers the image.

FLORENCE HENRI

Several recent studies have drawn attention to the presence of a community of expatriate women, who included writers Gertrude Stein, Alice Toklas, Djuna Barnes, and the photographer Berenice Abbott, in Paris during the interwar period.[25] The capital rivalled Berlin in offering these women from the United States and other countries greater artistic and personal freedom than they would have enjoyed at home. Florence Henri (1893–1982), who was born in the United States and raised in Europe, took up residence in Paris in the mid-1920s but continued to shuttle back and forth to Germany. Ambiguity continues to surround the subject of Henri's sexuality, about which she remained intensely private. While at various times she maintained friendships with the musician Michael von Zadora and art historian Carl Einstein, it seems that her most lasting relationship was with Margarete Schall, a fellow photographer. Henri initially trained as a painter in the studio of Fernand Léger and was later associated with the pro-abstract *Cercle et Carré* (Circle and Square) group. She took up photography following a period of study at the Bauhaus in 1926–27, where she attended lectures by Lázló Moholy-Nagy, a polemicist for experimental photography. During this time, Henri's painting evinced a late-Cubist idiom that edged toward geometric abstraction. Her abstract works employ overlapping transparent planes reflecting exposure to the work of Wassily Kandinsky and other Bauhaus artists. She is deservedly better known as an innovative photographer whose work was regularly shown in

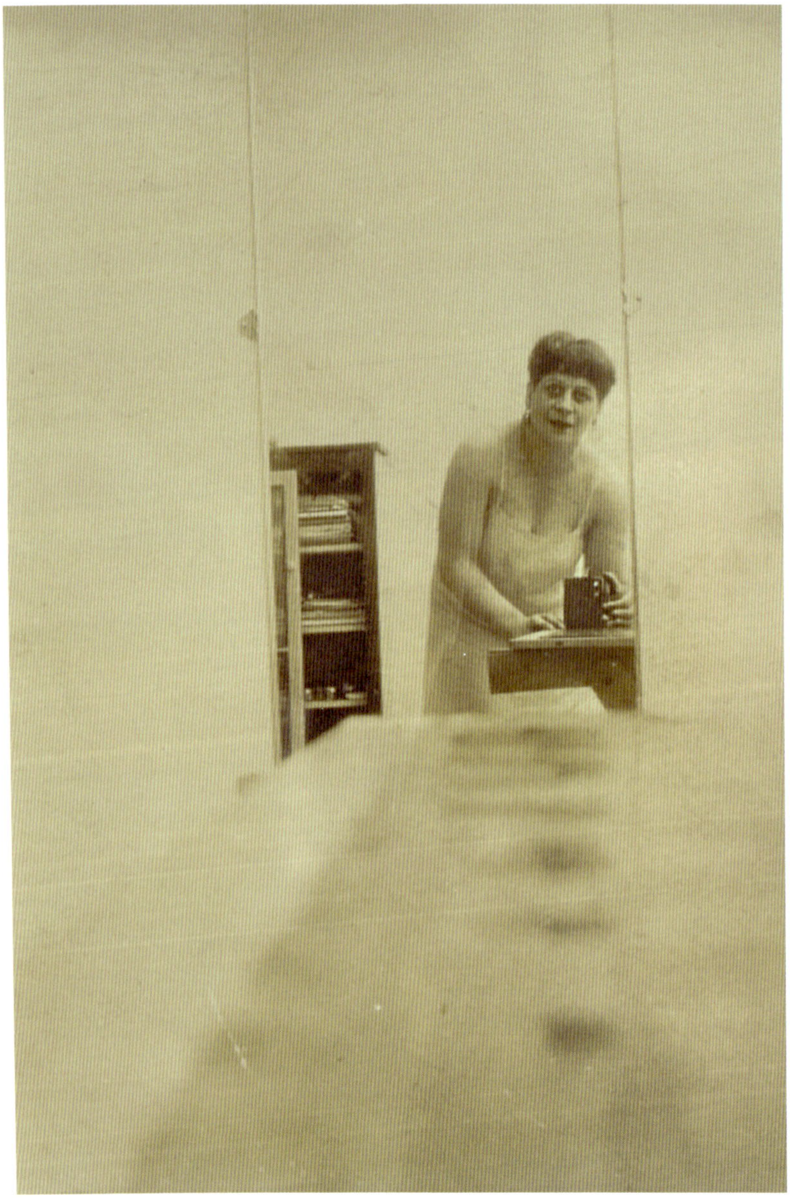

exhibitions of New Photography that toured Europe in those years including 'Fotografie der Gegenwart' (1928), 'Film und Foto' (1928) and 'Das Lichtbild' (1930). Her photographic oeuvre reflects the influence of Moholy-Nagy, who advocated the use of mirrors, and his wife Lucia. It covers a range of genres: portrait photographs of herself and other friends; the female nude; the city and modern life subjects including a series of shop windows. She is also known for still-life compositions that recall both Léger's use of close-ups and Purist 'type' objects in their obsession with repeated spherical forms (p.131). As noted, Henri was never associated with the surrealists, indeed the formalist *Cercle et Carré* group was notionally at loggerheads with surrealism, yet her work betrays commonalities that override these partisan allegiances. In 1928, shortly after taking up photography Henri produced an overtly experimental body of work where the essentially formal preoccupations of her teachers were deployed for a performative staging of identity. Mirrors are her invariable prop and the fracturing of space is similar to the kaleidoscopic effects of Léger's 1924 film *Ballet mécanique*. Henri takes great pains to absent herself from the field of the camera and only enters it at one step removed in the form of a mirror reflection. With the exception of a rare image showing her setting up a shot, the position of the camera doesn't coincide with Henri's own spatial coordinates, presenting the viewer with a conundrum as to where she really is. She plays a game of hide and seek which, as a visual strategy, we could conjecture is analogous to her obligatory discretion about her sexuality. In her comparison of Henri's 1928 *Autoportrait* (p.66) with Man Ray's *Homage to D.A.F. de Sade*, Krauss elicits a formal correspondence discerning in both images the superimposed form of a phallus. Without contradicting this reading, what I would rather draw attention to is the implied gender masquerade in Henri's 'ballsy' self-portrait. A male friend called Charly also appears in some of the photographs. In one such photograph, a *Double portrait* (1928, p.67), Margarete Schall and Charly peer into a wall-mounted mirror setting up competing axes of sameness and difference. One recognises the iconographic reference but is left wondering who is Echo and who is Narcissus here.

opposite: **Florence Henri** *Autoportrait*, 1927–28
below: **Florence Henri** *Double portrait*, 1927–28

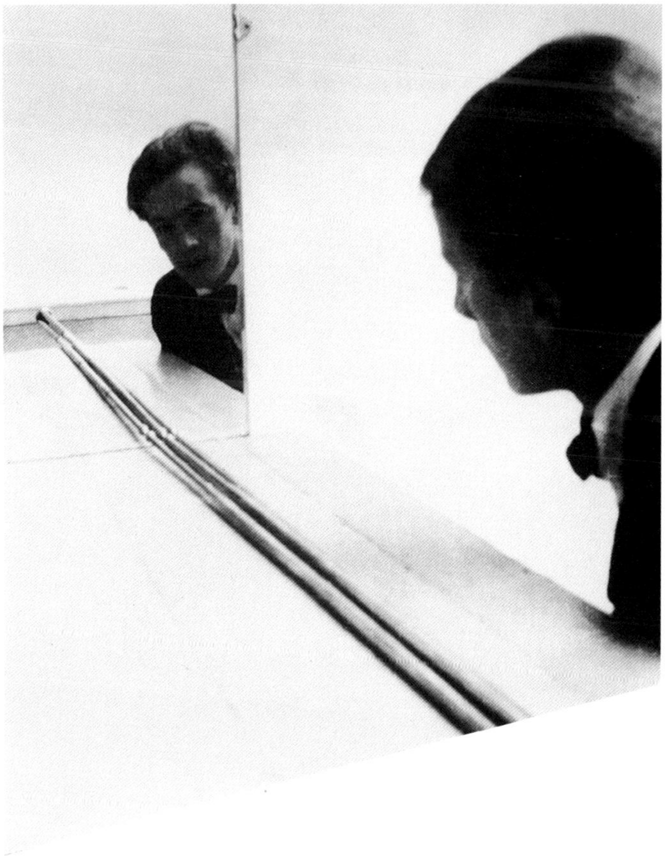

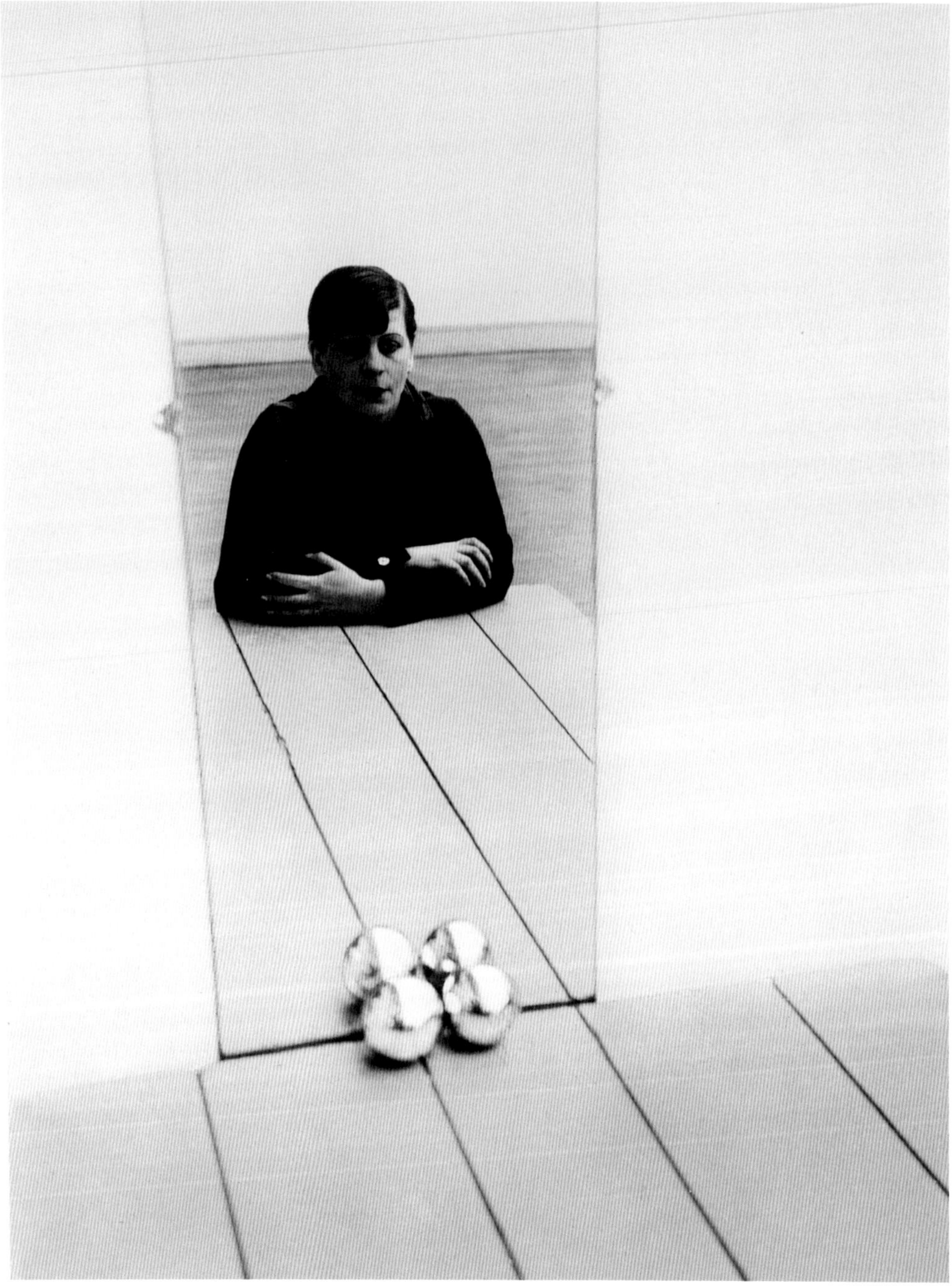

Florence Henri *Autoportrait*, 1928

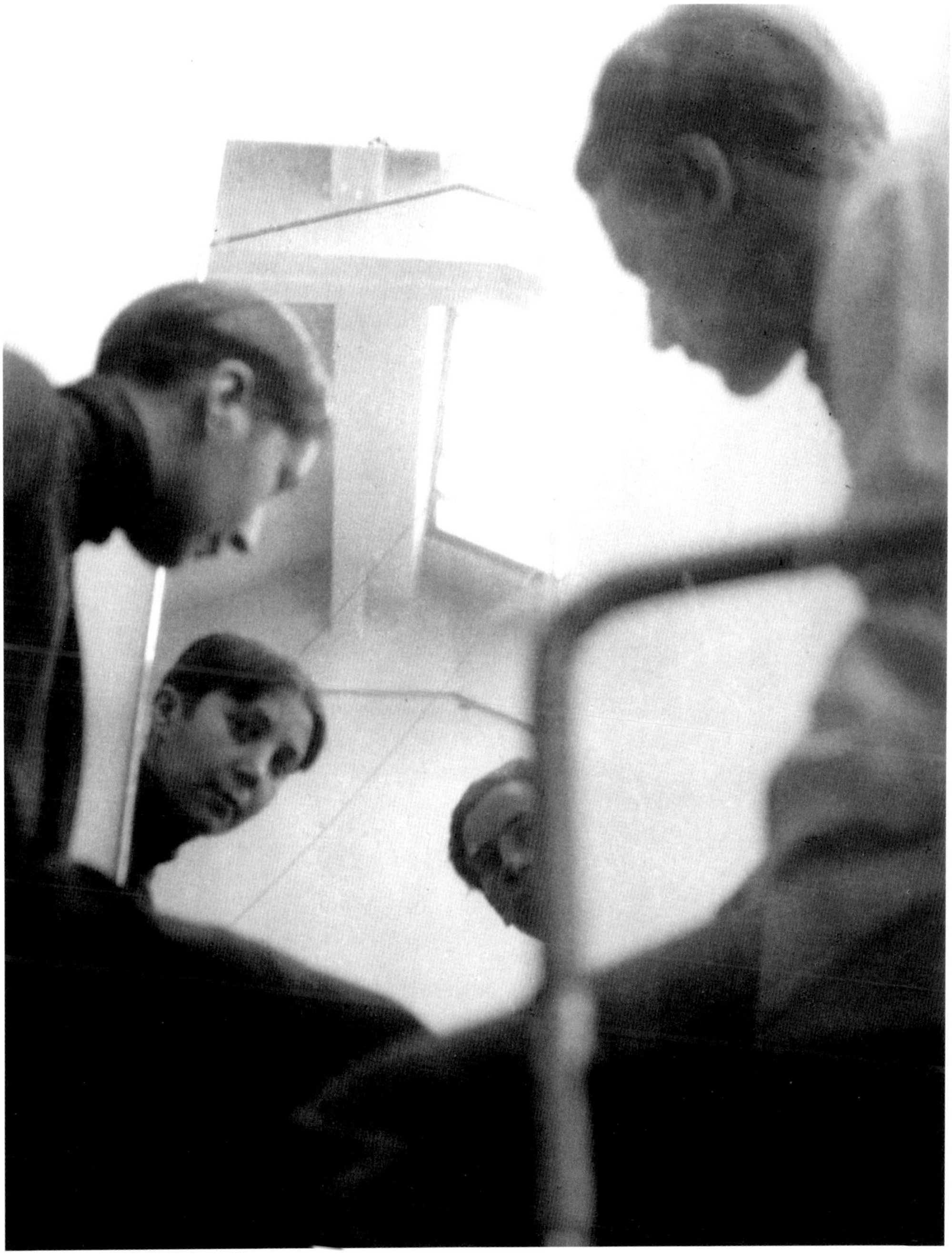

Florence Henri *Double portrait*, 1928

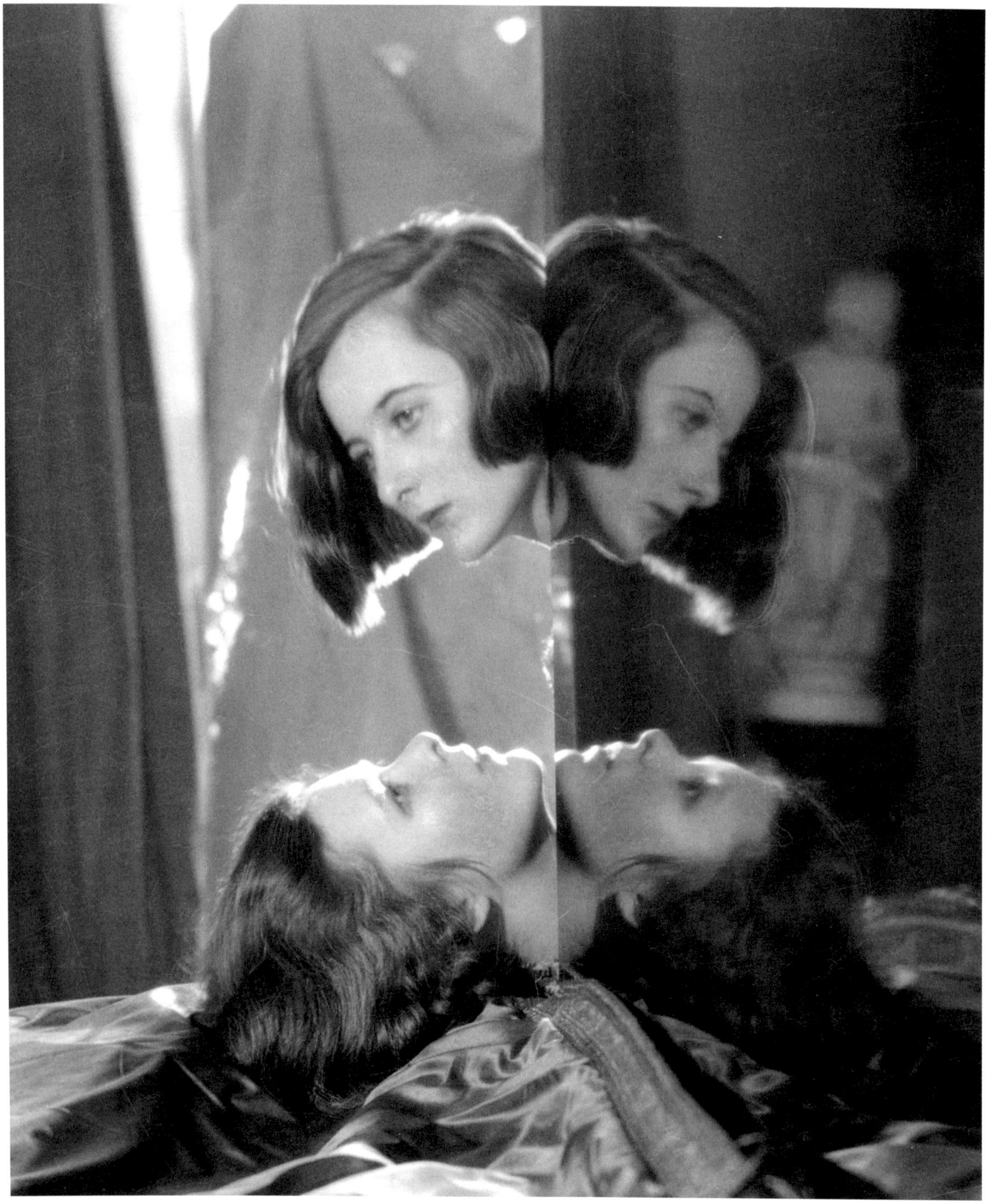

Cecil Beaton *Nancy and Baba Beaton*, c.1927

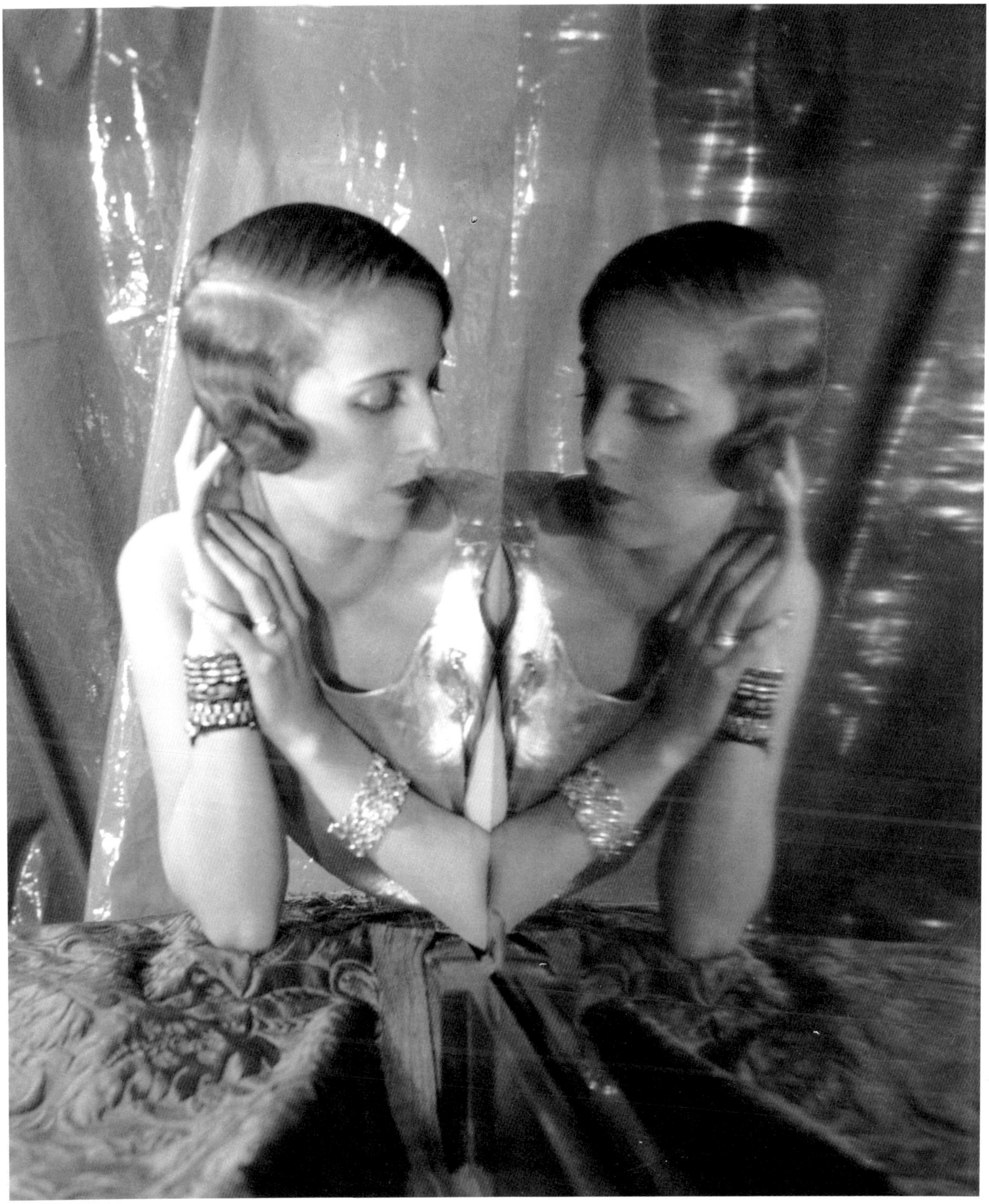

Cecil Beaton *Paula Gellibrand*, 1928

CECIL BEATON

Situating the work of English fashion photographer Cecil Beaton (1904–80) alongside the other photographers here, it is evident that many of the same photographic tropes are played out. Beaton's numerous portraits of the rich and famous abound with narcissistic tropes of mirror reflections, doubles and such like. It is a kind of signature style. Among his favourite subjects are his sisters Baba and Nancy, and he also had a penchant for photographing sets of twins.

'Beaton's beauties', in David Mellor's perfectly apt phrase, pay heed to the displacements and sublimations of polite high society.[26] A certain exceptionalism was, and still is, granted to gay men by the world of fashion; yet one has to understand Beaton's approach as respecting rather than challenging the limits of the milieu he inhabited. The extreme sensitivity of the issue of homosexuality for the English surrealists, with whom Beaton was more than peripherally involved, is shown in an extraordinary statement that punctuates an essay by Herbert Read at the time of the International Surrealist Exhibition at the New Burlington Galleries in London in 1936. Read was responding to J.B. Priestley's bigoted attack on the surrealists in a newspaper article. On the subject of homosexuality, Read insisted, 'the surrealists are not in the least prejudiced':

> They recognise that inversion is an abnormal condition due to a certain psychological or physiological predisposition for which the individual is in no way responsible. But they protest when such individuals form a sodality or freemasonry for the purpose of imposing their special ethos upon the social and intellectual life of the day. It leads in particular to an intolerance for women which is certainly no part of the surrealist creed.[27]

Their sexuality was undoubtedly a factor in what drew a considerable number of new adherents to surrealism in England, perhaps hopeful that it would be more sympathetic than it proved to be: John Banting, Cecil Beaton, Edward Burra and Francis Bacon (who was refused

below: **Cecil Beaton** *Gilbert and George*, 1974
opposite: **Cecil Beaton** *Gervase Griffiths, Reddish*, 1968

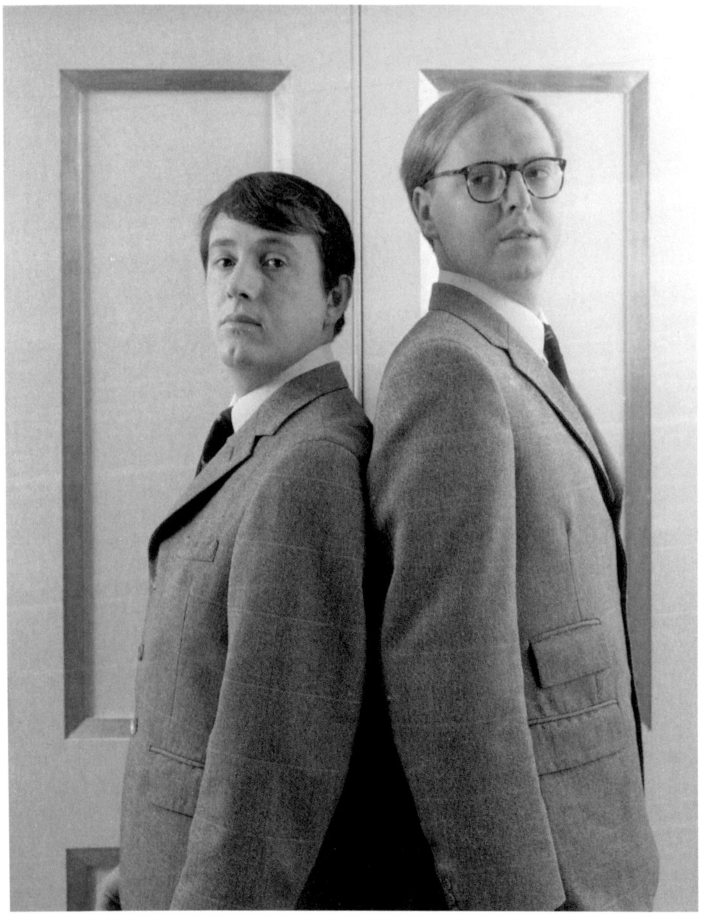

membership on these grounds) to name only the Bs. Without them the ranks of English surrealism would have been much thinner, but this issue is one about which, in deference to Breton, scholars of surrealism have chosen to remain tight-lipped.

One might conjecture that Beaton's female subjects give vent to a queer subjectivity by proxy. A photograph of Gilbert and George from 1974 belongs among Beaton's images of celebrities and, while hinting at the queer potential of the double, it is an exception within Beaton's photographic oeuvre that proves the rule. After a lifetime of displacing a narcissistic self-regard onto female subjects, Beaton in a late photo allows Narcissus, to speak in his own name. The 1968 image of a gangly Narcissus perched at the edge of an indoor pond was the culmination of a photoshoot in which a naked youth, Gervase Griffiths, was photographed frolicking in the gardens of Beaton's home, Reddish House. Ever since Wilhelm von Gloeden's late-nineteenth century postcard images of Sicilian boys, which this photograph recalls, homoerotic photography has taken cover under a classical myth.

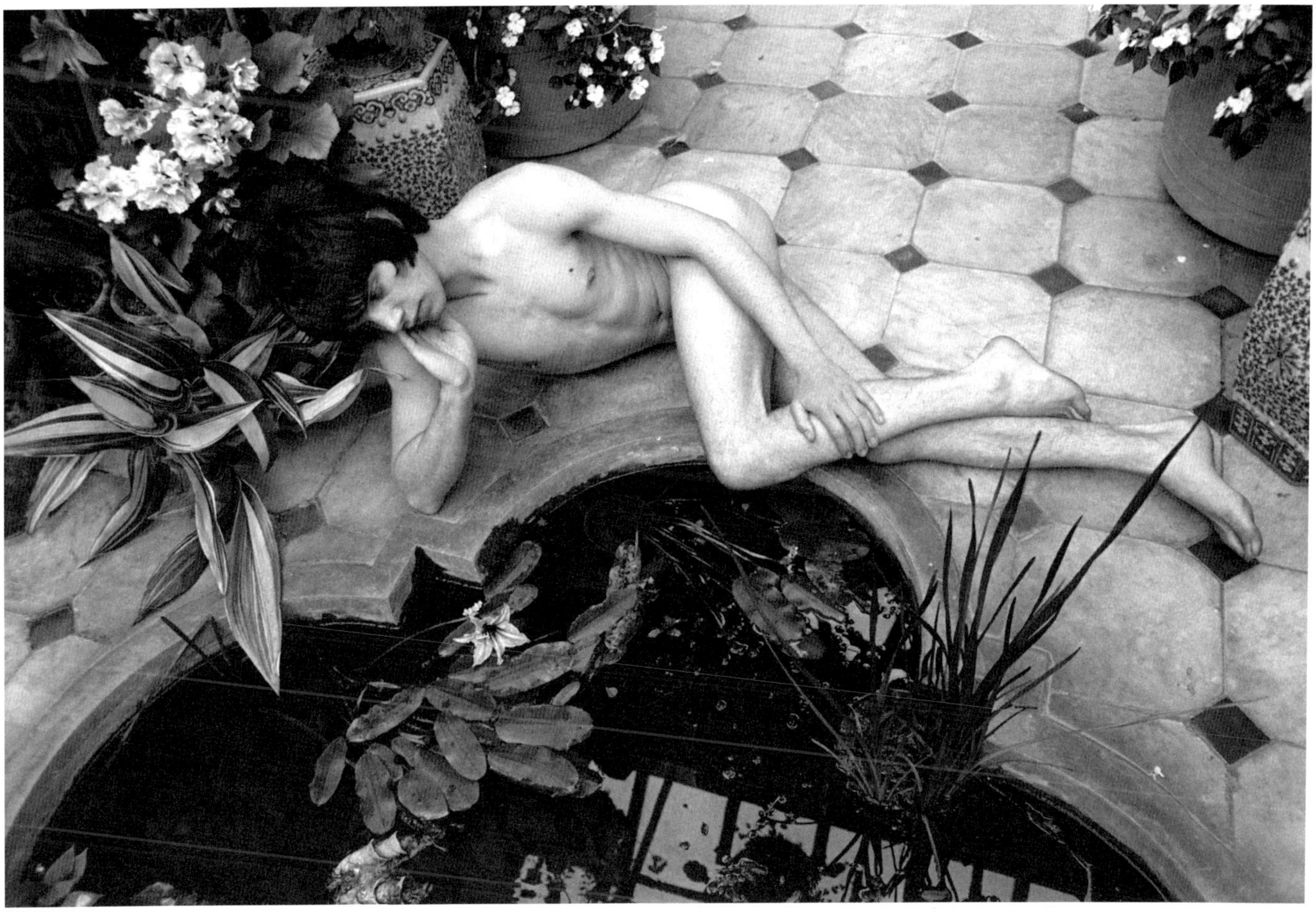

below: **Pierre Molinier** *Le lit et ses commodités* (The Bed and its Amenities), c.1968
opposite: **Pierre Molinier** *Pantomime narcisse* (Narcissus Pantomine), 1967

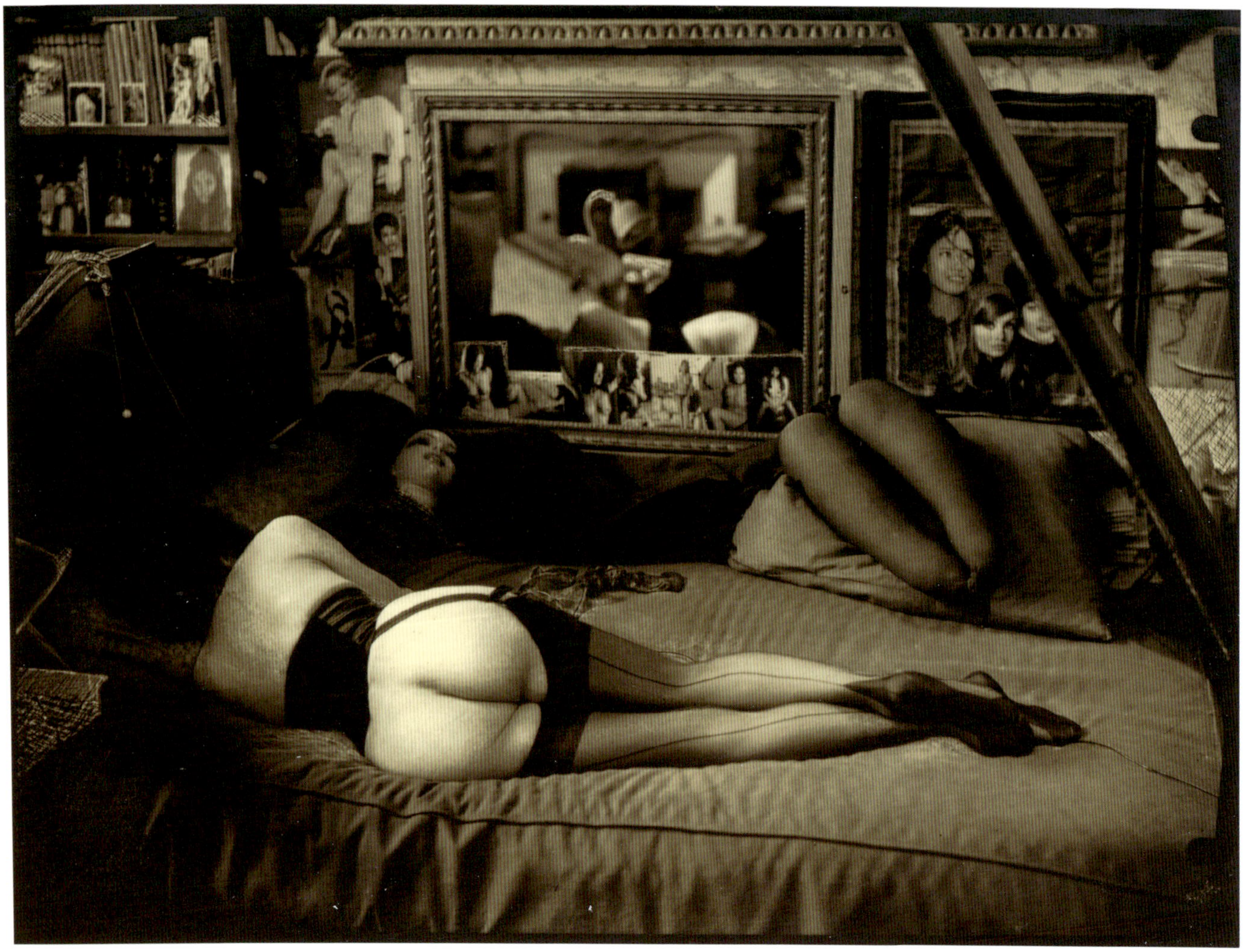

PIERRE MOLINIER

Adopting the title of one of his photographs, Pierre Molinier's (1900–76) oeuvre can be regarded as a 'Narcissus pantomime.' Its privileged terrain is autoeroticism. Once more, the mirror plays a crucial role in actualising Molinier's fantasy and providing a sort of externalised confirmation of it. A large double-sided psyche (a dressing mirror) that dominated the studio and another heavily framed mirror beside his bed were vital props for his photographic practice. The opening up of Molinier's archive reveals his extensive use of montage and his manipulation of negatives to build up in a gradual and stepwise fashion images that would then be re-photographed. He would often develop the same negative in recto and verso to create a mirror-like symmetry. The most surprising light is shed on multi-figure compositions that were built up in an additive fashion; in these images Molinier is the sole actor engaged in sexual couplings where he is at one and the same time playing male and female, active and passive, roles. Art historian Jean-Luc Mercié, who has studied the archive in some depth, remarks that 'photography embellishes, rejuvenates, and serves as an adjunct to narcissism.'[28]

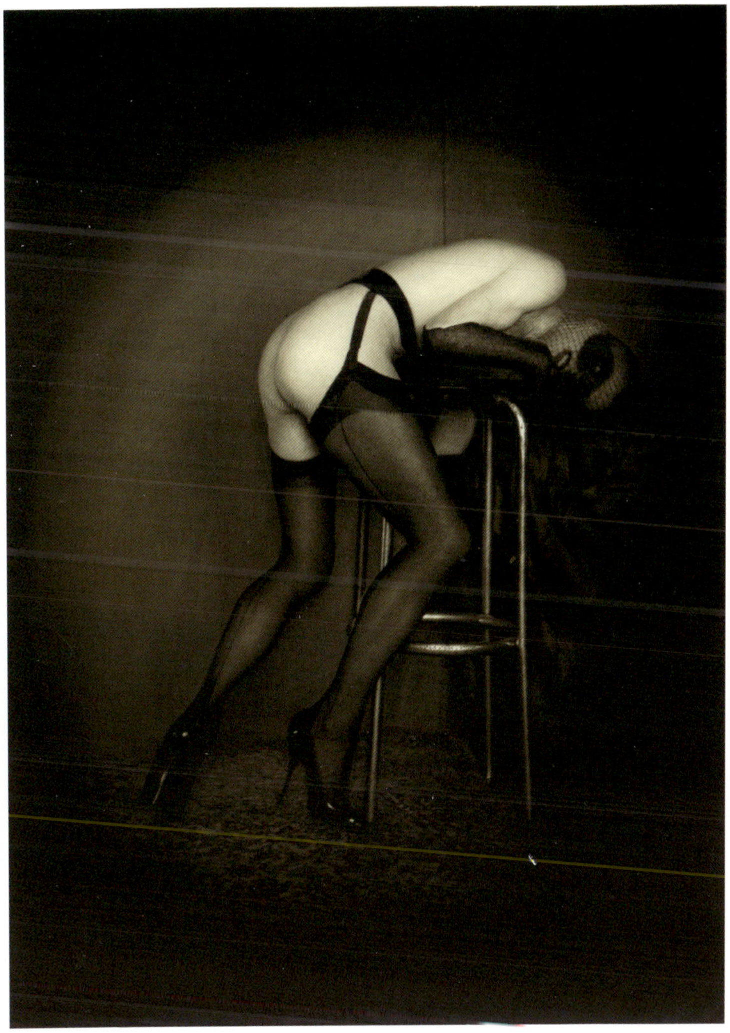

In spite of its normative assumptions, Janine Chasseguet-Smirgel's study of *Creativity and Perversion* (1985), can offer insights into the animating principles of Molinier's perverse universe.[29] Escaping the 'double bind' of gender difference is the pervert's fundamental goal, writes Chasseguet-Smirgel. The ease with which a photograph can reverse from positive to negative made it an ideal medium for Molinier's transvestism, enabling him to see himself as now a man, now a woman. In a similar way, the anus as a habitual focus for both Molinier's autoerotic pleasure and his camera lens, implies the elimination of sexual differences. Chasseguet-Smirgel refers to anality as the denial of not just maternal castration, but of the paternal phallus. That would seem to be the inference to be drawn from Molinier's 'éperon d'amour' (love spur) – a phallic spur attached to the back of his shoe with which he pleasures himself.

below: **Pierre Molinier** *Mes jambes* (My Legs), c.1967
opposite: **Pierre Molinier** *Luciano Castelli*, 1975

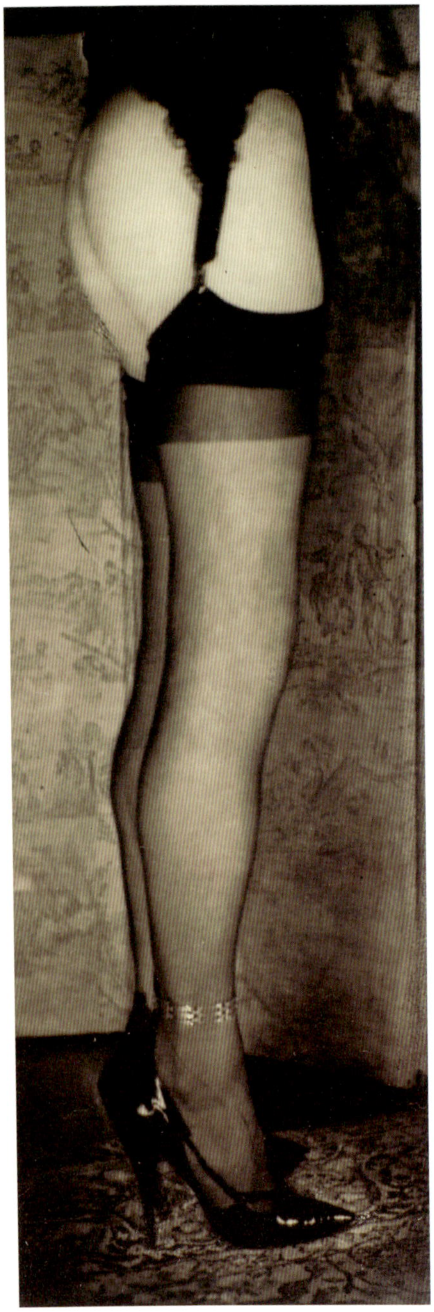

The pervert seeks to defy the Oedipal law and to overturn the authority of the father ('père-version'). Fetishism, a paradigmatic form of perversion, is literally a suspension of the Oedipal law. Molinier confessed a fascination for suspenders and stockings, for high-heeled shoes that tense the muscles, declaring: 'I don't approve at all of the new fashion for broad heels.' Another facet of Molinier's oeuvre that relates to perversion is his appetite for sacrilege. Sacrilege was very much the order of the day among the surviving surrealists such as Clovis Trouille, a defrocked priest and long-time member of the group, with whom Molinier was in contact with. 'Perversion is the equivalent of Devil religion,' writes Chasseguet-Smirgel.[30] She notes the anal attributes of the Devil and of those who consort with him, such as witches. The Devil is a rival to God the Father, a veritable negative of him. Molinier refashioned himself as a shaman in communion with Luciferian forces, apparently after reading Mircea Eliade's classic 1957 book *Sacred and Profane.* He produced an album of photomontages titled *Le Chaman et ses créatures* (The Shaman and his Creatures). Part of the appeal of shamans, one suspects, was their prerogative to switch gender, another link back to Narcissus as the epitome of androgyny.

There is a story yet to be told about the striking consonance of Molinier's late surrealism with the generation of the sexual revolution. A significant moment in this intergenerational dialogue was the publication of Xavière Gauthier's 1971 *Surréalisme et sexualité* (Surrealism and Sexuality). Gauthier had been inspired by Simone de Beauvoir to undertake a feminist critique of surrealism. Predictably, her book attracted an outraged response from the surrealist old guard, but it now seems highly prescient. A section analysed the surrealists' homophobia while at the same time cataloguing the perverse desires at play within surrealism. Her book is remarkably in accordance with present day taste in locating surrealism's most radical accomplishments in the perversity of Hans Bellmer and, especially, Molinier. This aspect of her project was not taken up, however, and her book was instead

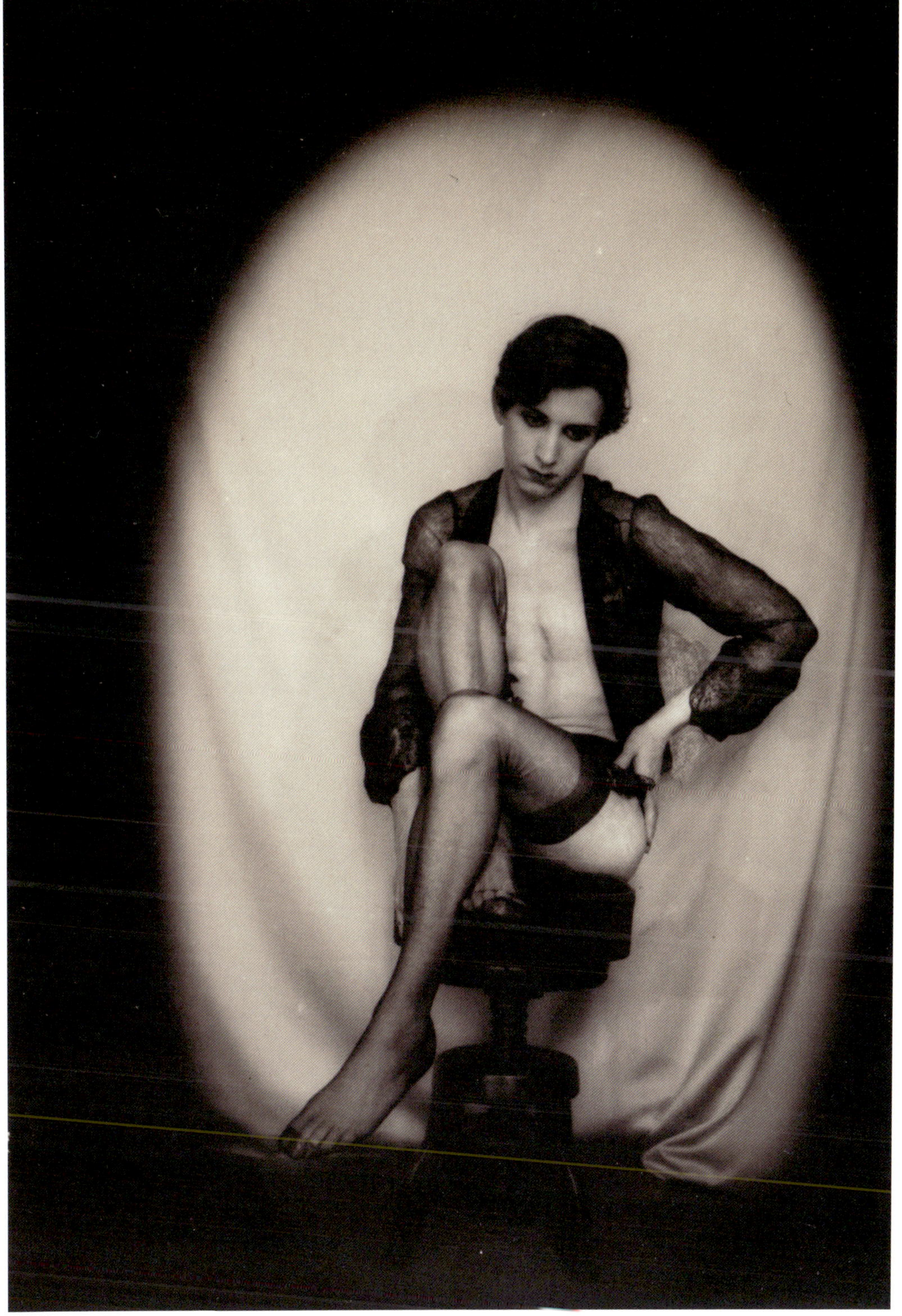

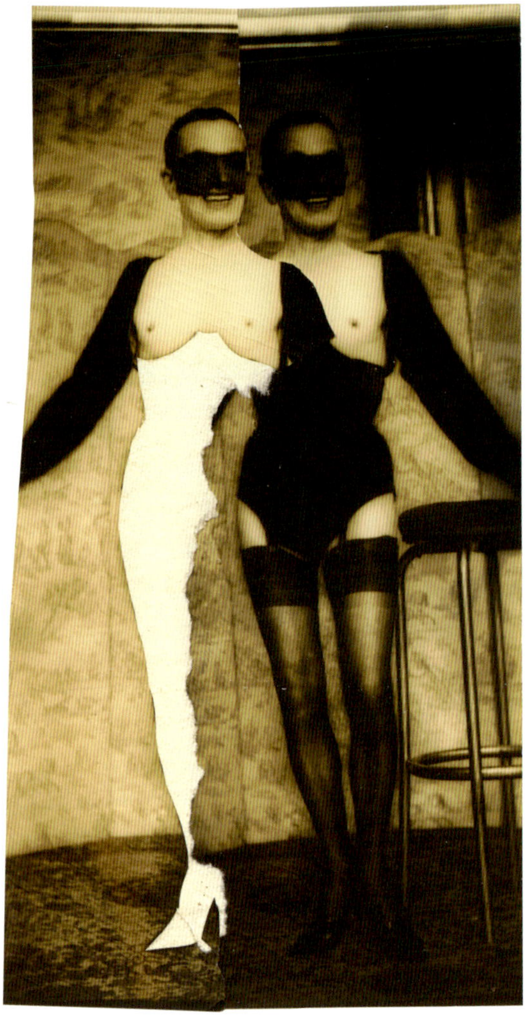

above: **Pierre Molinier** *Double autoportrait*, c.1965
opposite: **Françoise Molinier** Pierre Molinier's apartment photographed by his daughter the day after his suicide, 1976

a prompt to feminist approaches that have interrogated the surrealists' attitudes towards gender and their treatment of female artists, leaving aside considerations of sexuality for the most part. After the book's publication, Molinier wrote to Gauthier expressing his appreciation of what she had written about him. They struck up a correspondence that culminated in a visit by Gauthier and her companion, Jean Meunier, who eagerly took part in a photo-shoot with Molinier. Gauthier was just one of a roll call of visitors to Molinier's Bordeaux studio during his final decade. The group exhibition 'Transformer: Aspekte der Travestie' at Kunstmuseum Luzern in 1974, curated by Jean-Christophe Ammann, affords another illustration of how readily Molinier was assimilated to contemporary taste. Luciano Castelli, a young Swiss painter, was one of the other artists included in the show (p.75). He, too, began a passionate exchange of letters with the much older artist and eventually paid Molinier a visit in April 1975. 'Erosion of the double difference between the sexes and the generations is the pervert's objective', writes Chasseguet-Smirgel,[31] a comment that resonates with photographs of the androgynous Castelli cross-dressed and posed like a miraculously rejuvenated version of Molinier. The plainly narcissistic basis of Molinier's 'object choice' is a confirmation of Freud's analysis of da Vinci's life, that the boys who were the target of his affections in adult life were substitutes and revivals of himself in his own childhood.

Molinier's emulation of Narcissus was kept up until the end. A photograph of his studio taken by his daughter Françoise, the day after he committed suicide in 1976, shows the mirror before which the artist had 'shot' himself many times in the past. On this occasion, he did so with a loaded pistol. Since then, new generations of performance artists have drawn inspiration from his uniquely, transgressive oeuvre. The flowering of this trans-generational legacy ('legs' in French) has ensured Molinier a kind of immortality. He is in the process of becoming his own myth.

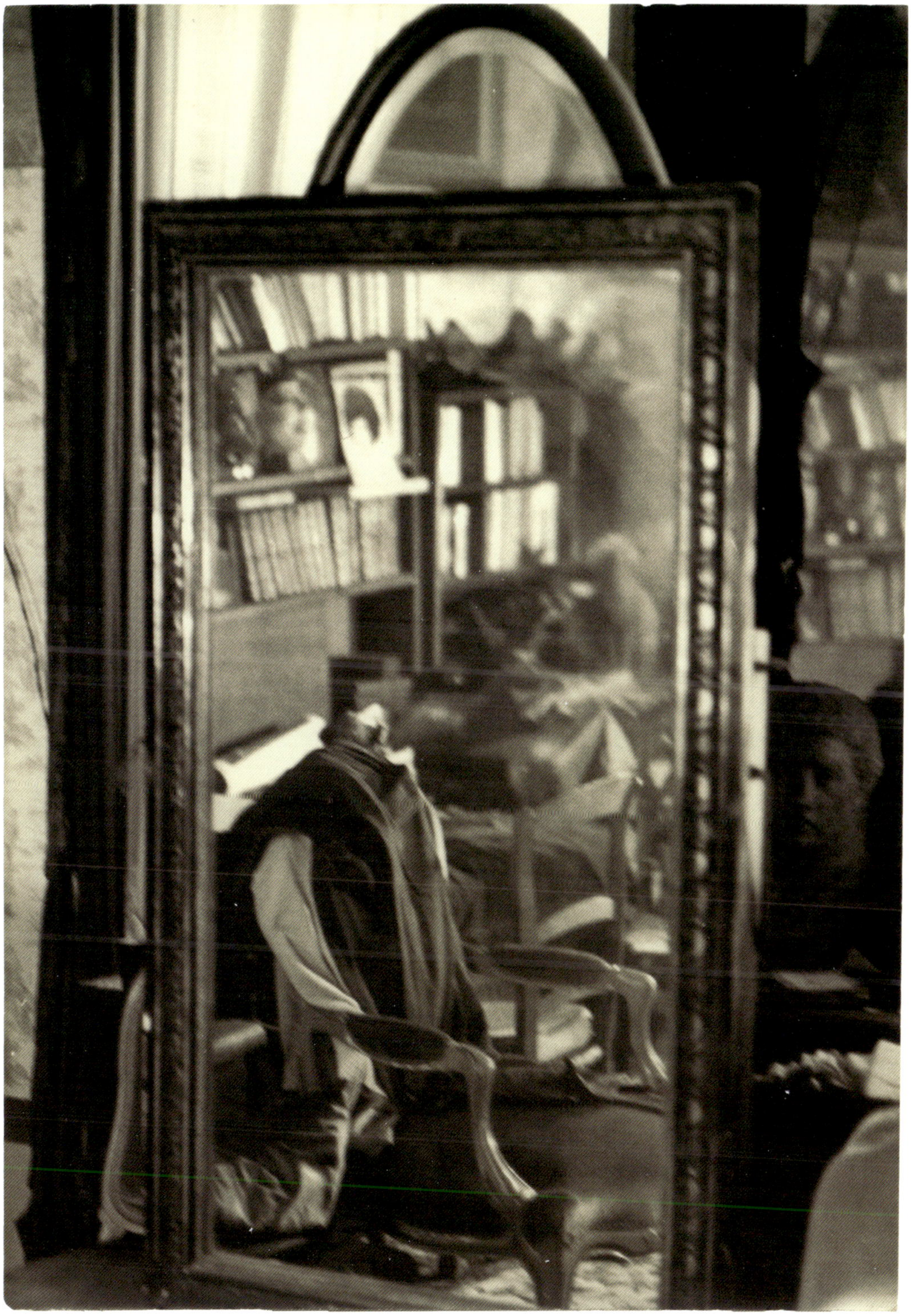

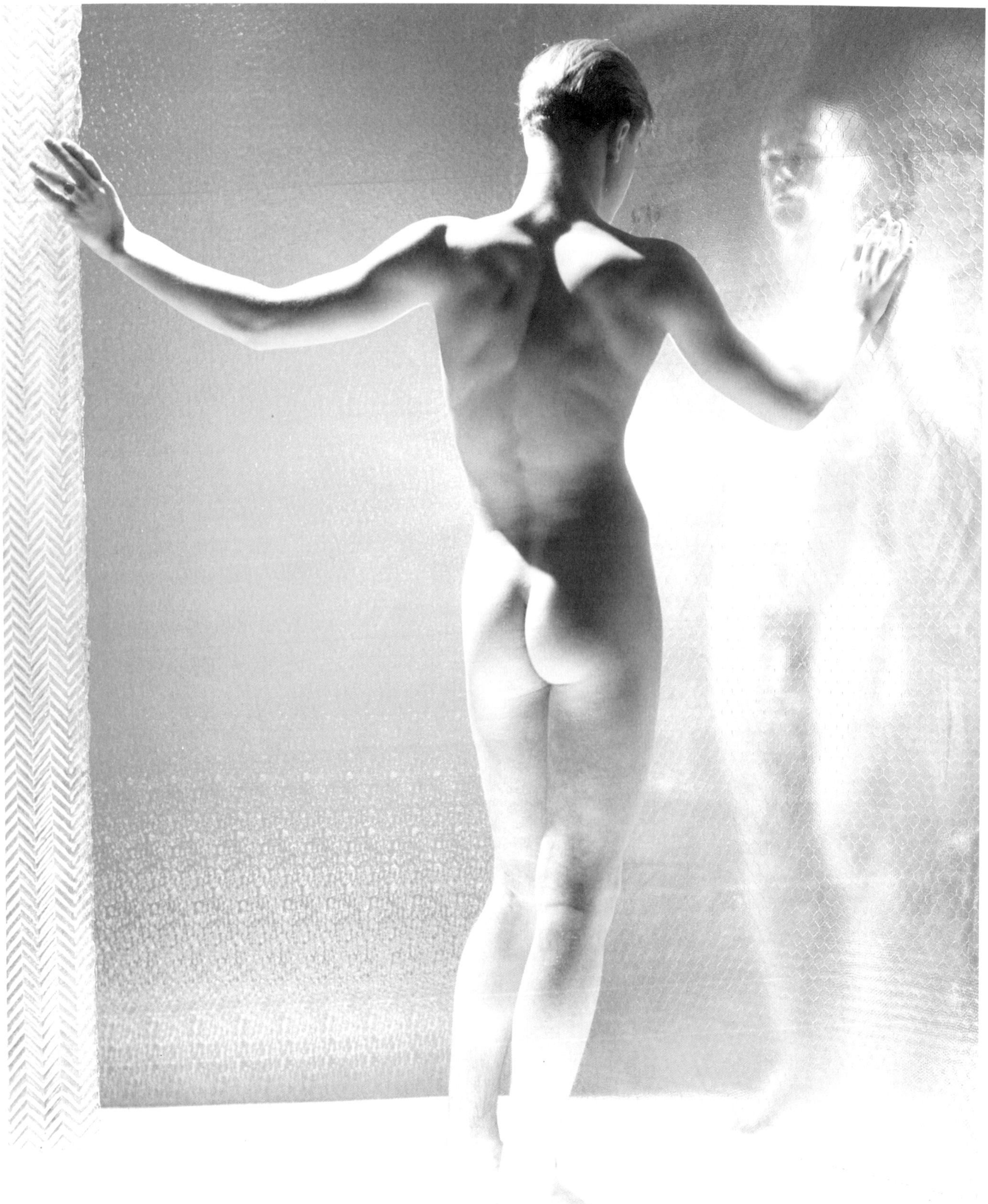

A NEW MYTH IN FORMATION

The usual view of surrealism is that it became progressively watered down and misunderstood as it moved away from Paris. Consideration of the issue of sexuality causes us to question the subordinate relation of periphery to centre, and to recognise that in the far-flung locations where surrealism was adopted in the 1930s and later the movement was opened up to new and unforeseen emancipatory agendas, as was the case with the circle of mostly gay writers and photographers associated with the New York-based surrealist magazine *View*. Charles Henri Ford (1913–2002) and Parker Tyler, co-editors of *View*, were the authors of what is deemed the first gay novel in the United States, *The Young and Evil* (1933).

Asked for his opinion about Breton in a late interview, Ford exclaimed: 'Puritan, puritan, puritan. His stupid anti-homosexuality ….'[32] Ford, who had spent several years in Paris in the later 1920s shows his awareness of the tensions caused by sexual politics in the Parisian avant garde and speaks of those who were openly or covertly gay within the French group. In the same interview, he also talks about his fondness for Dalí. One senses a power play between Breton in wartime exile from Europe, out of his element and vulnerable, and the young pretender. Ford was aware of Breton's antipathy for the film-maker Jean Cocteau (1889–1963), who had a close relationship with the poet Raymond Radiguet from 1918, yet that didn't prevent him from running an issue of *View* on Cocteau. Ford also published a book of Breton's poems, *Young Cherry Trees Secured Against Hares* (1946), with a cover image by Marcel Duchamp which, he notes mischievously 'made Breton into a drag queen – [Duchamp] stuck his face onto the Statue of Liberty.' Michael Taylor argues that Duchamp, as de facto leader of the surrealists in exile, acted as peacemaker and go-between: the artist with a female alter-ego was able to fraternise as easily with Ford as with *VVV*, a rival publication to which Breton lent his support.

In October 1943, *View* ran a 'Narcissus' special issue. It had a cover by André Masson, who had treated the Narcissus theme in paintings in 1934 and 1937 (see chapter 5).[33] The issue contained essays by Wallace Fowlie, a professor of French literature, as well as Ford and Parker Tyler. Narcissus was an

below: *View magazine*, vol. 3, no. 3, October 1943, 'Narcissus' special issue (cover by André Masson)
opposite: **George Platt Lynes** *Chester Nielson with J.Ogle (behind glass)*, 1937

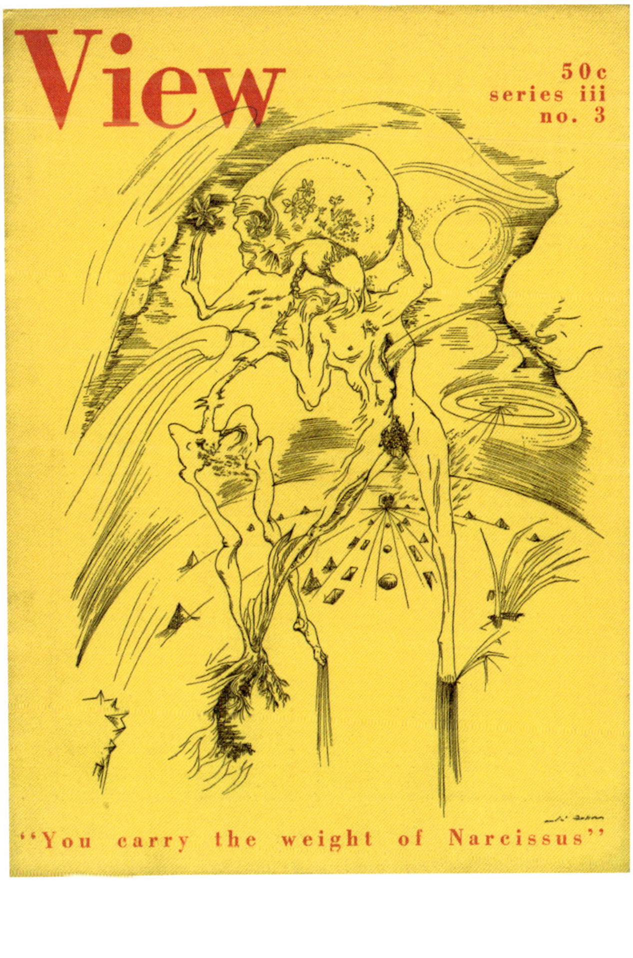

autobiographical myth for another contributor, the expatriate Greek surrealist Nicolas Calas. Narcissus is also a conspicuous theme in Tyler's film criticism and poetry: *The Granite Butterfly: A Poem in Nine Cantos* (1945) was notable for its explicit admission of the author's sexual orientation. The eighth canto of this ambitious, albeit somewhat opaque, blend of Freudian and other mythic topoi is dedicated to Narcissus.[34] One begins to suspect the presence of a Narcissus cult amongst this group of devotees.

The advocacy of Narcissus amounts to a dissident intervention into a debate about myth in late surrealism. In 1942, *VVV* ran an inquiry 'Concerning the Present-Day Relative Attraction of Various Creatures in Mythology and Legend.' The same year, Breton compiled an album 'On the Survival of Certain Myths and On Some Other Myths in Growth or Formation' that appeared as an insert in the catalogue of the 1942 'First Papers of Surrealism' exhibition in New York. The subject of myth in the present day was taken up again the same year in Breton's major essay on Max Ernst for *View*, subtitled 'a new myth in formation.' Some of the ideas being floated, such as Breton's myth of the 'grand transparents' – beings that lead a parallel existence shadowing occupants of the real world – are quite outlandish and foster an impression of surrealism's obsolescence as a cultural movement. Narcissus, maybe because of its Freudian currency, strikes one as a more viable contender. A preoccupation with myth at this moment drew Breton closer to Georges Bataille, the dissident surrealist writer. The loss of a mythic world-view, as a corollary to the decline of the sacred, was a salient theme in Bataille's writings in the late 1930s. He laments that 'the old house of myth appears no less deserted than the "picturesque" rubble of temples.'[35] The matter of the 'absence of myth' would continue to be debated by Breton in his contribution to the 1947 International Surrealist Exhibition in Paris. The hold exercised by Narcissus over the modern imagination stands out as a major counter-example to the dominant trend towards decline of myth in modernity.

The Narcissus theme is especially salient in the photography of George Platt Lynes (1907–55) who belonged to the *View* coterie. Platt Lynes's portrait of René Crevel (p.54), taken on a visit to Paris in 1928, slyly inserts between the subject and his reflected self another reflection, that of the photographer aiming his camera, a further example of the *en abyme* discussed earlier. The dual reflections of Crevel and Platt Lynes create an inter-subjective rapport, a sort of shared mythos, within the space of the photograph. A later photograph by Platt Lynes of two friends from 1937 poses one of them behind a frosted pane of glass in such a way that at first sight the one appears to be a reflection of the other (p.78). This is Narcissus with Narcissus, to borrow Cahun's expression.

The Narcissus myth stages an erotics of looking at a beautiful male body – a structure of viewing, and of visual seduction, that is replicated by the male or female beholder of an artwork depicting the theme. This renders the subject a threat to hetero-normative codes of behaviour. The addition of Echo is one of the means whereby artists have sought to allay the danger: the male viewer is permitted to see Narcissus as desirable, but through her eyes, which preserves a heterosexual structure of desire. Charles Henri Ford's self-portrait as Narcissus (c.1937) plays with these codes of viewing.

Artists treating the theme of Venus at her toilet, such as Velázquez in the *Rokeby Venus*, play a trick with mirrors. When we look at such an image we tend to think that the female subject is looking at her own reflection, as the theme of Narcissus and its adaptation to representations of female vanity would seem to imply. In fact, a sleight of hand is involved. The swivelling of the mirror, which allows us a privileged view of her face, means that Venus would not be able to see herself but would see us instead, the 'hidden' viewer and interloper into her boudoir. Whether artists do this deliberately, to create an interaction with the beholder, or whether it is done inadvertently, is a matter for conjecture.[36] What we can say, however, is that Ford gives the mirror an extra twist in his self-portrait as Narcissus. Drawing upon a pictorial iconography that

Charles Henri Ford *Narcissus*, c.1937

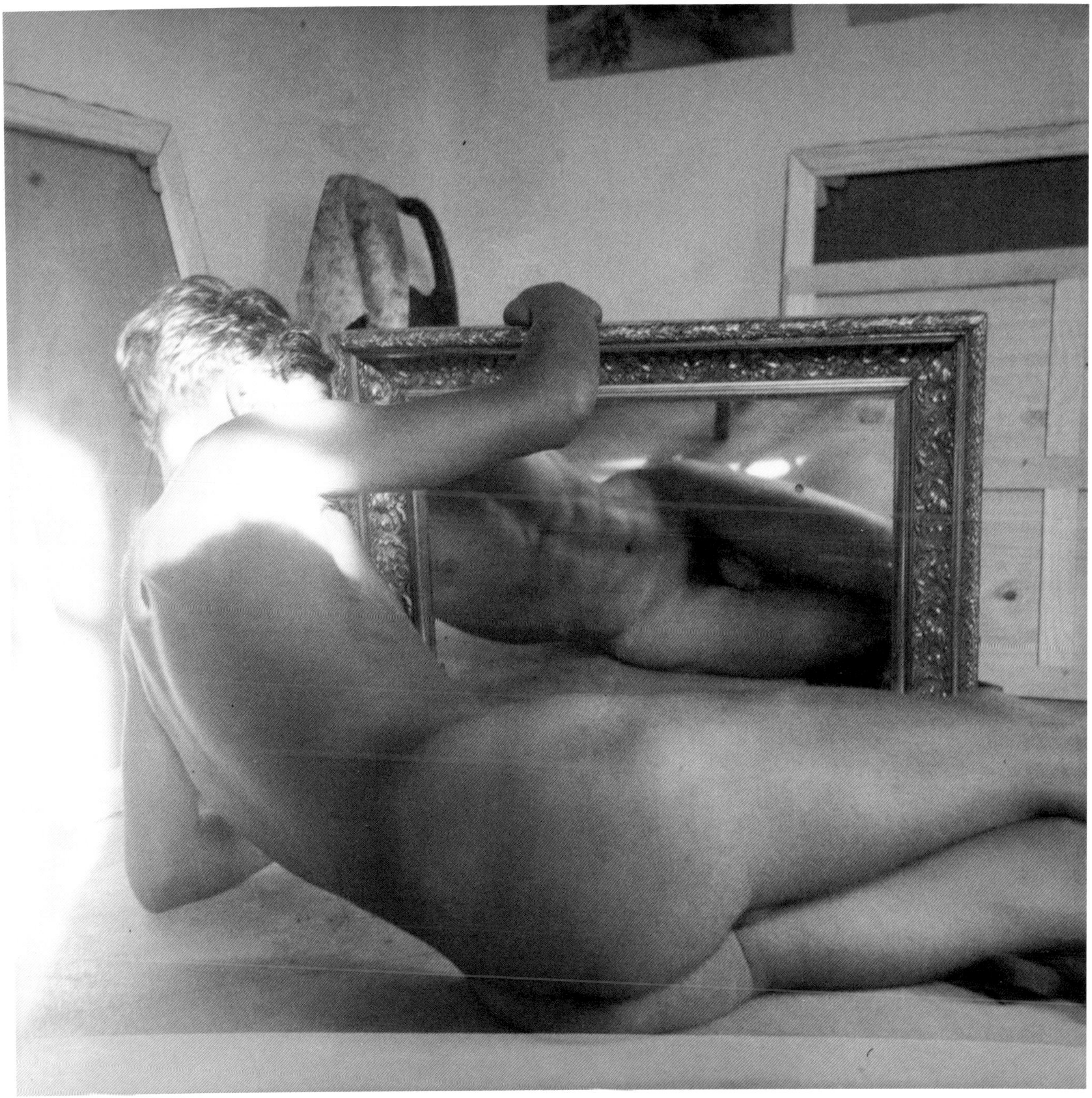

symbolises vanity (female narcissism, in other words) Ford positions himself as the putative object of a desiring male gaze. There's a playful subversion at stake in this deflection of a painterly stratagem familiar from the tradition of Western high painting by a lowly photograph. The presumptive male viewer finds himself lured in and led astray by Ford's gender boundary-crossing. Whether straight or gay, one's gaze is queered. The frisson Ford proposes to the viewer is like that of seeing the Roman marble sculpture of the sleeping Borghese Hermaphroditus in the Louvre. One is lulled into thinking that the figure lying prone on a mattress is yet another eroticised female nude, until one moves around to the other side and makes the surprised discovery of male genitalia. The viewer is caught out by Ford in a similar way.

By contrast with the arch and agile humour of Ford, Platt Lynes's beefcake nudes can appear peculiarly graceless. The companions who shed their clothes to pose for him have perfectly toned and gym-fit bodies, but somewhere along the way the erotic in the homoerotic is lost. One wonders what Alfred Kinsey, who acquired a tranche of these images in connection with an unrealised study of homosexual artists, made of them. During the period, there was a fast-growing market for magazines that pandered to a gay audience under the guise of a celebration of physical culture. Platt Lynes's photos are the high art tip of this iceberg. A common ploy of such photography, both the high art and mass culture varieties, is to supply the figure with classical garb, a sort of fig leaf which, without necessarily covering over the nudity, sanctions it by referencing classical Greece. This game of cat and mouse with the censor may be one practical reason for the recruitment of myth and of Narcissus in particular. One can point to numerous Platt Lynes equivalents in Europe, such as the German Herbert List and the Frenchman Raymond Voinquel. Voinquel took some photographs during the Occupation of a young man propping up a birch beside a pond to illustrate Paul Valéry's *Le Narcisse* in 1940 that are surprising in their homoerotic appeal.

Ford and Platt Lynes had none of Breton's animosity to Cocteau. In fact, Cocteau was an important role model for them. They took very seriously his conception of the artist or film-maker as someone who turns everything he touches into poetry. It was a time, Ford recalls, when one could use the word poet without blushing. The Narcissus theme crops up everywhere in Cocteau's films, comprising a personal myth on a par with the importance of Orpheus to the film-maker. As James S. Williams, an astute commentator on Cocteau's films, notes of the 1930 *Le Sang d'un Poète* (The Blood of a Poet) – the first part of Cocteau's 'Orphic Trilogy' which is followed by *Orphée* (Orpheus) in 1950 and *Le Testament d'Orphée* (The Testament of Orpheus) in 1960 – the two myths are often merged: 'The film asks to be read as a collage of styles and influences, from its blending of the Orpheus and Narcissus myth in the figure of the poet who drowns in his own image.'

The myth, as recounted in Ovid's *Metamorphoses*, tells the story of Orpheus, the greatest of all the musicians, who had such skill that he could charm any living thing. He fell in love with the nymph Eurydice, who tragically died. Bereft, Orpheus follows Eurydice to the underworld where his music persuades Hades and Persephone, the King and Queen of the underworld, to allow Eurydice to follow him back to earth, but only on the condition that Orpheus doesn't look back during the return journey. Orpheus tragically fails and in looking back loses Eurydice forever. Although this is a story of heterosexual love, at this point Ovid's telling of the myth states that Orpheus, due to his sadness, shrinks thereafter from the love of women preferring instead 'to centre his affections on boys of tender years, and to enjoy the brief spring and early flowering of their youth'.[37] Like Narcissus he spurns the attention of women 'many [of whom] were fired with a desire to marry the poet'.

In Cocteau's *Orphée* the myth is set in contemporary Paris and as in the myth, Orphée (Jean Marais) follows his wife Eurydice (Maria Déa) into the underworld after her tragic death. However, in Cocteau's retelling Orphée escapes the underworld with his wife and they are able to continue their life together. The Narcissus myth is also explicitly evoked in a scene from the film in which Orphée is reflected in a pool of water (p.84), and is also referenced in the fact that Orphée descends to the underworld through a mirror. As we have seen, Cocteau was anathema to Breton and kept aloof from the surrealist group. Nonetheless, Cocteau was a key source of inspiration

Jean Cocteau still from *Orphée*, 1950

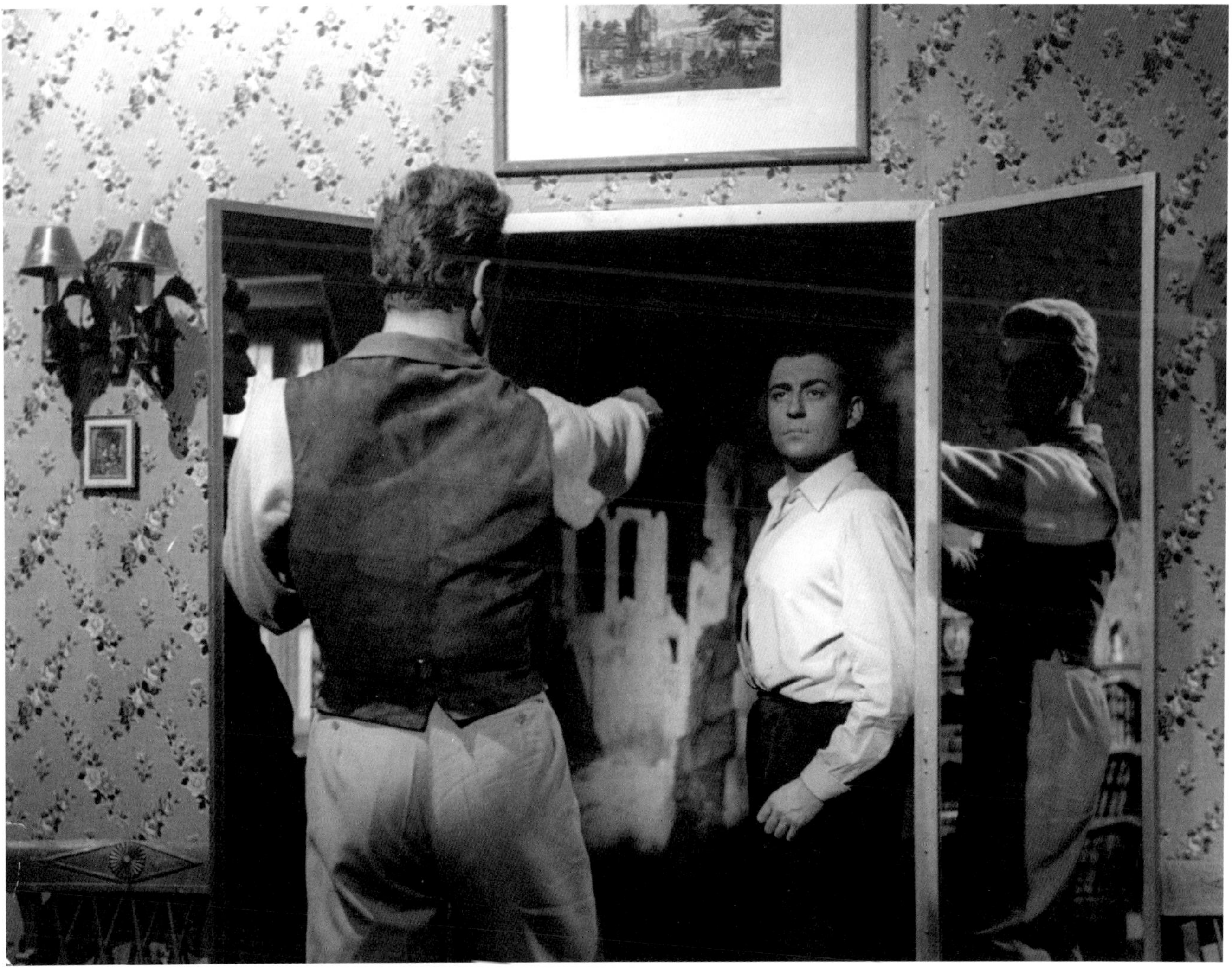

for many later figures, especially in the United States, who claimed an allegiance to surrealism though him.

Cocteau was indeed a major influence upon the writer and playwright Jean Genet's only ballet, *'Adame Miroir* (1948), which makes use of a hall of mirrors in a sumptuous palace as a dream-like *mise-en-scène* exploring themes of the self and its doubles. A contemporary reviewer described the action thus:

> At the beginning, Roland Petit … does a solo, Massine-like, full of zest, cap in hand. The two sailors, one standing up, the other lying down, go through identical movements, and this gives the strange illusion of a real figure and its reflection. The sailors link hands by a rotating movement [to] give the impression of a slow-moving wheel so that the picture appears to be projected from a mirror above them. Suddenly, a hooded figure breaks in on the sailors' dual dance … He separates the sailors and starts shadowing one … The three figures are then drawn irresistibly together … With brutal suddenness … the hooded Death figure … stabs the sailor to death and by a quick movement, discarding his cloak, he himself appears to be a reflection of the sailor. Then he … slinks down the gallery of mirrors and fades out.[38]

The idea for the ballet came to Genet after he saw a palace of mirrors in a fair at Montmartre. As Genet explained, the title began as the preposterously camp 'Madame Miroir' but pronounced with a working-class accent it sounded more like 'adame' – a word in which,

below: **Jean Cocteau** still from *Orphée*, 1950
opposite: **Willard Maas** stills from *Narcissus*, 1956

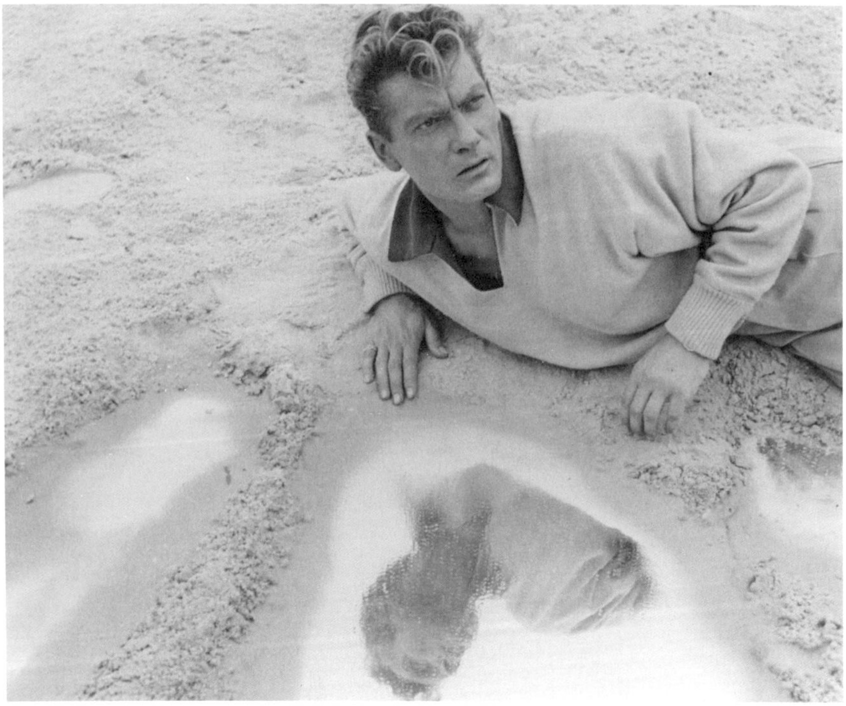

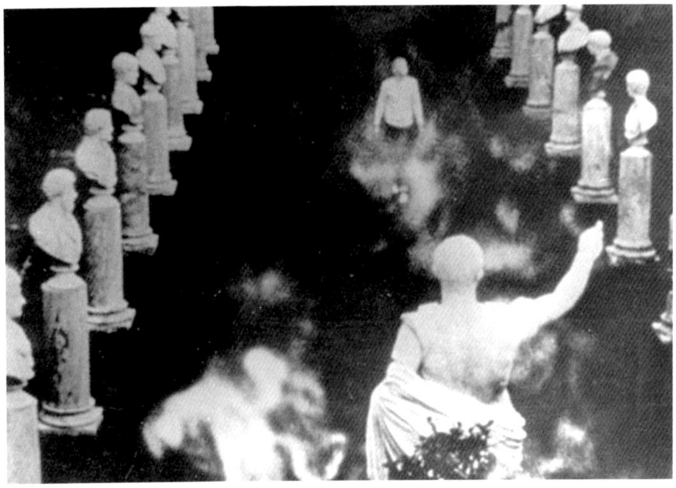

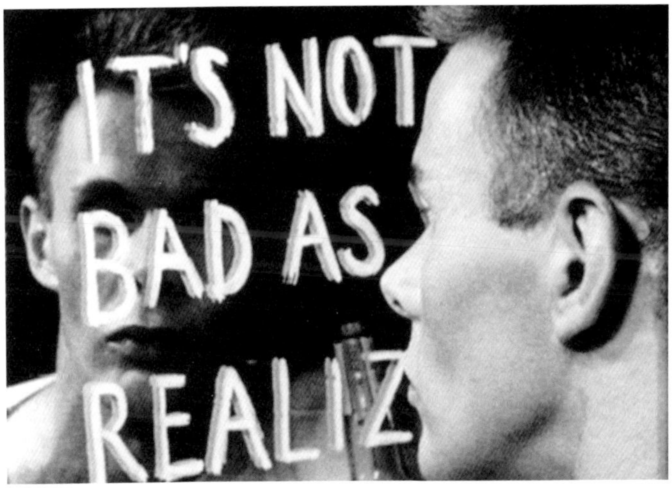

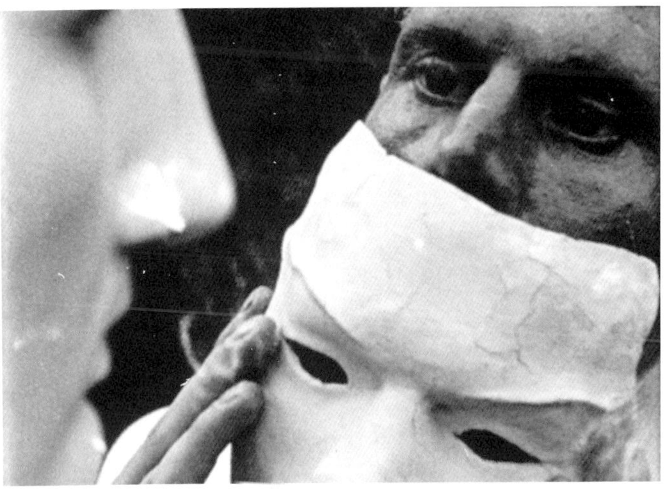

he says, 'a feminine past and possibility could also be read.'[39] The connotative equivalence of Adam and Narcissus would have been familiar to him from Gide.

In his survey of *Underground Film* (1971), Parker Tyler remarks cryptically: 'The film camera therefore turns out to be the chief auteur – that camera which has a wonderful faculty for being Narcissus's pool.'[40] A photo-essay inserted into the book is a two-page spread highlighting the Narcissus theme in a selection of films. Tyler visually tracks the evolution of the hero from the laurel-crowned poet of *Le Sang d'un Poète* in 1930 to the neckerchief-wearing hustler in Andy Warhol's *Flesh* in 1968, elevating Cocteau's position as fountainhead for a generation of alternative film-makers. The recourse to myth as the expression of a poetic sensibility, one aspect of Cocteau's influence, is best exemplified in Tyler's opinion by the films of Gregory Markopolous. The Gryphon Film Group, of which Markopolous was a part, is noteworthy for its full-blooded engagement with Greek myth.[41] *Narcissus* (1956), a film by another member of the Group, Willard Maas (1906–71), is a Cocteau-like retelling of the myth in a modern setting. In Maas's film Narcissus is a solitary ragpicker living on the margins of society, filmed against a picturesque backdrop of ruined buildings – the very obverse of a brash modernist vision. As described by the film-maker, *Narcissus* is:

> A film poem, a re-telling of the Greek myth in modern terms. In the traditional pool the water has become muddy and Narcissus finds that mirrors are more rewarding for the study of his changing reflections.

> There are three mirrors, each reflecting a dramatic study in self-love. The first, love that deserves the adoration of the opposite sex; the second, homosexual love that investigates itself and its own sex; the third, love that insures one a place in the present and history.

The film is replete with borrowings from, and knowing allusions to, Cocteau. Its episodic, dream-like character would seem to reflect the specific influence of *Le Sang d'un Poète*. A solemn voiceover intones: 'The excitement of dreams, the excitement of reality. There are no frontiers where one leaves off and the other begins.' Each of the dream sequences begins with Narcissus gazing into a mirror – a mirror which, much as in Cocteau's *Orphée*, is the gateway to another world.[42] A starfish in the first dream and a row of Roman portrait busts on columns in the third dream are motifs purloined from Cocteau. The mythic overlay notwithstanding, the film reads as a fairly transparent allegory of gay life in the 1950s. Narcissus is an isolated and sensitive soul with an eye for beautiful rather than useful things. In retribution for having rejected Echo, he is pursued to his junk yard shack by a gang of toughs who beat him savagely with a spade and take particular delight in destroying his few precious belongings, girlish lace and assorted trinkets. Following this 'queer bashing', the distraught Narcissus drowns himself. The film thus gives an ominous update to the original meaning of the myth as a warning. This was, after all, the era of McCarthyism. In its deference to European art house film, one senses that Maas is not only distancing himself from mainstream film, but also rejecting a dominant American identity from which he felt alienated due to his sexuality. As with Cocteau's *Orphée*, which is set in post-war France, the inclusion of jarringly anachronistic elements within a modern setting undermines the here and now by introducing an alien time that signifies a simultaneous belonging and yet not belonging.

The obtuseness of Maas's *Narcissus* is indubitably a function of the artful negotiation of repression in a pre-emancipation era. From a later period, the camp stylizations and visual pyrotechnics of James Bidgood's Cocteau-inspired *Pink Narcissus*, shot entirely in his New York apartment between 1963 and 1970, flaunts a self-aware queer sensibility. José Rodriguez-Soltero's *Jerovi* (1965), another film from the same era of an emergent gay conciousness, outs itself and its director, in part through its recruitment of Narcissus, a figure now firmly typecast as queer. The scene of Rodriguez-Soltero masturbating over his reflection in a pond culminates a gaudily-coloured and fantastical evocation of the Narcissus myth.

NOTES

1. André Gide, *Si le grain ne meurt* (If It Die), (1926), (Paris: Gallimard, 1966), p.206.
2. Rosalind Krauss, 'The Photographic Conditions of Surrealism,' *October* 19 (winter 1981), pp.3–34.
3. See Édouard Roditi, 'The Homophobia of André Breton,' *Christopher Street*, no. 113, July 1987, pp.17–24. Roditi was important as an American translator of Breton's writings.
4. Salvador Dalí, in *The Collected Writings of Salvador Dalí*, ed. Haim Finkelstein (Cambridge: Cambridge University Press, 1998), p.191. Dalí's radical assertion finds unexpected support in Freud. Observing that the most disgusting perversions may be considered as an idealisation of the sexual instinct, Freud adds: 'The omnipotence of love is perhaps never more strongly proved than in such of its aberrations as these.' Sigmund Freud, 'Three Essays on the Theory of Sexuality', *Pelican Freud Library*, vol. 7, trans. James Strachey (Harmondsworth: Pelican Books, 1977) p.75.
5. Salvador Dalí, *Diary of a Genius*, trans. Richard Howard (London: Hutchinson, 1966).
6. The latter are insightfully explored in David Vilaseca, *The Apocryphal Subject: Masochism, Identification, and Paranoia in Salvador Dalí's Autobiographical Writings* (Bern: Peter Lang, 1995).
7. Essentialism holds that masculinity and femininity are composed of fixed, generally innate characteristics.
8. See Dawn Ades, 'Surrealism, Male-Female', in *Surrealism: Desire Unbound*, ed. Jennifer Mundy (London: Tate Publishing, 2001), pp.171–196.
9. Joan Riviere, 'Womanliness as a Masquerade', *The International Journal of Psycho-Analysis*, vol. 10 (1929), pp.303–313.
10. Ernest Jones, 'The Early Development of Female Sexuality,'

The International Journal of Psycho-Analysis, vol. 8 (October 1927), pp.459–472.

11. Ibid.
12. Oscar Wilde, *The Picture of Dorian Gray* (1890), (Harmondsworth: Penguin, 2000), p.137.
13. Jay Prosser, 'Transsexuals and the Transsexologists: Inversion and the Emergence of Transsexual Subjectivity,' in *Sexology in Culture: Labelling Bodies and Desires*, ed. Lucy Bland and Laura Doan (Oxford: Polity, 1998), pp.116–131.
14. The confusion of same-sex desire with a cross-gendered identification with a person of the opposite sex persists in the concept of bisexuality, as we saw above.
15. See Laurie Monahan, 'Radical Transformations: Claude Cahun and the Masquerade of Womanliness,' in *Inside the Visible: An Elliptical Traverse of 20th Century Art in, of, and from the Feminine*, ed. Catherine de Zegher (Cambridge and London: MIT Press, 1996), pp.125–143.
16. Abigail Solomon-Godeau, 'The Equivocal "I": Claude Cahun as Lesbian Subject,' in *Inverted Odysseys: Claude Cahun, Maya Deren, Cindy Sherman*, ed. Shelley Rice (Cambridge and London: MIT Press, 1999).
17. See Craig Owens, 'Photography "en abyme",' *October* 5 (summer 1978), pp.73–88. Krauss acknowledges this article as having an important bearing on her thinking; it lies behind her foregrounding of reflections, doubles, and so forth in her definition of surrealist photography.
18. Admittedly, the Gidean image of the poet as a solitary, contemplative Narcissus sits uneasily with Cahun's political engagement.
19. Bram Dijkstra, *Idols of Perversity: Fantasies of Feminine Evil in Fin-de-Siècle Culture* (Oxford: Oxford University Press, 1986), p.144.
20. Sigmund Freud, 'Leonardo da Vinci and a Memory of His Childhood', *Pelican Freud Library*, vol. 14, trans. James Strachey (Harmondsworth: Pelican Books, 1985), pp.191–192.
21. See Michael Warner, 'Homo-Narcissism; or, Heterosexuality,' *Engendering Men: The Question of Male Feminist Criticism*, eds Joseph Boone and Michael Cadden (New York and London: Routledge, 1990), pp.190–206.
22. Julia Kristeva, *Tales of Love*, trans. Leon S. Roudiez (New York: Columbia University Press, 1987), p.126.
23. See Tirza Latimer, *Women Together/Women Apart: Portraits of Lesbian Paris* (New Jersey: Rutgers University Press, 2005) chapter 3. '"Narcissus and Narcissus": Claude Cahun and Marcel Moore', and Jennifer Shaw, 'Narcissus and the Magic Mirror,' in *Don't Kiss Me: The Art of Claude Cahun and Marcel Moore* (London: Tate Publishing, 2006), pp.33–45.
24. An inscription on one of the collages in *Aveux non avenus* reads: 'Beneath this mask another mask. I will never be finished removing all these faces.'
25. Shari Benstock, *Women of the Left Bank: Paris, 1900–1940* (Austin: University of Texas Press, 1986). See also Florence Tamague, *History of Homosexuality in Europe, 1919–1939* (New York: Algora Publishing, 2004).
26. David Mellor ed. *Cecil Beaton* (London: Weidenfeld & Nicholson, 1986).
27. Herbert Read, ed. *Surrealism* (London: Faber and Faber, 1936), p.85. This volume included a contribution by André Breton.
28. Jean-Luc Mercié, *Pierre Molinier* (Paris: Les presses du réel/Kamel Mennour, 2010).
29. Janine Chasseguet-Smirgel, *Creativity and Perversion* (London: Free Association Books, 1985).
30. Ibid., p.9.
31. Ibid., p.2.
32. 'Charles Henri Ford: Catalyst Among Poets', interview by Asko Kitaori. *Modern American Poetry* www.english.illinois.edu/maps/index.htm.
33. The Masson cover image belongs to a suite of eight pen and ink drawings titled *Mythology of Being* that was published in book form in New York in 1942, and re-published in *Mythologies* (Paris, 1946), where it is assigned a date of 1939.
34. Marjorie Perloff undertakes an enlightening analysis in *William Carlos Williams Review*, 22, no. 1 (spring 1996), pp.103–111.
35. Georges Bataille, *Visions of Excess: Selected Writings, 1927–1939*, trans. Allan Stoekl (Minneapolis: University of Minnesota Press, 1985), p.232.
36. Marco Bertamini, Richard Latto, and Alice Spooner, 'The Venus effect: people's understanding of mirror reflections in paintings,' *Perception*, 32 (2003), pp.593–599.
37. Ovid, *Metamorphoses*, trans. Mary M. Innes (Harmondsworth: Penguin, 1955), book X.
38. Elsa Brunelleschi, cited in Janet Rowson Davis, 'Ballet on British Television 1948–1949, Part II: Grand Ballet Season and the French Connection 1948–1955', *Dance Chronicle*, vol. 15, no. 2, 1992, pp.153–190.
39. Jean Genet, *Fragments of the Artwork*, trans. Charlotte Mandell (Stanford: Stanford University Press, 2003), p.1.
40. Parker Tyler, *Underground Film: A Critical History*, (London: Secker & Warburg, 1971).
41. See the authoritative article by Juan Suárez, 'Myth, Matter, Queerness: The Cinema of Willard Maas, Marie Menken, and the Gryphon Group, 1943–1969,' *Grey Room* 36 (summer 2009), pp.59–97.
42. Rabun M. Taylor explains the function of the mirror in the Orphic cult of Dionysus as 'an initiatory threshold into an alternate state of being' and a route to self-transformation. Rabun M. Taylor, *The Moral Mirror of Roman Art* (Cambridge: Cambridge University Press, 2008).

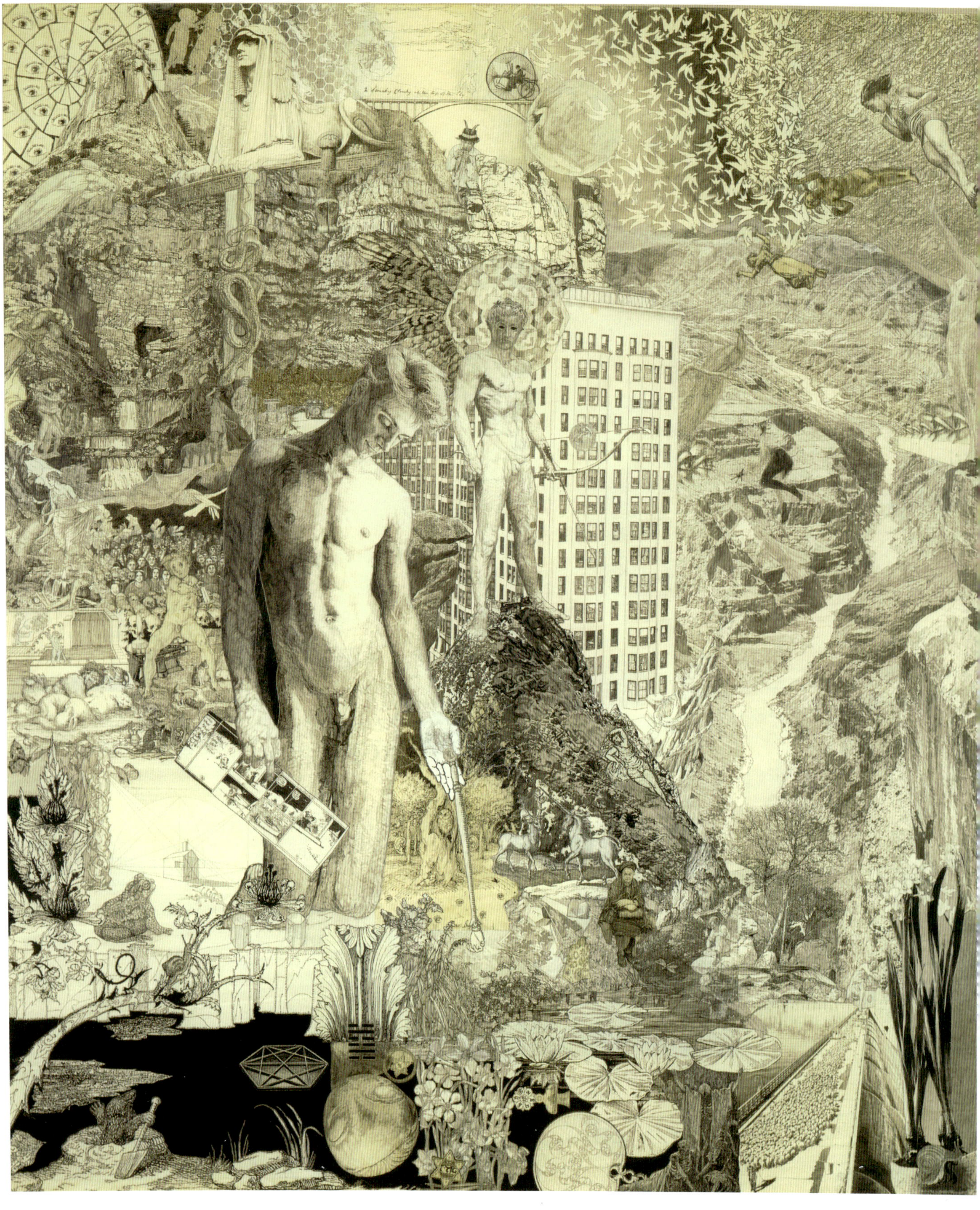

Jess *Narkissos*, 1976–91, pencil on paper and paste up

CHAPTER THREE
HOMOEROS UNPROFANED

> Through all the torture overtaking me in passing,
> another flower, not of evil, shone.
> Robert Duncan

Narkissos (1976–91) is the masterwork of San Francisco-based artist Jess (1923–2004), whose collage practice was in part inspired by a gift of Max Ernst's 1934 collage novel *Une semaine de bonté* (A Week of Kindness) from his partner, the poet Robert Duncan. Jess's ultimate ambition for the work is recorded in a notebook where he spoke of: 'seeking finally to maintain intense homoeros unprofaned, sensuous, joyful-fearful.' The arduous labour involved in reaching that goal is scarcely conveyed by the laconic inscription that appears below Jess's initials at the bottom right of the picture:

> Imagined '59 Collected '59 –'73 Sketched
> & Pinned up '76 – '79 Translated and
> Pasted up '78 –'79 Developed '79 –'91.

Extending over three decades, *Narkissos* was the best part of a life's work. More than ten years were spent in preparation before Jess was ready to embark on the picture. His research, which is documented in a ring binder notebook that he kept during this time, was utterly exhaustive.[1] No stones were left unturned as he made copious notes from books consulted in the San Francisco Public Library. Jess also compiled a dossier of Narcissus images and his own descriptions of historical works on the Narcissus subject, as well as a reservoir of source images, catalogued by subject, only a relatively small proportion of which eventually found their way into *Narkissos*. Covering the period 1959 to 1990, the notebook is fascinating as an example of art as research, and an invaluable aid to decoding the complex web of images and meanings that comprise the work.

Narkissos was executed in several stages. After amassing all the images he would need, Jess then pinned them to a board in the positions they would occupy in the larger work (p.91). The next stage, which Jess called 'translation', involved scaling up the found images by drawing them by hand on sections of paper and pasting them onto the support. As all his source images are reproductions of one sort or another, Jess skilfully imitated the medium in question, whether photograph or engraving, in order to preserve the heterogeneous look of a collage. Some sections of the paper have been coloured with washes so that they appear yellowed or browned. The resultant work, completed between 1976 and 1991, is most accurately described as a hand-drawn collage. Jess envisaged *Narkissos* as just a provisional step in a process in which the final stage would have been to make a second version in oil paint. This would have been the culminating picture in a series of *Translations*, all of which utilise found images and are painted in thick impasto with incised contours, a 'paint by numbers' style. Jess was forced to abandon this work, subtitled *The Last Translation*, at the stage of having traced it freehand in graphite on primed linen. This pendant, now in the Museum of Modern Art, New York, though unfinished is still rather majestic: a shimmering, mirror-like replica of *Narkissos*.

In 1966, at a point where he had already begun thinking about the Narcissus myth, Jess produced six collages cut from a single larger work that he called *Echo's Wake I–VI* (1961/66). The title pays tribute to – echoes – his beloved James Joyce. It also references the nymph Echo, who features in Ovid's version of the myth. As a punishment from the goddess Juno, Echo was condemned to repeat the last words spoken to her. Thus, when she makes to throw her arms around Narcissus, he flees from her, crying out: 'I would die before I would have you touch me!' To which Echo retorts: 'I would have you touch me!' The obligatory economy of her means does not stop Echo from turning the repeated fragment into a new expressive whole, expressive of her desire. As Jacques Derrida notes, Echo's 'ruse' is to turn citationality into an inventive and original medium whose message is there to be heard by whoever cares to listen.[2]

In a sense, Jess's entire oeuvre, not just *Narkissos*, was produced in Echo's wake. Literally everything Jess did was second-hand. Its originality lies in the inventive use of quotation, the 'ruse of Echo' transposed to a visual register. Jess's collage practice is entirely premised on the recycling of pre-existing cultural fragments, to the extent that he is now regarded as a forerunner of Pop and appropriation art. Jess preferred the term 'paste-up' to collage because it preserves something of the child-like delight in cutting and pasting. Playful humour and paradox are of the essence in Jess's oeuvre. *Narkissos* is no exception in playfully reversing the order of originality implied in the hand-drawn and the merely reproduced.

Narkissos is a vast echo chamber, an assemblage, a comprehensive resumé of the visual history and interpretation of the Narcissus myth. Everything in the work is a citation taken from another source. Even Jess's signature, shortened to the initials 'JS', was a found image. Adopting Derrida's coinage, it is a kind of *échographie*, a drawing or writing that is a series of echoes; or, in Roland Barthes's apt phrase, 'a tissue of quotations drawn from the innumerable centres of culture'. Densely-woven allusions to myth, psychoanalysis, and children's nursery tales reflect the incredibly erudite literary household that Jess shared with Duncan. They would often entertain themselves with a sort of cultural studies *avant la lettre*, as Jess recalled:

> I am interested in the path of an image, particularly a certain spiritual or mystical path that I might discover. Robert and I would often discuss a particular image from reading or television and follow its line back in time using our library here. We would always be fascinated by how the imagination travels through time, the image being a constant vehicle.[3]

Jess tracked down the Narcissus legend in Hollywood movies and Krazy Kat cartoons, as well as tracing it back in time. The format is that of a table where all these different narratives, and the successive moments from a single narrative – Narcissus and the flower that he will become – are simultaneously present. His method is a syncretism that draws things together on the basis of analogy. Jess bewilders the would-be interpreter with a surfeit of information. Lost in a hall of mirrors, we grasp for some threads that might permit us to navigate a course through its confusing profusion and proliferation of appropriated images and meanings.

Jess *Pinning Board for Narkissos*, undated
paper, images and texts pinned to board

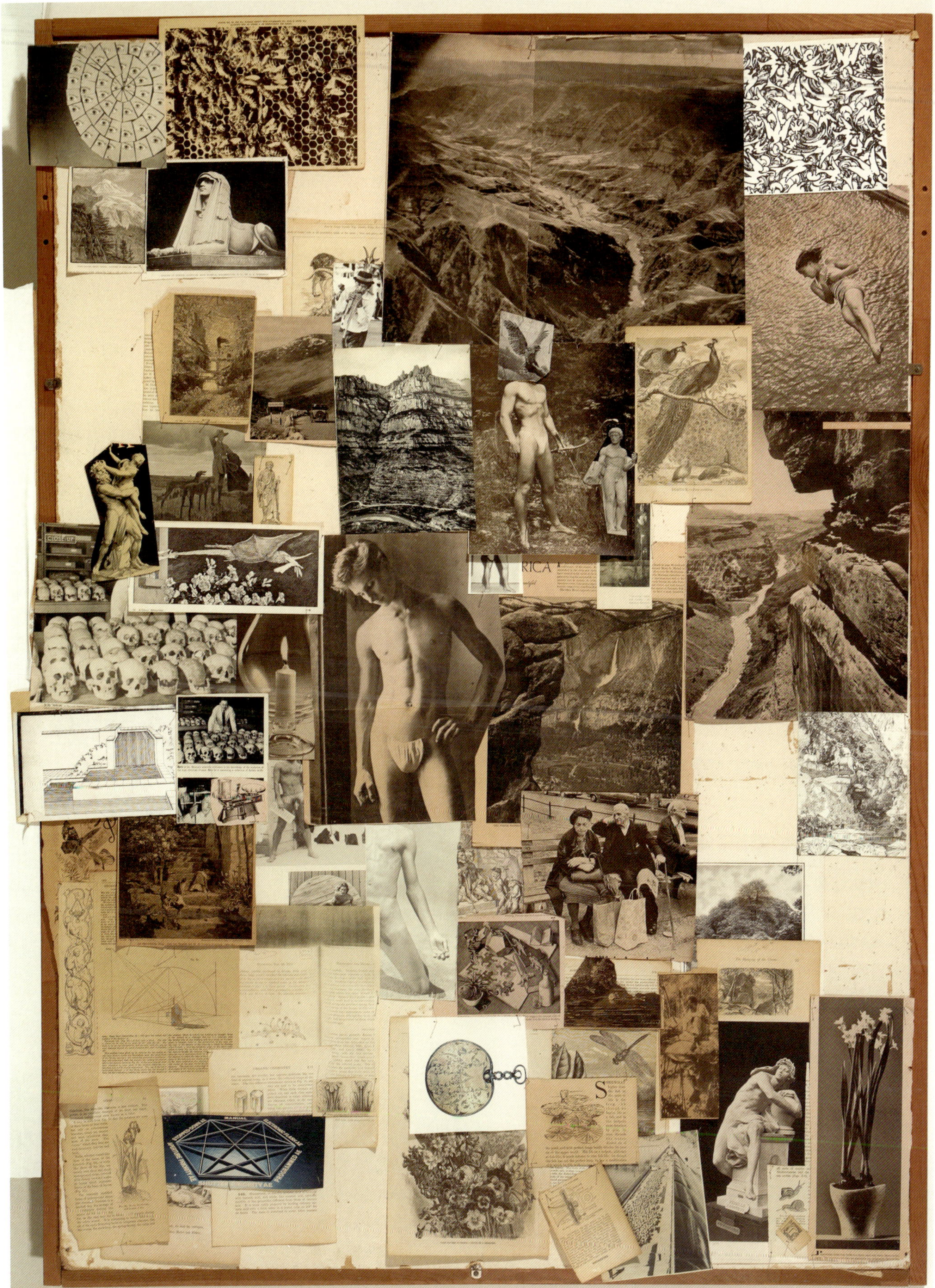

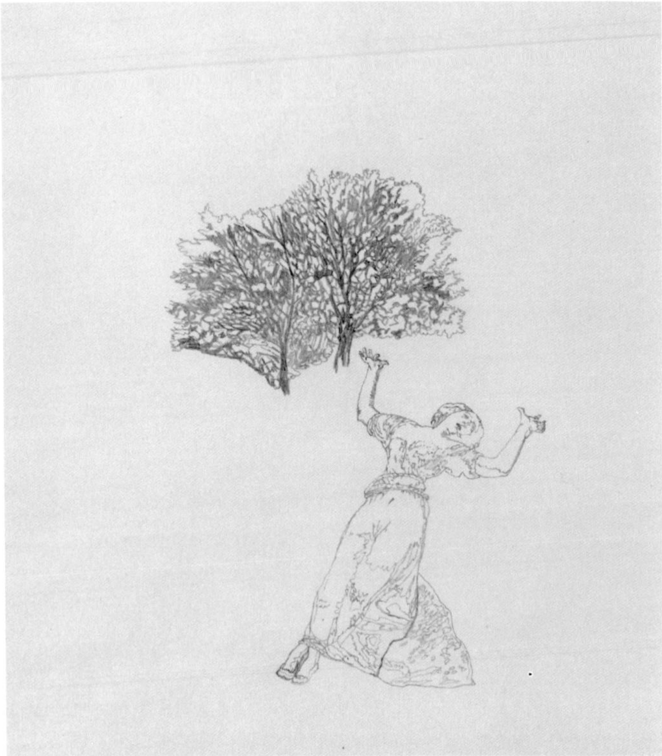

Jess *Study for Narkissos IV*, undated, pencil on paper

Mirroring, as a cardinal element of the Narcissus myth, almost constitutes the core of his cosmogony, a view that was reinforced by Jess's scientific background in chemistry. A kind of mirror symmetry akin to that of our left and right hands is found throughout nature, even down to the molecular level.[4] Stereoisomers (also termed enantiomers) are molecules that are mirror images of one another. They are non-superimposable but have identical physical properties, except for the direction in which they rotate polarised light. A structure of reflection, where each thing has its potential reverse or inverse, is thus a principle common to nature and man. Jess underlined the point by including in *Narkissos* a diagram of enantiomorphic crystals from a chemistry textbook.

As the poet Michael Palmer astutely shows in a detailed analysis of the picture, the upper and lower sections of *Narkissos* as a whole are related by a structure of mirroring.[5] Jess's researches had acquainted him with Neoplatonist thought, which viewed the world we perceive with our senses as the reflection of a higher, immaterial reality. Thomas Taylor, in the c.1790 study *The Eleusinian and Bacchic Mysteries*, a source consulted by Jess, relays the philosopher Plotinus's view of the Narcissus fable as a parable of what happens when one is too much attached to the material world and led astray from one's spiritual nature:

> For by Narcissus falling in love with his shadow in the limpid stream we may behold an exquisitely apt representation of a soul vehemently gazing on the flowing conditions of a material body, and in consequence of this, becoming enamoured with a corporeal life, which is nothing more than the delusive image of the real man, or the rational and immortal soul.[6]

AS ABOVE, SO BELOW

Each and every iconographic element in *Narkissos* has its double or echo. There is a pervasive structure of mirroring as well as numerous actual mirror reflections to be discovered by the attentive viewer. A fascination with reflections and doubles, with inversions and reversals, runs through Jess's oeuvre. A striking illustration of this is seen in the section at the upper right of the picture where the American Olympic diver Pat McCormick, one of several figures who represent Echo, has been upended. With arms crossed over her chest to make a dive, she now looks like a saint ascending to the celestial vault. Jess constantly alters the ways we look at things.

The motif of error is very salient in the Platonic and subsequent Christian tradition of Narcissus readings. As a result of his 'immoderate attachment to this unsubstantial mockery and gliding semblance of the real soul', Narcissus is changed into 'a vegetative condition of being, into a beautiful but transient flower, that is, into a corporeal life, or a life totally consisting in the mere operations of nature.'[7] Not content with this second-hand account by Taylor, Jess also read and copied out the relevant passages from Plotinus's third century *Enneads* and the much earlier seventh-century BC *Homeric Hymn to Demeter*, which recounted the rape of Persephone. The abduction of Persephone to Hades, was understood by Neoplatonists in terms similar to the drowning of Narcissus – as a descent of spirit into matter.

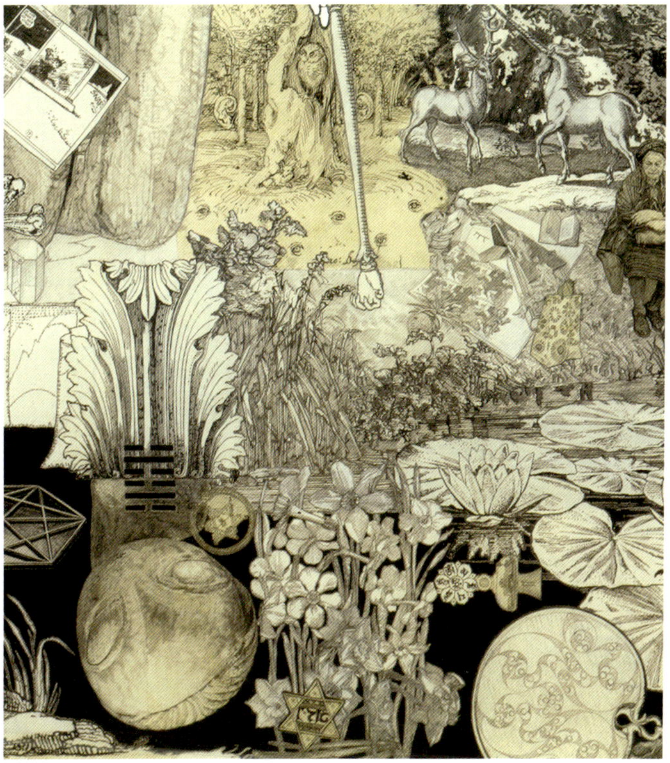

Jess detail of *Narkissos*, 1976–91

It would be hasty, though, to align Jess with the idealist Platonic viewpoint. In fact, he studied Hans Jonas's 1958 classic study of Gnosticism, a violently anti-idealist and heretical strand of thought whose influence was continued in a number of the occult and hermetic writers of particular interest to Jess.[8] Jess concentrated on the section of Jonas's book which analysed the *Poimandres* of Hermes Trimegistus. He also took notes from the *Poimandres* itself, using an English translation by G.R.S. Mead (one of the founders of theosophy) from 1906. Jonas explains that the *Poimandres* is unique in deploying the Narcissus myth to express an idea with a far wider currency in Gnostic thought namely: 'the idea that either the cosmogonic process or the sinking of the Soul, or generally the downward movement of a divine principle, was initiated by a reflection of the upper Light in the Darkness below.'[9] In this account, light becomes enamoured of the dark, is drawn down into it, and in consequence, 'a radiation, reflection, or image of the Light [is] projected into the Darkness below and there held fast.'[10]

Jess found an ingenious solution for visualising this schema. The motifs distributed over the surface of the pond at the bottom of the painting shine out from the dark like stars in a night sky.[11] At the centre of this inverted firmament is a sort of lunar eclipse borrowed from a Narcissus sculpture by Constantin Brancusi and used by Jess to represent Narcissus's reflection. Scattered around it are a number of hexagrams (six-pointed stars) obtained from some quite obscure sources. An entire section in Jess's image bank is dedicated to 'Enigmatics Signs Contradictions' and another to 'Symbols'. A six-pointed geometric figure, known as the Star of David or the Seal of Solomon, the hexagram

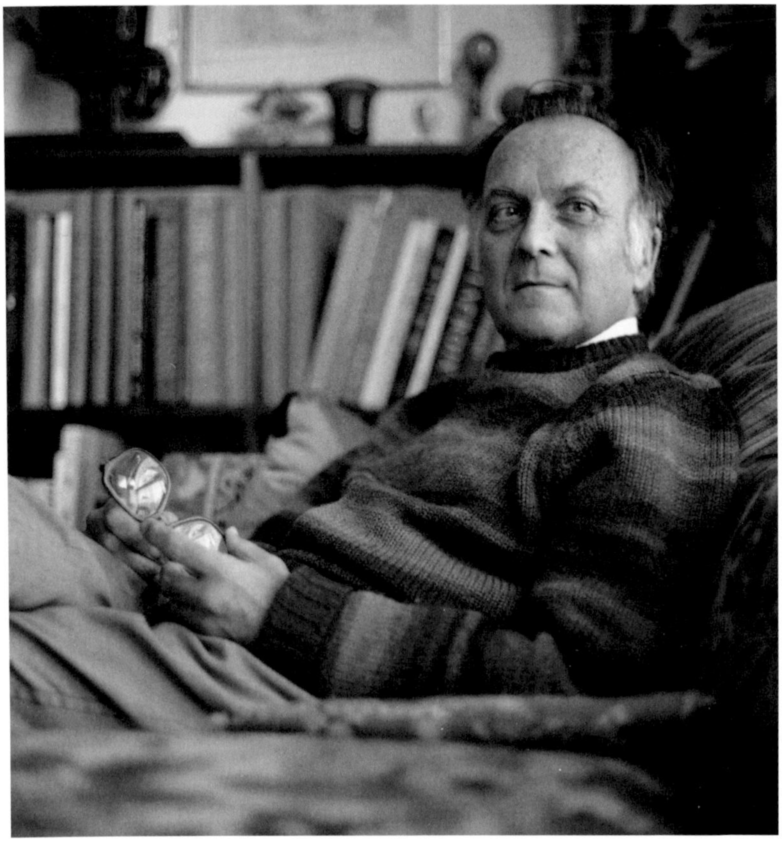

Allen Ginsberg Robert Duncan, San Francisco, 1984

vertical hierarchies of high and low, elevated and base. Let's not forget also that the narcissus flower is a six-pointed star shape like a hexagram (Jess certainly didn't).

As with Dalí, it is tempting to think of Jess's Narcissus as a myth shared. Jess certainly partook of Duncan's incredible erudition and his magpie approach to synthesizing myth with other systems of ideas. Peter O'Leary, author of the 2002 *Gnostic Contagion: Robert Duncan and the Poetry of Illness*, believes that Narcissus and related ideas of doubling are key to Duncan's personal mythography.[12] Owing to an eye injury, Duncan literally saw double. His adoptive parents were adherents of theosophy and as a result he grew up thoroughly versed in esotericism. Such literature was a mainstay of Jess's quest as well.[13] His notebook contains long screeds laboriously copied from hermetic and theosophic sourcebooks, among them Taylor's *The Eleusinian and Bacchic Mysteries* and G.R.S. Mead's *Thrice Greatest Hermes* (which included the *Homeric Hymn to Demeter.*) The three volumes of the latter can be seen on the bookshelves in many pictures of Jess and Duncan's home.

Taylor's translations of Greek texts were widely read by the Romantic poets, notably William Blake, and by Mead, who was secretary to Helena Blavatsky, the founder of the Theosophical Society in New York in 1875. Taylor explains the connection of the Narcissus myth and flower with the Eleusinian mystery rites. The

is a symbol in many world religions, as well as in freemasonry, theosophy and alchemy. It is therefore an effective shorthand evoking the systems of belief that cohere in Jess and Duncan's cosmogony. The hexagram consists of interlocked equilateral triangles, one pointing up and the other down, hence it represents the adage 'As above, so below' which is a fundamental tenet of Jewish Kabbalah. It thus embodies the compositional principle governing the whole work in which upper and lower sections mirror one another. This structure, inherited from the Gnostics who were considered heretics in their own day, has the potential to subvert ceremonies based in the ancient city of Eleusis centred on the cult of Demeter, the godess of the harvest and the earth, and her daughter Persephone. The myth tells how Persephone was gathering flowers when she was abducted by Hades and carried off to the underworld, an event represented in Jess's *Narkissos* by a drawing of Gianlorenzo Bernini's seventeenth-century marble sculpture, which appears to the left of Narcissus's shoulder towards the left hand side of the frame. Eros, the smaller of the two main figures in Jess's composition, also played an important part in the Eleusinian rites, whose secret essence is kept alive within the hermetic tradition.

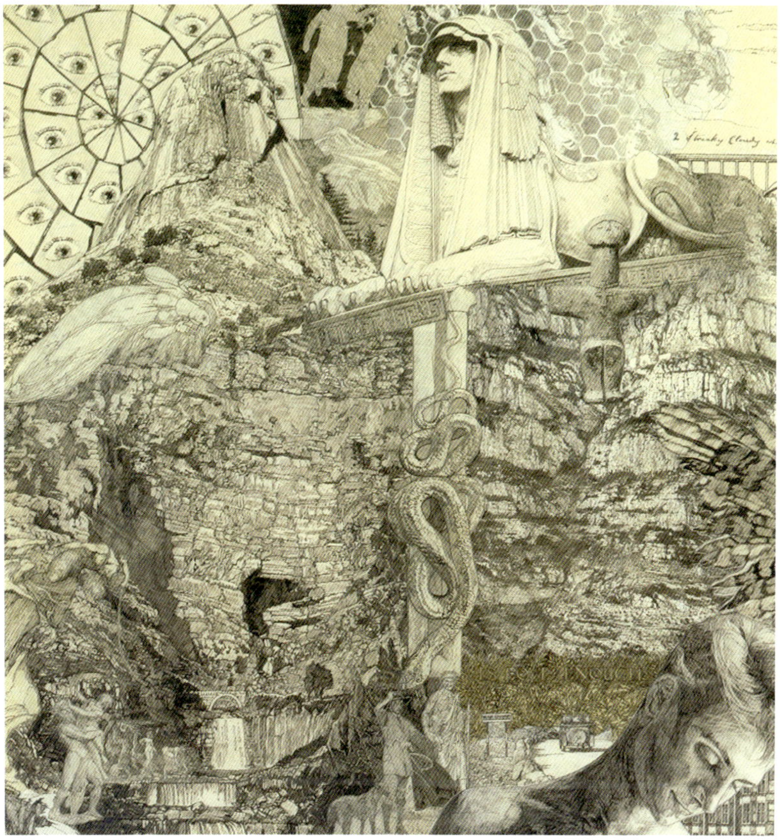

Jess detail of *Narkissos*, 1976–91

Beyond the specifics of Gnostic beliefs, Duncan and Jess were, it seems, deeply attracted to the idea of knowledge ('*gnosis*') as a revealed mystery. One is inclined to see the idea of secret or hidden knowledge accessible only to adepts, prominent in the Eleusinian mysteries as well as in Gnostic sects, and their attraction to more recent non-mainstream systems of thought, as connected at some level with their sexuality. Like Freud's analysis of da Vinci, it may have been the search for a personal answer to this enigma that drove Jess's unquenchable thirst for knowledge. Not for nothing is the inscrutable sphinx, placed at the upper left side of the painting, a member of his *dramatis personae* for *Narkissos* from the very earliest sketch (p.106). There may also have been one other reason, more specific to the San Franciscan counter-culture, for Jess's inordinate interest in the Eleusinian rites. No less than six handwritten pages are copied from *The Road to Eleusis* (1978) by Gordon Wasson, Albert Hofmann and Carl A.P. Ruck, which put forward an argument that hallucinogenic drugs were consumed by participants in the rites. Jess, a trained chemist, pored over the pharmacological evidence. In his notebook for *Narkissos* he cites one of the contributors to the volume, who points out that the narcissus flower was so-named because of its narcotic properties and concludes that Persephone's abduction can be interpreted as a drug-induced seizure.

NARCISSUS OR NARKISSOS

Reverting to the Greek spelling 'Narkissos' enabled Jess to sidestep the pejorative connotations that the Narcissus myth had accrued in the Christian tradition and more recently. Furthermore, it differentiated his use of the myth at a time when narcissism had become a general catchphrase for the American malaise, notably in Christopher Lasch's bestselling *The Culture of Narcissism*. There may be another reason for Jess wanting to hark back to antiquity as well. The modern rediscovery of Greek homosexuality, an important factor in asserting a more positive gay identity, tends to be identified nowadays with Kenneth Dover's landmark *Greek Homosexuality* (1978) and the work of Michel Foucault comparing modern and ancient concepts of homosexuality, but this process of recovery had begun in Victorian England with studies by John Addington Symonds and subsequently Edward Carpenter.[14]

The evidence that this literature informed Jess's conception of the myth is found in the ways in which his treatment of the Narcissus subject departs from traditional representations. He completely reverses the relative maturity of Eros and Narcissus from the standard iconography where Eros or Cupid is typically depicted as a small child. How Jess has chosen to portray them could reflect an awareness of Greek pederasty. The German classicist, Paul Brandt, writing under cover of the pseudonym Hans Licht in the early 1930s, explained:

> The word most frequently used [for Greek love], 'paederasty' (παιδεραστία), comes from παις (boy) and ἐραν (to love), and consequently denotes the spiritual and sensual affection for a boy, though it should be noted, as will later be more fully shown, that the word 'boy' is not to be understood offhand in the modern colloquial sense. In the Greek language the word 'paederasty' had not this ugly sound it has for us to-day, since it was regarded simply as an expression for one variety of love, and had no sort of defamatory meaning attached to it.[15]

Greek homosexuality was an institutionalised social practice, not the expression of an individual preference or orientation as now. *Erastês* and *erômenos* are the commonly accepted terms for the two pederastic roles. The *erastês* was a man who had reached maturity – in imagery showing pederastic relationships on Greek pottery he would be bearded and probably in at least his early twenties – while the *erômenos* would be younger, generally an adolescent boy. The *erômenos* would later marry and neither partner would be exclusively homosexual; both would be expected to produce children within a marriage. Whether or not there was a reciprocal attraction between the partners and the nature of their sexual relations is debated.[16] One explanation of the practice is that it served an initiatory function as a rite of passage to adulthood.

Bernard Sergent, a proponent of this view, argues that the origins of the Narcissus myth lie in this initiatory practice.[17] Supporting this concept, he notes that the earlier version of the myth of Narcissus by Conon contains no mention of the spurned female lover, Echo, but only a male suitor, Ameinias, and the description of Narcissus's love is more overtly homoerotic. The myth in its earlier, so to speak, uncorrupted form was grouped together by Sergent with the myths of Hyacinthus and Cyparissus, also retold by Ovid in *Metamorphoses*, beautiful youths who die and are transformed into a plant bearing their name. Hyacinthus is loved by Apollo but is killed while competing with the god at throwing the discus, and is turned into a purple flower, a hyacinth. Cyparissus, 'the handsomest of the Cean boys' accidentally kills a stag that had been given to him by Apollo and is so filled with grief that he begs Apollo for death. His wish is granted, and he is turned by the god into a cypress tree. Sergent argues that the theme of metamorphosis in all three myths represents the act of initiation: 'Like a plant, the *erômenos* dies, because like a plant he will be reborn, though on a qualitatively different plane.'[18] Narcissus, as the myth has come down to us, is an inversion of the paradigm because Narcissus rejects the *erastês.* 'He rejects love, not only homosexual love but also heterosexual, as shown by the famous story of the nymph Echo, desperately in love. He is a paradigmatic asocial character. His function is to articulate what must not be done.'[19] Narcissus is a kind of gay outlaw. The German philosopher Herbert Marcuse puts a positive gloss on his refusal (see below).

Jess's keen interest in this subject is evidenced by the fact that he was at work on another picture entitled *Apollon-Hyakinthos* when he first conceived *Narkissos.* Jess's notebook shows that he was well aware of the different versions of the myth. In contrast with images such as Waterhouse's painting which privileges Echo and Narcissus (p.20), in *Narkissos* the two main protagonists are male. In accordance with the pederastic model, we can see the older Eros and the plainly younger, epicene Narcissus as *erastês* and *erômenos* respectively. Although not especially prominent, Ameinias is also present in the composition behind and to the left of Narcissus. The source image is a seated nude boy by the Italian Mannerist painter Pontormo, which Jess culled from a volume by Brandt Aymar on *The Young Male Figure* (in paintings, sculptures and drawings from ancient Egypt to the present). Jess has armed him with a sword, derived from the marble sculpture of the *Dying Gaul* (a Roman copy of a Hellenistic bronze) in the Capitoline Museum, Rome, which he thrusts in the direction of Narcissus, offering him the handle. *A Shrine to Ameinias* is one of the poems in Duncan's 1968 collection *Bending the Bow.* As noted, Jess also includes a representation of Echo in this composition. This even-handedness is consistent with Jess and Duncan's syncretic approach to myth, though *Narkissos* can be understood as tracing the myth back through its various historical overlays to a more original homoerotic meaning.

Jess *Study for Narkissos I*, undated, pencil on paper

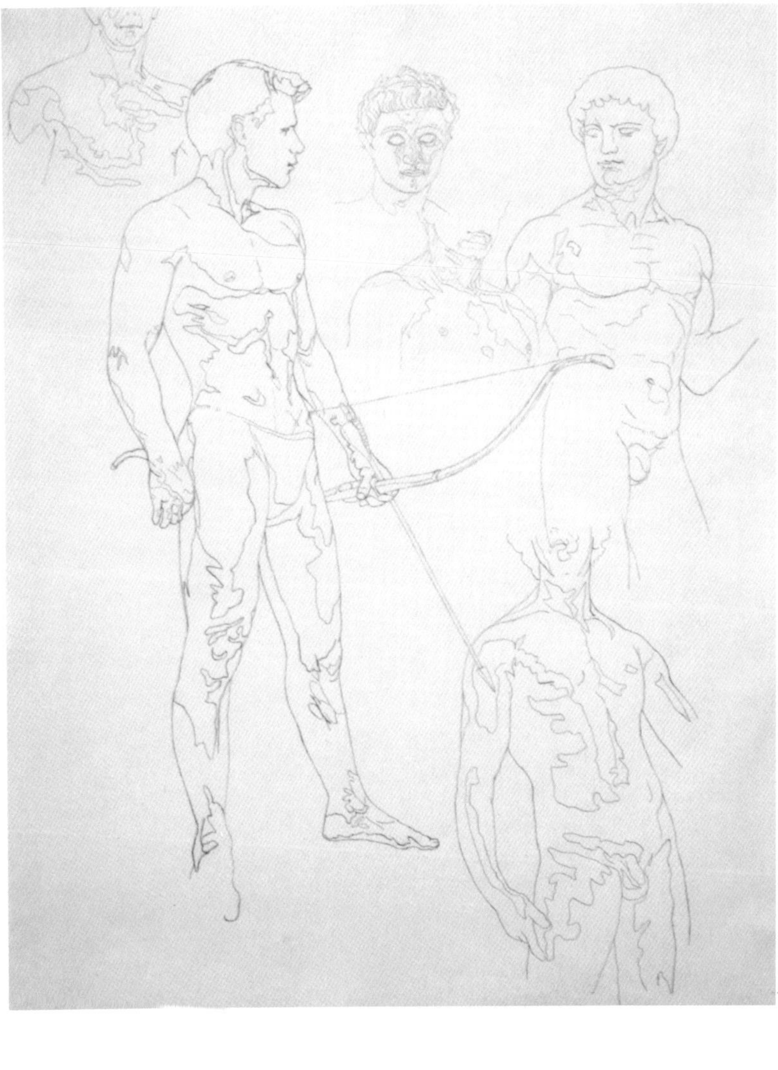

THOM GUNN

Dear Jess, here's the poem for your Narcissus dossier, if it looks useful. Thanks for a lovely lunch.

XXX
Thom

Once in a Dark Restaurant

Once in a dark restaurant I caught the eyes of another
they stared back at mine with unflagging interest.
Another! no it was my own eyes from a recessed mirror.

I and the reflected self were identical twins,
alike yet separate, two flowers from the same plant.

In Caravaggio's Narcissus the bottom half of the painting
reflects the top half
but for us there is a difference:
the face above is in profile, even to the lashes,
but from the three-quarters face below both eyes glare up.
Narcissus however cannot see himself as we can;
as he leans over the surface, absorbed, he sees
only the other -- male delicacy, rounded arms,
a hunk of auburn hair tumbled forward, lips parted
in awe, in craving
And reaches down toward him.

He escapes, he does not escape, he is the same, he is other.
If he drowned himself he would be one with himself.
If he drowned himself he would wash free into the world,
placid and circular, from which he has been withdrawn.
He would at last be of it, deep below the mirror
his white limbs braided with a current
where both water and earth are part of the whole flow,
and would come to rest on a soft dark wave of soil
to root there and stand again
one flower,
one waxy star, giving perfume, unreflecting.

Among the miscellany of documents filed in Jess's *Narkissos* notebook is a poem by Thom Gunn. It was a gift from the author to Jess for inclusion in the dossier of literature on Narcissus. The typed poem is prefaced by a brief personal note in which Gunn thanks Jess for a 'lovely lunch'. The title of the poem is *Once in a Dark Restaurant*, and the opening stanza recounts an event that we are led to believe had occurred to Gunn in a dimly-lit restaurant. His wandering gaze catches the attention of another man seated in the distance. An exchange of looks occurs and more than one appetite is aroused before Gunn soon realises that he is looking at himself in a mirror. 'I and the reflected self,' he writes, 'were identical twins, alike yet separate, two flowers from the same plant.' The theme of twinning in relation to Narcissus is one that we have encountered before. Gunn introduces the Narcissus myth proleptically by subtly referencing a flower. The poem he gave to Jess differs from a published version mainly in the second stanza, which is an ekphrasis of Caravaggio's *Narcissus.*[20] The relatively recent transformation of Caravaggio into a gay icon has gone hand in hand with this picture's inexorable rise to stardom.[21] In the published form of Gunn's poem, the explicitness of the reference to Caravaggio is gone. I am inclined to think that the version he gave to Jess came first, though it is not inconceivable that it was the other way round. Gunn may have revisited the poem and reinstated a link with Caravaggio especially for his artist friend.

below: **Caravaggio** *Narcissus*, c.1597–99, oil on canvas
opposite: Letter from Thom Gunn to Jess including a poem *Once in a Dark Restaurant* from Jess's notebook for *Narkissos*, 1959–90

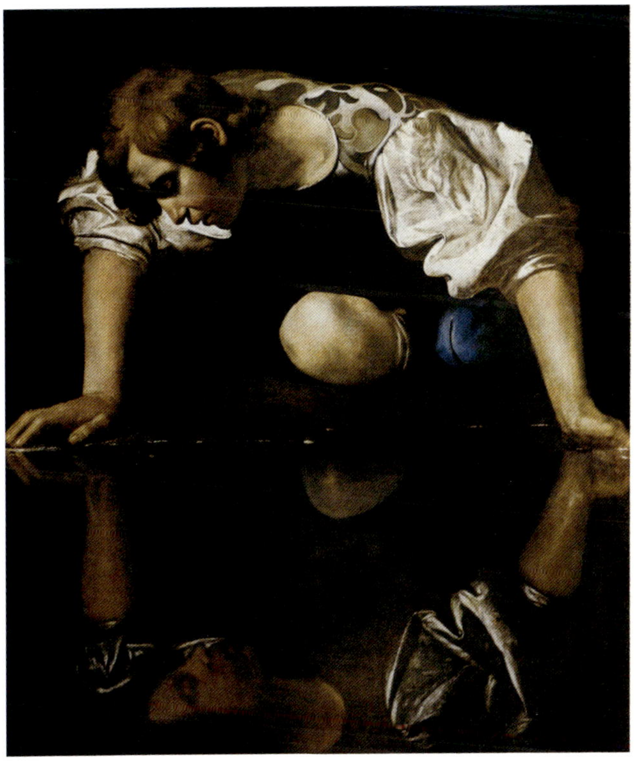

As has been noted in the discussion of Dalí's *Metamorphosis of Narcissus*, the Narcissus myth is remarkable for the parallelism of visual and poetic traditions that feed off each other. Ekphrasis brings to a climax the reciprocity of text and image. The author of a number of ekphrastic poems, it is likely that Gunn would have known the Narcissus ekphrasis found in Philostratus's collection of essays from the third century, *Imagines* (Images). Philostratus conveys an acute awareness of seeing and being seen. His text closes with a marvellous description of Narcissus alone with his reflection, which contains an incisive observation about how our view of Narcissus differs from his view of himself. The beholder's privilege is to be seduced into identifying with Narcissus and yet still be able to withdraw to a more omniscient viewpoint. Gunn picks up on this discrepancy, remarking that: 'Narcissus however cannot see himself as we can.' Maybe Gunn meant to suggest that Caravaggio's Narcissus could not recognise the homosexual nature of his desire as we can with historical hindsight.

Stephen Bann detects the influence of Philostratus on the way in which Caravaggio has portrayed his subject.[22] It seems that the artist may have taken into consideration a description of Narcissus's golden locks in a passage that lingers unduly over the youth's hair:

> There would be much to say about the hair if we found him while hunting. For there are innumerable tossings of the hair in running, especially when it is blown by a wind; but even as it is the subject should not be passed over in silence. For it is very abundant and of a golden hue; and some of it clings to the neck, some is parted by the ears, some tumbles over the forehead, and some falls in ripples to the beard.[23]

Placing these works in sequence, we can see that Gunn's poem is a commentary on a painting that in all probability was inspired by a text that is a description of a painting, a criss-crossing back and forth from text to image to text and back again. Gunn himself explicitly paraphrases Philostratus when he refers to a hunk of auburn hair 'tumbled' forward. The *Imagines*, which the narrator says are addressed to a boy, were meant to enlighten as well as entertain, and it has been claimed that, in accord with Greek pederasty, they are instructive in the codes of homoerotic viewing. Certainly Philostratus doesn't miss a trick in his blow-by-blow description of the youth's physical charm. Aside from the tousled hair, Philostratus describes Narcissus resting in a contrapposto pose that has the effect of showing off his buttocks. With respect to the hair, the main index of homoeroticism, he states that the subject ought not be passed over in silence – an admonition that Gunn seems not to have ignored, since his own poem began, as we saw, with a cruisy exchange of looks.

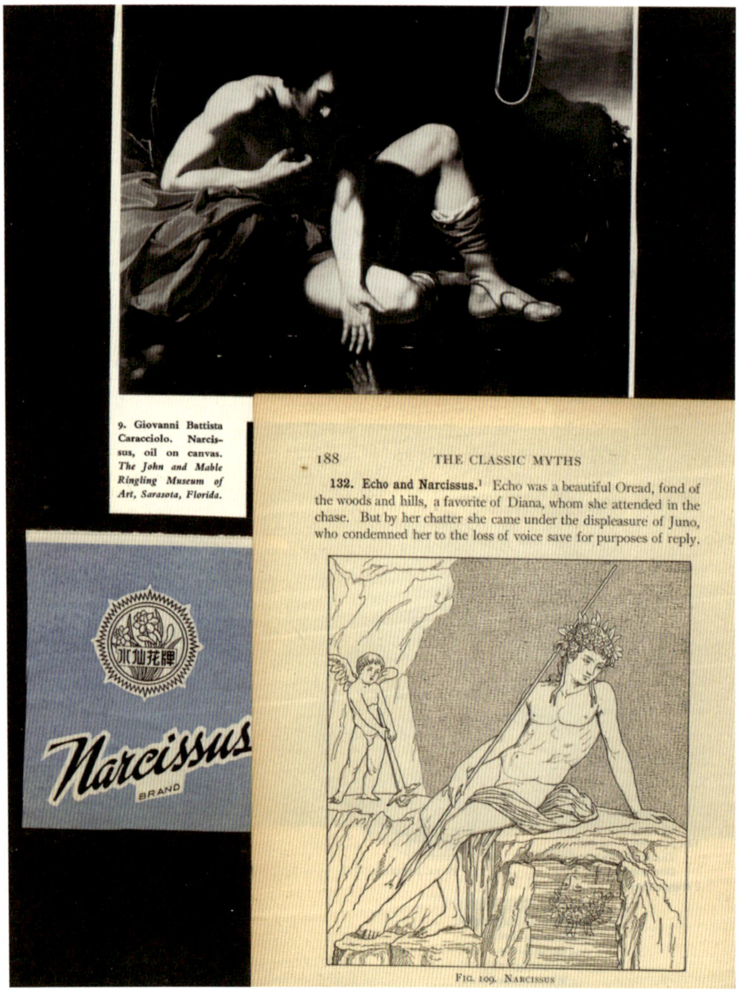

'In Caravaggio's *Narcissus*,' Gunn writes, 'the bottom half of the painting reflects the top half.' As noted, *Narkissos* has precisely this structure, as do the three stanzas of Gunn's poem in a sense. Moving down the page, the last section refers to the drowning of Narcissus. Gunn tries hard to conceal his erudition behind a laconic style, but even so we can recognise this as an invocation of the Neoplatonist and Gnostic readings of the myth which were so influential upon his friend Jess:

> If he drowned himself he would wash free into
> the world,
> placid and circular, from which he has been
> withdrawn.
> He would at last be of it, deep below the mirror
> his white limbs braided with a current
> where both water and earth are part of the whole
> flow, …

Against the grain of Neoplatonism and the Christian morality tale of the Fall, the movement of the poem down the page contrarily affirms downwardness. If we think of Caravaggio's *Narcissus* as the anchor for the poem, it accords with modern understandings of Caravaggio as realist, materialist and anti-idealist. In relation to the negotiation of gay identity that subtends so much of Gunn's poetry, it also reveals how a structure of reflection or inversion can be used to a political end to destabilise hierarchical notions of high and low, elevated and base. Gunn ends by recapitulating the motif of the flower, a narcissus – 'one waxy star' – perfectly analogous to Jess's inverted image of a starry firmament in the inky black pond.

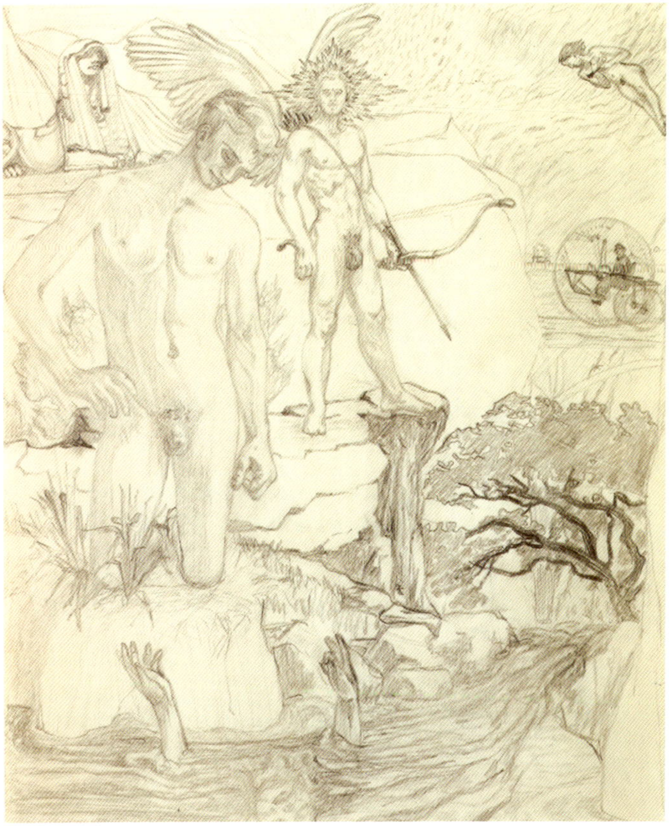

opposite: Page from Jess's notebook for *Narkissos*, 1959–90
right: **Jess** Compositional drawing for *Narkissos*, 1964
pencil on paper

below: **Jess** *Study for Narkissos II*, undated, pencil on paper
opposite: **George Minne** *Kneeling Youth*, 1898, bronze

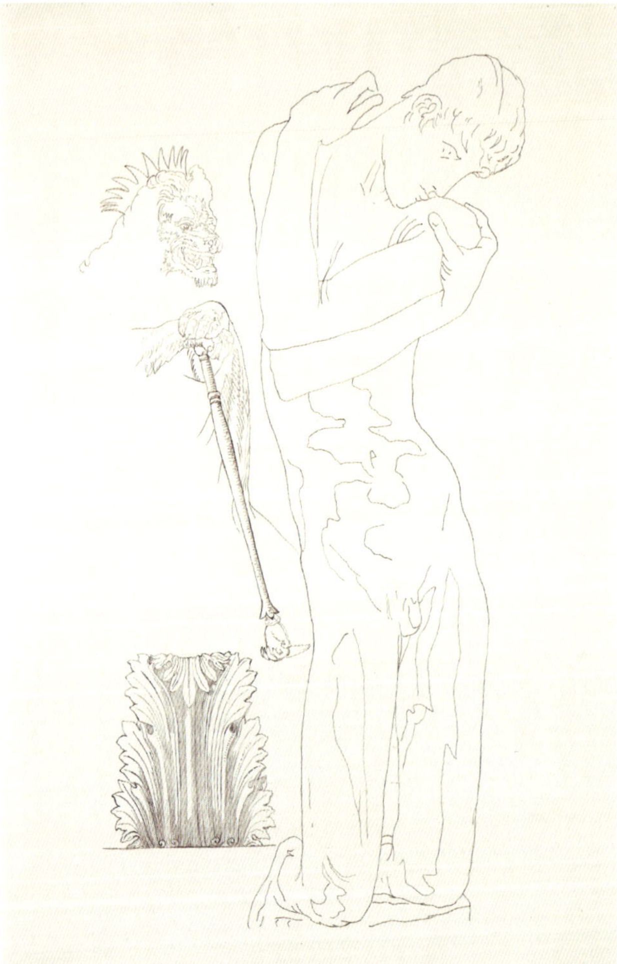

ART NOUVEAU REVIVAL

Art Nouveau ranks high in Susan Sontag's definition of camp in her well-known essay of 1964. Duncan and Jess were certainly not immune to its seductions: a Tiffany lampshade, visible in Jess's portrait of Duncan, was one of their prized possessions. We can be more specific about its significance for them, however. As we have seen repeatedly, a detour through the *fin de siècle* is characteristic of surrealist and post-surrealist art that seeks to give a voice to dissident sexuality. Compounded of a plethora of references to Art Nouveau and symbolism, *Narkissos* is no exception. Indeed, the figure of Narcissus is based on *Kneeling Youth*, one of a series of sculptures in bronze, marble and plaster made around the turn of the century by the Belgian sculptor Georges Minne (1866–1941), regarded as a high point of symbolist statuary.

In a letter to his dealer, informing him that work on *Narkissos* is forging ahead at last, Jess – evidently in good spirits – writes:

> I'm taking a break this morning from translating Beardsley's pen-line into a pencil-component for *Narkissos* (left foreground). This fragment from his 'Siegfried' drawing will elegantly entertain that Wagnerian Freudianism which dominates most of the modern interpretations of Narcissus.[24]

The Art Nouveau revival of the 1960s has been abundantly documented in a 2010 exhibition at the Musée d'Orsay in Paris.[25] In the wake of a retrospective exhibition at the Victoria and Albert Museum in London in 1966, which subsequently travelled to California, Aubrey Beardsley's influence upon what the d'Orsay exhibition termed *psychadélisme* was enormous, spawning lookalike record covers, poster designs and book illustrations.[26]

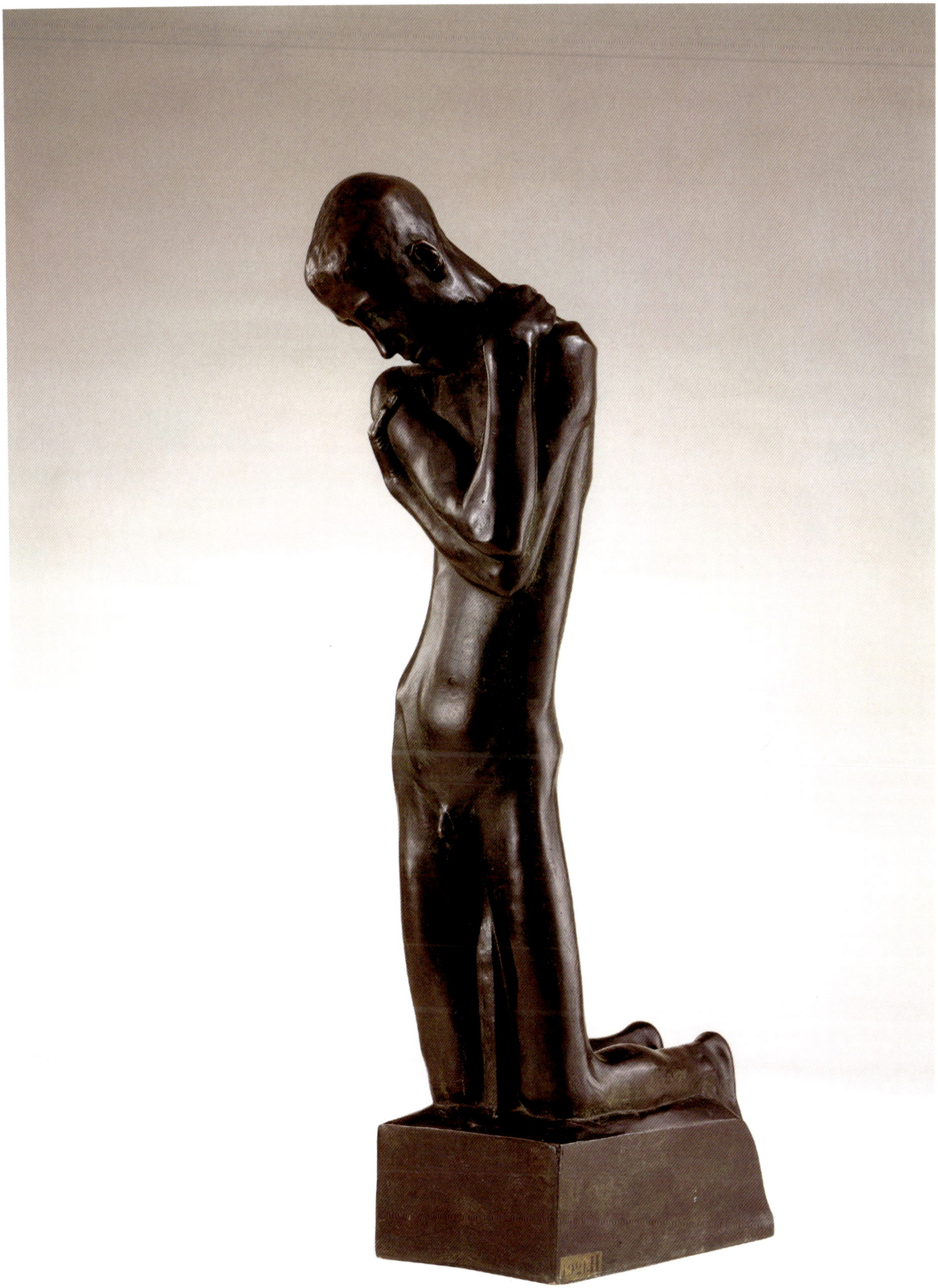

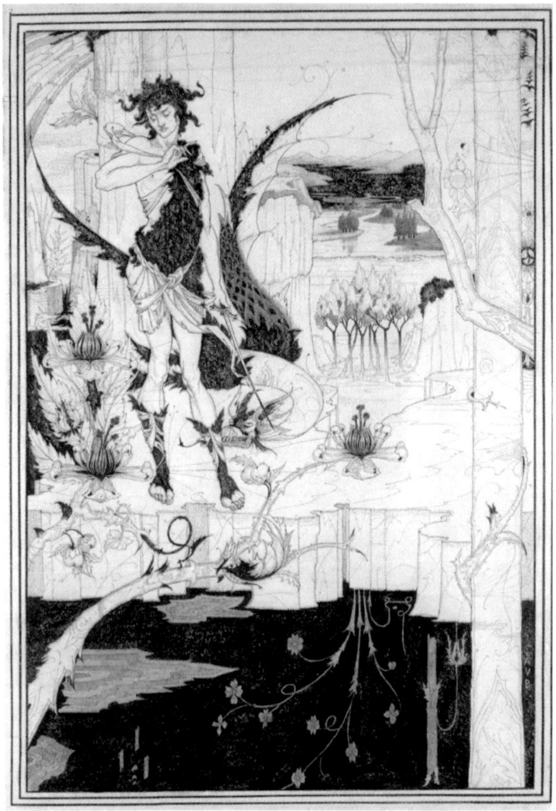

Aubrey Beardsley *Siegfried, Act II*, 1892, pen, ink and wash

London and San Francisco were the main hotspots for this phenomenon. An over-refined aesthetic reeking of perversity, combined with the youthfulness of its creator who tragically died of tuberculosis before his twenty-sixth birthday, gelled with the spirit of the 1960s and made Beardsley a byword for trendy decadence. While Beardsley's fey, knock-kneed *Siegfried* is no Narcissus, there is a conspicuous overlap in the stock iconography of youth, flower and pond that Jess may well have discerned.

Oscar Wilde, more than anyone, was responsible for crystallizing the equation of the Narcissus subject and same-sex passion at the time. During his trial, *The Picture of Dorian Gray* (1890) was raked over for evidence of encrypted homosexual desire. The same text is the subject of a lengthy analysis by Otto Rank in a chapter on Narcissus in his 1914 psychoanalytic study of *The Double*.[27] Dorian, he finds, is explicitly characterised as the Narcissus of Greek myth. In the novel, Dorian is painted by the artist Basil Hallward who portrays him in that very guise: 'You had leant over the still pool of some Greek woodland, and seen in the water's silent silver the marvel of your own face.' Dorian's infatuation with his portrait is excessive, pathological – narcissistic in Rank's diagnostic lexicon – and, following a line of reasoning familiar from Freud's da Vinci analysis, shades into Dorian's close friendships with young men that are 'attempts to realise the erotic infatuation with his own youthful image.'[28] Rank finds in Dorian's obsession with his portrait a parallel with a motif that is a staple of the medical literature on sexual inversion, or becomes so after Wilde, namely kissing one's image in a mirror. In Wilde's 1894 prose poem *The Disciple* the pool mourns the death of Narcissus, an example of a pathetic fallacy in which the sentiments of the poet, as a devotee of Narcissus, are transposed to the pool. Jess, a latterday disciple, does likewise in the two compositional studies (pp.101, 106) where arms reach out from a stream as if to return Narcissus's embrace. Somewhat reminiscent of the ghoulish reflection in Waterhouse's *Echo and Narcissus* (p.20), this so to speak 'naturalistic' motif subsequently changes into a Brancusi head and an acanthus leaf pattern, the latter substituting for the upraised arms but it is evident that the pool can still be seen as an independent 'actor' in the myth.

With good reason, Jess subtitled *Narkissos* a 'homage to Moreau'. The French symbolist painter Gustave Moreau treated the Narcissus subject on at least a dozen occasions from the mid-1870s, but especially in the 1890s. The iconography of Narcissus in Moreau's work is to some extent interchangeable with that of Orpheus, both of them surrogates for the artist. Moreau was also the author of a Narcissus poem that may be regarded as a textual, ekphrastic counterpart to his paintings on the subject in which he expresses a pantheistic, eroticised fusion with nature. The presence of the sphinx from Jess's first sketches for *Narkissos* may also owe something to Moreau. In paying homage to Moreau, Jess causes us to attend to the 'queerness' of a surrealist precursor who, in his own day, attracted loyal support from a group that included the novelists Joris-Karl Huysmans, Jean Lorrain, Marcel Proust and Wilde.[29] Jess's notebook contains a description of an especially dainty Narcissus with a wasp-like waist by Moreau that caught his eye in a volume of homoerotic art.[30] A knotted loincloth equips this gender indeterminate figure with a prosthetic phallus. Another Moreau *Narcissus* belonged to the writer and collector Robert Lebel, who was Duchamp's first biographer and a friend of Breton's – a picture with a perfect surrealist provenance. As recently as 1967, this picture was exhibited as *Venus and Cupid*, which is not at all surprising given the feminine delicacy of the figure. In both these works, Moreau has casually tipped upright a pose that he used elsewhere for the reclining Venus, without making any adjustment to the body.

The literary historian Alan Sinfield argues that before the Wilde trials in 1895, effeminacy was an unstable signifier of same-sex desire. By definition, it is a failure to meet accepted standards of manliness. Excessive emotionality, a weakness for beauty, and the artistic temperament were some of its traits. Before the mid-1890s, effeminacy was liable to be put down to men spending too much time in the company of women.[31] The majority of Moreau's depictions of Narcissus, notable for their gracefulness, fall right on the watershed where a link begins to be forged between the feminised male and sexual inversion. The notion of the androgyne, as a term applied to Moreau's gender ambiguous bodies, intersects with the development of views about homosexuality. Surveying various theories of causation, in the second volume of his *Studies in the Psychology of Sex* (1897) Havelock Ellis is inclined to the view that sexual inversion is an embryonic form of hermaphroditism. He finds evidence for the innateness of bisexuality in studies of embryogenesis, as well as psychology, lending support to a concept that harks back to the Greek myth of Hermaphroditus. Jess alludes to these ideas in the form of the alchemical androgyne. He uses an emblem from the *Musaeum Hermeticum*, a compendium of alchemical texts published in Germany in the seventeenth century, which depicts the meeting of a magnificent stag (representing the sun) and unicorn (the moon) in a forest clearing – a symbol, like the androgyne, for the alchemical fusion of opposites. It may be significant that he placed this image right beside the androgynous Narcissus.

Jess *Study for Narkissos III*, undated, pencil on paper

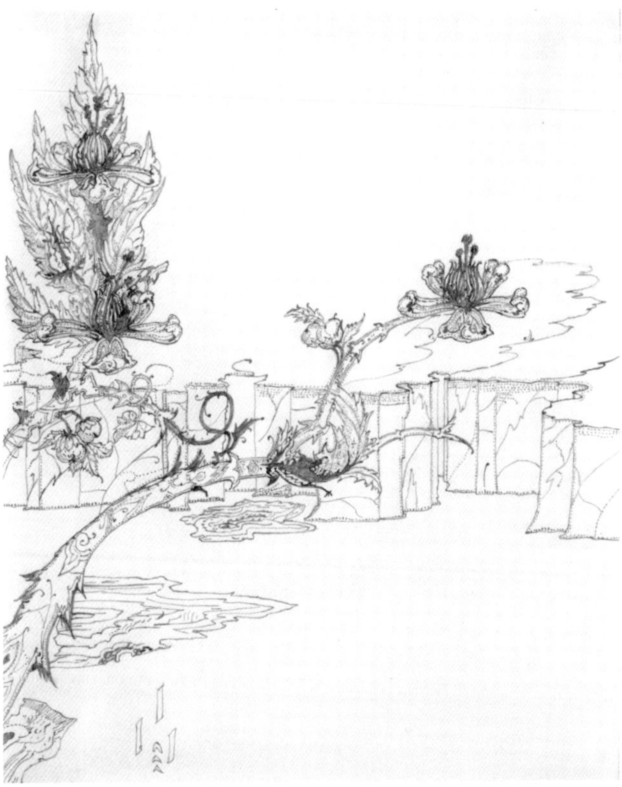

Jess surrounded the head of his figure of Eros with an aureole – a halo – that turns out to be yet another erudite reference to symbolist art. The source for the form of this luminous circle of light is one of Charles Filiger's *Chromatic Notations* from around the turn of the century – oil paintings featuring proto-abstract, fractal-like patterns that look to be based on colour charts. One has to imagine that, had Jess finished the painted version of *Narkissos*, colour would have radiated out from this central point in the composition. Filiger, an obscure member of the Pont-Aven School (the group of French symbolist painters centred on Paul Gauguin in the 1890s), was the subject of an article about him supported by André Breton who also had a sizeable collection of his work. New research by the art historian Jill Fell has shown that Breton was following in the footsteps of the French playwright Alfred Jarry – best known for the play *Ubu Roi* (1896) which was very influential for the surrealists – who had gone out of his way to promote Filiger.[32] She speculates that Jarry, ever a champion of the unconventional, knew about Filiger's homosexuality and had sympathy for the young artist's struggles with this. A stabbing, rumoured to be the tragic outcome of an altercation following a sexual liaison, was the event that precipitated Filiger's departure in 1890 from Paris for remote Brittany. Breton, naturally, remained silent on this score, if indeed he knew of it, and seems rather to have appreciated the naive mysticism of Filiger's work. He may have seen the work as belonging with his outsider art collection as the element of pattern-making is not dissimilar. There is no indication that Jess was aware of Breton's interest in Filiger, let alone that he knew about Filiger's sexuality, but it shouldn't be ruled out either since Jess and Duncan were great Jarry fans, to the extent of naming a gallery they opened in San Francisco to showcase their own work and that of their friends after the monstrous protagonist of *Ubi Roi*, Père Ubu. Their championing of Jarry's work is another instance of the queer reclamation of a surrealist precursor, analogous to the cult of the nineteenth-century French poet Arthur Rimbaud in the postwar generation of American poets and film-makers.

For Jess, who sought his own reflection in the mirror of Beardsley's pond, the *fin de siècle* may well have seemed a more congenial era than his own, affording a glimpse of how hedonism and decadence might be the basis of an enlightened and radical politics. In focusing selectively on figures from a surrealist pantheon whose sexuality went unacknowledged by the surrealist group, he and Duncan reconfigured avant-gardism as a project for sexual liberation.

Jess Compositional drawing for *Narkissos*, 1959, pencil on paper

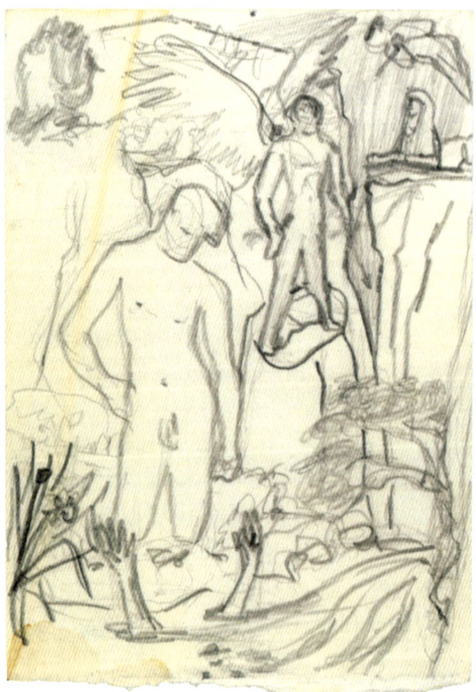

EROS AND NARCISSUS

Dominating the composition, and almost unchanged from Jess's earliest, most rudimentary sketch, are the paired figures of Narcissus and Eros. As previously noted, Jess reverses their ages as traditionally depicted, opting for a chaste, desexualised Narcissus (less obviously pubescent than in his original sketches), and a contrastingly strong, virile Eros who stands astride a rocky promontory near the centre of the picture. Eros's muscular physique is like an outgrowth of the rock upon which he stands. Both figures are composites of imagery culled from quite diverse sources, including *The Young Physique*, a proto-gay magazine. Jess takes an arm from here, a leg from there, a procedure that is as much about meaning-creation, and opening channels between the raw libidinal energies of gay culture and the arena of high art, as it is about the soldering together of a viable human form.

Eros dominates in Jess's conception of the theme. I conjecture that Herbert Marcuse's 1955 *Eros and Civilization*, which has a chapter on 'The Image of Orpheus and Narcissus', afforded the basis for an understanding of Narcissus as the affirmative expression of homoeros.[33] Jess copied out long passages from it by hand.[34] In the myth Narcissus was punished for having defied Eros by refusing the solicitations of would-be suitors, but Marcuse says that Narcissus did not love only himself; after all, he didn't realise that the lovely youth he saw reflected was himself. Citing the fusion with nature implied in the Freudian concept of primary narcissism, and literary treatments of the myth, Marcuse discovers in the Narcissus myth the basis of an expanded conception of the libido. 'Eros here signifies a quantitative and qualitative aggrandizement of sexuality', Marcuse remarks. Of even greater importance for Jess is his description of narcissistic love as an emphatic negation of 'the repressive order of procreative sexuality' or what he terms 'the Great Refusal.' In Jess's visual formulation, Eros and Narcissus have plainly resolved their antagonisms, indeed the imploring look of Eros in the direction of his younger companion might lead one to surmise they were a pair of lovers.

Marcuse's notion of a 'great refusal' turns out to be applicable to Jess in a very personal sense. Born Burgess Collins, Jess stopped using his surname in the late-1940s after a falling out with his family, evidently over his sexuality. Not long after they had been introduced, in one of the first letters to his dealer, Jess appends a postscript with a plea: 'In regards to my artist-nomer please always give it as Jess (simply). I know it gives supercilious distress sometimes to reviewers and pedants, but I mean all that the elision implies.'[35] The boyish Narcissus is a positive identificatory figure for the artist who rejected his family name and with it the adult world. Permitting ourselves to indulge in some speculation, such as Jess and Duncan might have done, it is tempting to think of the winged Eros as playing Tinkerbell to Narcissus as Peter Pan, the boy who famously refused to grow up. Jess made numerous borrowings from Victorian and Edwardian children's book illustrations. The assorted animals that he placed around the pool in the secluded grove where Narcissus paused to rest conjure up a magical haven, a sort of Neverland. Reversing the terms of the comparison, perhaps a historical ancestry could be traced for J.M. Barrie's characterisation of Peter Pan and Wendy in the artistic iconography of Narcissus. Peter Pan inherits the asociality of the mythic prototype in his inability or refusal to reciprocate Wendy's love, and more generally in his great refusal 'à la Marcuse' of the world of adults, but escapes the wrath of the god who punished Narcissus for his vanity.

A concern that surfaces in Jess's correspondence with his dealer is his wish to avoid any hint of pornography, which he evidently saw as a danger besetting his project. Feeling vindicated after a visit by art historian Peter Selz, who didn't find Jess's paintings at all pornographic, Jess picks up what had evidently been the subject of a previous conversation:

Gustave Moreau *Hercules and the Lernaean Hydra*, 1875/76, oil on canvas

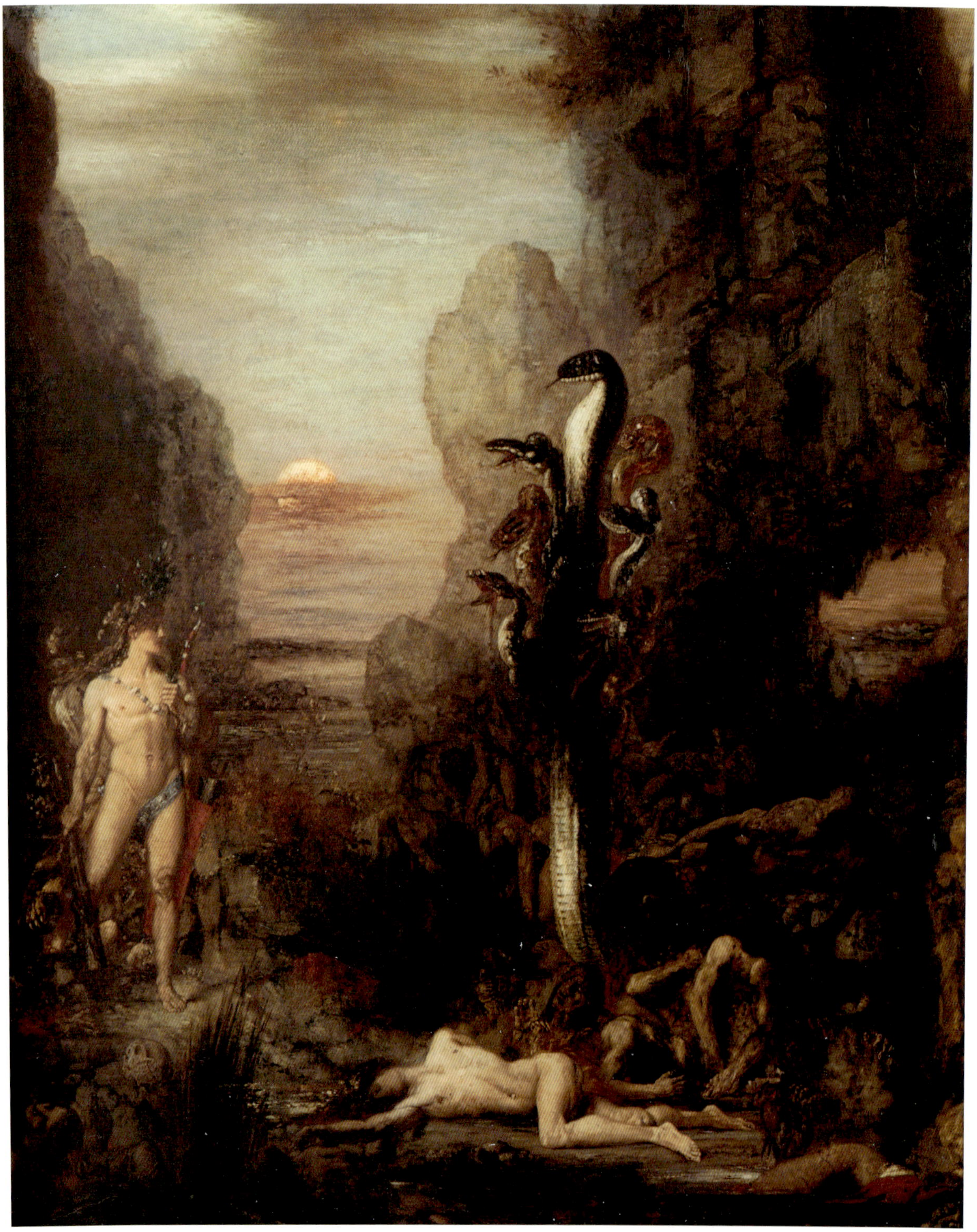

Well, I know you didn't either; but these paintings aren't of the same kind as the Schiele you mentioned, rather I believe they are a breakthru [sic] for everybody, so that romantic painting can accept a return of Eros and a freer worship of life in art.[36]

The final remark allows us to see *Narkissos* as consistent with an overall sublimatory trend.[37] Marcuse is the originator of the term 'desublimation', which has enjoyed a tremendous vogue in theoretical debates over the last decade or so, eclipsing the fact that in *Eros and Civilisation* he endorses a principle of non-repressive sublimation. Where Marcuse speaks only of Eros as an undifferentiated quantity, albeit enlarged beyond a purely heteronormative desire, it is notable that Jess specifies 'homoeros'. The kneeling pose of Narcissus, which lends a devotional piety to the work, and Eros's halo reinforce the impression that Jess intended *Narkissos* as a hymn to sacred – i.e. unprofaned – Eros.[38]

SLAYING THE HYDRA

It is no exaggeration to say that *Narkissos* was Jess's life's work. To do justice to its complexity would require far more space than this essay permits but, in concluding, I would like to signpost another image that, while not actually a part of the final work, makes its presence felt. Its importance for him is underlined by the fact that Jess chose to replicate the original dimensions of the painting, Gustave Moreau's *Hercules and the Lernaean Hydra* (1875/76) in his *Narkissos*. The ultra-intellectual Jess would surely not have overlooked a parallel between the Greek myth of Hercules overcoming the Hydra and the Norse myth of Siegfried and the dragon, illustrated by Beardsley (p.104) and retold by Wagner in the *Ring Cycle*. Painted at a time of national insecurity in the aftermath of the Franco-Prussian war, Moreau presented a lugubrious vision of Hercules, a demigod and one of the greatest of the Greek heros, confronting the fearful Hydra, the scene of this unequal contest strewn with victims.

For Jess, we conjecture, the significance was more personal. Freud interprets the hero as 'someone who has the courage to rebel against the father and has in the end victoriously overcome him.'[39] This supports our reading of Jess's repudiation of the name of his father (*nom du père*), a father whose despotic authority could be seen as symbolised in the phallic form of the Hydra in Moreau's painting.[40] It would be a mistake, though, to limit our interpretation of the multi-headed serpent to just a single meaning. Assuredly, more than one foe had to be defeated along the path to realising Jess's vision of Eros triumphant.

Duncan, Jess's partner, bravely outed himself in an essay that is considered a landmark in gay history.[41] 'The Homosexual in Society,' was written in 1944 before Duncan and Jess had met. However, it may be significant that Duncan revisited the essay in 1959, adding a preface and notes that provide a sort of running commentary, thus looking back, as it were, from a moment in time that coincides with Jess's initial study for *Narkissos*. Duncan states: 'I felt in writing the essay that I must gather forces and weight to override some adversary', a comment that resonates with my notion of Jess as a diminutive, child-like Hercules confronting an overbearing Hydra, the odds of success stacked against him. An emancipatory agenda can also perhaps be inferred from Jess's incorporation of Gustave Doré's 1865 engraving of *The Visions of Ezekiel* showing three skeletons, one robed and with arms stretched upwards, at the bottom edge of *Narkissos*. The prophet Ezekiel's vision of skeletons being restored to life by God was seen as a message of hope for the people of Israel in exile.

If *Narkissos* is fundamentally about a struggle to represent identity using myth as a vehicle, the inordinate length of time Jess spent on this project and his continual procrastination may be taken as symptomatic of the difficulty of the task. 'My biggest debt is the *Narkissos* painting; but, altho [sic] you can't yet be shown a single paintstroke, it is many years underway and grows richer for its continuing germination', he writes to placate a dealer impatient to see his outlay begin to bear fruit. Duncan's essay makes clear that his identity-politics were anchored in a quest for complete transparency of the self to representation. Any opacity is regarded as evasion or mystification to be swept aside. Yet the contradictions besetting such a project are immediately evident from the attraction of both Jess and Duncan to occult systems of thought. While the heroic character of Jess's undertaking is undeniable, and the grandeur of the results self-evident, what the myth of Narcissus tells us is that we can never be identical with the image we see reflected in the mirror, and that the truer image of desire may be the ripples that spread out across the pond obliterating the coherent self-image – or, in the case of *Narkissos*, the myriad ramifying pathways that defy attempts at a unitary interpretation.

NOTES

1. The notebook belongs to Odyssia Skouras who, together with her husband Federico Quadrani, supported Jess throughout much of the time that he worked on *Narkissos*.
2. Jacques Derrida, *Pregnances – Quatre lavis de Colette Deblé* (Paris: Brandes, 1993). I am thankful to Fréderique Joseph-Lowery for bringing this to my attention.
3. *Jess: A Grand Collage, 1951–1993* (Buffalo, New York: Albright-Knox Art Gallery, 1993), p.26.
4. Jess was a keen reader of popular science books. Martin Gardner's *The Ambidextrous Universe: Mirror Asymmetry and Time-Reversed Worlds* (New York: Basic, 1964) was a reference for him, as it was for Robert Smithson (see chapter 4).
5. Michael Palmer, 'On Jess's Narkissos', in *Jess: A Grand Collage, 1951–1993*, pp.93–103.
6. Thomas Taylor, *The Eleusinian and Bacchic Mysteries: A Dissertation* (c.1790), (New York: J.W. Bouton, 1891), p.150.
7. Ibid.
8. Hans Jonas, *The Gnostic Religion: The Message of the Alien God and the Beginnings of Christianity* (Boston: Beacon Press, 1958).
9. Ibid., p.161.
10. Ibid.
11. The metaphor is present in Ovid: 'As he lay on the bank, he gazed at the twin stars that were his eyes.' Ovid, *Metamorphoses*, trans. Mary M. Innes (Harmondsworth: Penguin, 1955), book III.
12. Peter O'Leary, *Gnostic Contagion: Robert Duncan and the Poetry of Illness* (Middletown: Wesleyan University Press, 2002), pp.77–79 and pp.134–139.
13. Jess's notebook is filled with running, sometimes acerbic commentaries on his reading. At one point, he chides the author of a popularising psychoanalytic study (see note 34): 'on looking into the book's index: there are no references to Jung, Plotinus, Iamblichus, Proclus, NeoPlatonic, Plato, Mystic, Gnostic, Hermes, Poemandres, etc., yet she has asserted that she exhaustively sifted man's previous understandings of Narcissus! & this is a "Scientist", who is not by any means ill-meaning'. I read Jess's remarks as a reproach to myself from an artist whose imagination was nurtured by Narcissus for more than three decades.
14. John Addington Symonds, *A Problem in Greek Ethics: being an inquiry into the phenomenon of sexual inversion, addressed especially to medical psychologists and jurists* (1883),(London: The Areopagita Society, 1908).
15. Hans Licht [pseud. Paul Brandt], *Sexual Life in Ancient Greece* (London: Routledge & Keegan Paul, 1932), p.413.
16. See James Davidson, *The Greeks and Greek Love: A Radical Reappraisal of Homosexuality in Ancient Greece* (London: Weidenfeld and Nicolson, 2007).
17. Bernard Sergent, *Homosexuality in Greek Myth* (London: Athlone Press, 1987), pp.81–101.
18. Ibid., p.99.
19. Ibid., p.83. See below for Marcuse's affirmation of Narcissus's refusal.
20. See 'Behind the Mirror' in Thom Gunn, *Collected Poems* (Farrar, Straus & Giroux, 1995). I am grateful to John McAuliffe for sharing his thoughts about the poem with me.
21. See Nicholas Chare, 'Sexing the Canvas: Calling on Medium,' *Art History*, 2009, n. 34, p.687.
22. Stephen Bann, *The True Vine: On Visual Representation and the Western Tradition* (Cambridge: Cambridge University Press, 1989).
23. Philostratus, *Imagines* (London and New York: W. Heinemann Ltd; G.P. Putnam's Sons, 1931), book I, chapter 23, p.91.
24. Jess, letter to Federico Quadrani (4 November 1977). Bancroft Library, University of California, Berkeley.
25. 'Art Nouveau Revival 1900. 1933. 1966. 1974' (Paris: Musée d'Orsay, 2010).
26. Surveying the underground film scene, Parker Tyler, writing in 1971, notes: 'Among the pictorial arts there is the relevant case of Aubrey Beardsley, whose works are having a pop revival in our current period of psychedelic vision.' Parker Tyler, *Underground Film: A Critical History*,

(London: Secker & Warburg, 1971), p.123.

27. Otto Rank, *The Double: A Psychoanalytic Study* (1914) Chapel Hill: University of North Carolina Press, 1971), chapter V, 'Narcissism and the Double'.
28. Ibid., p.71.
29. See Pierre-Louis Mathieu, *Gustave Moreau Aquarelles* (Paris: Seuil, 1984), p.92. My interest is less in trying to prove 'the latent homosexuality of the painter' (Mathieu) than in showing how the work of this surrealist precursor might have been viewed differently by queer subjects.
30. Cecile Beurdeley, *L'Amour bleu* (New York: Rizzoli, 1978), p.49.
31. Alan Sinfield, *The Wilde Century: Effeminacy, Oscar Wilde and the Queer Moment* (New York: Columbia University Press, 1994), pp.25–47.
32. Jill Fell, 'The Fascination of Filiger: From Jarry to Breton,' *Papers of Surrealism*, no. 9 (spring 2011), np.
33. Herbert Marcuse, *Eros and Civilization: A Philosophical Inquiry into Freud* (1955), (Boston: Beacon Press, 1966).
34. Aside from Marcuse, Jess consulted only a limited number of psychoanalytic sources, notably a book for a lay readership by Grace Stuart, *Narcissus: A Psychological Study of Self-Love* (London: Allen & Unwin, 1955). His reading in this area is far outweighed by the aforementioned readings of Gnostic and hermetic sources.
35. Jess, letter to Federico Quadrani (15 February 1968).
36. Jess, letter to Federico Quadrani (10 February 1972).
37. Of relevance here is Freud's account of sublimation as desexualised homosexual libido.
38. The cult of love in classical Greece was centred on the city of Thespiae where Eros was worshipped in the form of a rock. Narcissus was also a native of Thespiae.
39. Freud, 'Moses and Monotheism', *Pelican Freud Library*, vol. 13, p.248.
40. One would have to admit that the picture is somewhat ambiguous in this regard and that the kneeling pose of Narcissus, which symbolises a willing supplication before a paternal principle – God or the father as in certain depictions of the prodigal son – gestures towards a reconciliation.
41. See Thom Gunn's explication of homosexual themes in Duncan's poetry, in *Robert Duncan: Scales of the Marvelous*, edited by Robert J. Bertholf (New York: W.W. Norton & Co., 1980), pp.143–160.

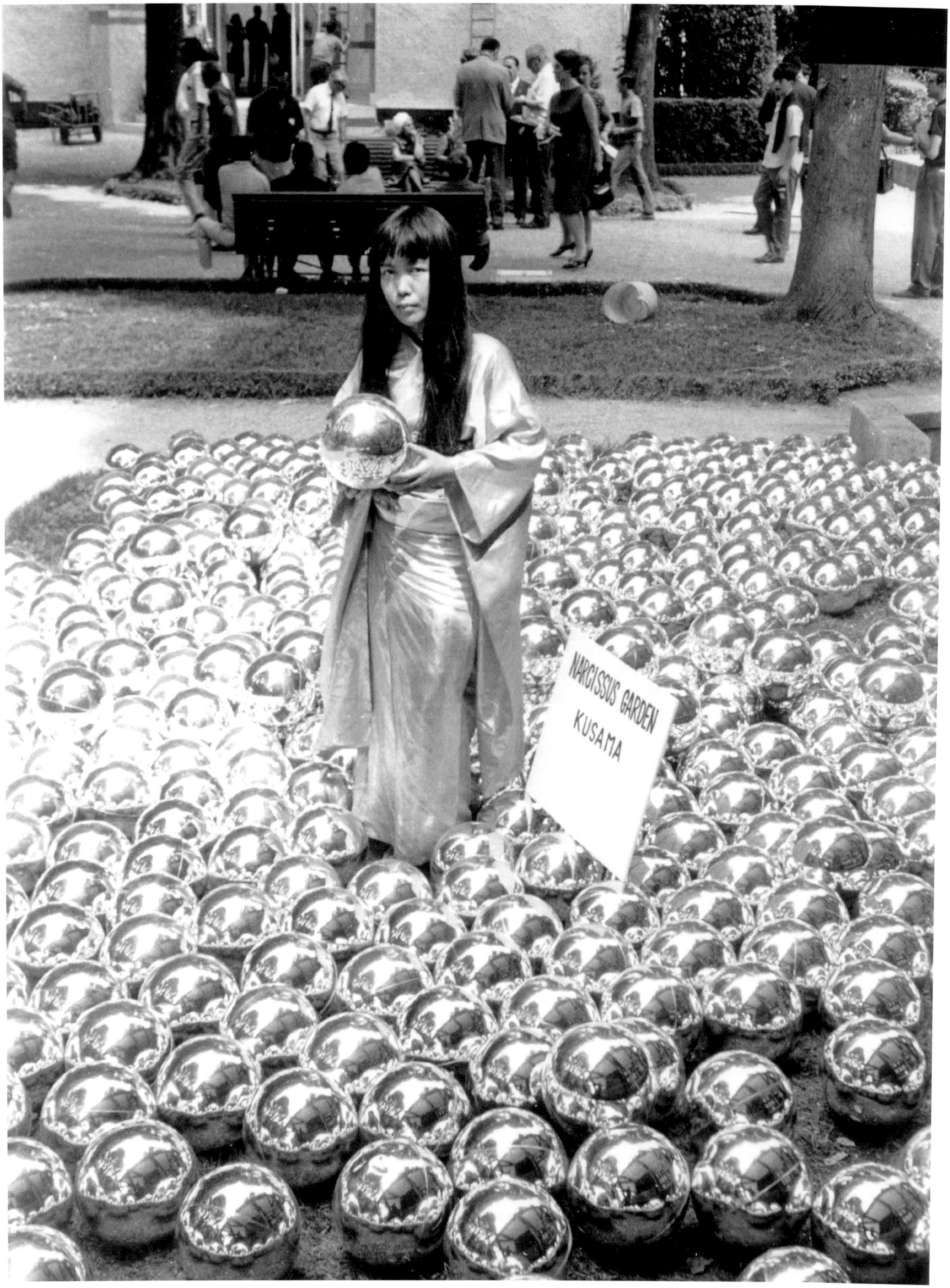
NARCISSUS GARDEN
KUSAMA

CHAPTER FOUR
NARCISSUS GARDEN

The fable is born simply from the image offered by the plant bent over the water.
The legend in its entirety seems to have arisen from a personification of the plant.
Larousse, *Grand dictionnaire du XIXe siècle.*[1]

The Narcissus myth is inseparably linked with the history of the flower described by Theophrastus in his early-fourth century BC botanical treatise *De Historia plantarum* (Enquiry into Plants). Nineteenth-century mythographers believed the myth could be explained by the properties of the narcissus, which is so-named because of the presumed narcotising properties of its powerful scent, hence the association with sleep, unconsciousness and death. Aside from the myth of Narcissus, the flower also features in the story of Persephone's abduction to the underworld. The Western symbolism of the flower and the garden and their relevance to the myth of Narcissus stretch back to the Biblical figure of Adam and the Garden of Eden. Adam has sometimes been compared to Narcissus, prior to the separation of the sexes and the introduction of Eve. In Eastern art, the Narcissus flower is ubiquitous but its symbolism is entirely different, and it is in Japanese artist Yayoi Kusama's seminal work *Narcissus Garden* (first shown at the Venice Biennale in 1966) that the Eastern and Western symbolic meaning of the narcissus flower are brought together.

This chapter will explore the hypothesis that the eighteenth-century study of botany is a realm in which one finds elaborated a notion of polymorphous eroticism that percolates down to the twentieth century and into the visual culture of surrealism. Immanuel Kant, in his 'Analytic of the Beautiful' (1790), puts aside the flowers reproductive function in order to extol it as an example of free beauty.[2] For surrealist artists and writers, by contrast, botany is the route to a de-sublimatory release of a polymorphous sexuality. The ubiquity of Kusama's flower imagery, and its relation to a pan-eroticism that permeates her sculpture and spatial installations, highlights the importance of the symbolism of the flower not only in Kusama's work, but in wider relation to the Narcissus theme.

Yayoi Kusama Installation view of Kusama with *Narcissus Garden* at the Venice Biennale, 1966

THE SEX OF PLANTS

In the 1890s, Gustave Moreau wrote a text that phantasises a state of erotic fusion of Narcissus with entangling vegetation. The origins of this erotic relationship between man and nature, and the analogies made between humans and plants, can be found in Ovid's *Metamorphoses* and the various stories of Narcissus, Hyacinthus and Cyparissus.

These ideas are reinvigorated within botanical science where a link between plants and eroticism was firmly established during the eighteenth century, a development that has major repercussions for art and visual culture of the late-nineteenth and twentieth century. The German botanist Rudolph Jakob Camerarius demonstrated in his 1694 *De sexu plantarum epistola* (Letter concerning the sex of plants) that stamens and pistils were respectively the male and female sexual organs of flowering plants, however, a detailed understanding of the role of these organs, and of pollen in the process of fertilization, would have to await another century and a half. Building upon these foundations and inspired by Sébastien Vaillant's 1718 *Discours sur la structure des fleurs* (Discourses on the Structure of Flowers), Carl Linnaeus introduced a system of botanical classification based upon the number and arrangement of pistils and stamens in *Systema naturae* (The System of Nature), a major landmark in botanical science which was published in 1735:

> One has given the name sexual system to this method, because its principles rest upon the sexual organs of plants; that is to say, the stamens considered as the male parts, and the pistils considered as female parts.[3]

An adherent of the Linnaean system became known as a 'sexualist'. In response to Linnaeus, Julien Offray de La Mettrie extended the comparative method beyond the reproductive organs, mapping a rigorous one-to-one comparison of human anatomy and plant structure in *L'Homme plante* (Plant Man, 1748), a pendant to his better-known essay *L'Homme machine* (Machine Man) of the same year. His purpose in proving such equivalences was to situate man in nature rather than as ruling over it. La Mettrie also discussed at length the process of generation in plants, noting that the plant kingdom includes the only hermaphrodites that are capable of fertilising themselves.

These eigthteenth-century developments in botany contributed to a growing perception of the plant kingdom as pervaded by eroticism. A frontispiece to Robert John Thornton's *The Temple of Flora* (1799), a magnificent opus produced in accordance with the precepts of Linnaean botany, depicts a cupid armed with bow and arrow, inspiring plants with love. From his lips emanate the rhyming couplets:

> And thou, divine LINNAEUS! trac'd my reign
> O'er Trees, and Plants, and Flora's beauteous Train
> Prov'd them obedient to my soft Controul.
> And gaily breathe the aromatic soul.

A genre of pornographic writing quickly sprang up in Linnaeus's wake, exploiting the botanical analogies with female or male genitalia. Looking ahead to any number of surrealist pictures employing flower and plant imagery as metaphors for the female sex, Philogynes Clitorides facetiously recorded the natural history of a newly-discovered plant, the *Frutex vulvaria*:

> ... a flat low shrub, which always grows in a moist warm valley, at the Foot of a little Hill, which is constantly water'd by a Spring, whose Water is impregnated with very saline Particles, which nevertheless agree wonderfully well with this Shrub; it is guarded round about with Fibrillae, or Capillary Tendrils, of the same Nature, and Use, with those at the root of the *Arbor Vitae*.[4]

Linnaeus was a devout Christian and presented a highly moralised vision of the plant kingdom, though others saw in his system an opportunity to challenge social convention. Erasmus Darwin's poem, *The Loves of the Plants* (1789), which, according to the historian of science Londa Schiebinger, brought the eroticisation of botany 'to full bloom', would provoke a backlash for its alleged licentiousness.[5] Up until that point, the vegetable world had mirrored the polite mores of eighteenth-century Europe. Where Linnaeus's sexual system teems with respectable marriage metaphors, the dissenter Darwin, who was also influenced by stories of free love in the Pacific Islands recounted by James Cook and other explorers, extols an amoral nature. Monogamy, it has been discovered, simply doesn't apply to the vegetable world. Formerly, botany had been thought an area of scientific endeavour suitable for women, but *The Loves of the Plants* changed all that. The art historian Asia Haut notes that 'its provocative scenes of plant polygamy caused some to condemn it as an example of botany at its most licentious, whose open advocacy of free love stood as a direct threat to feminine virtue.'[6] As a result, botany as a popular science declined during the nineteenth century, eclipsed by a sentimental Victorian language of flowers. A return of the repressed, when it later occurs in surrealism, is observed primarily in the work of its women artists.

In the course of an essay full of praise for Art Nouveau, Dalí suddenly declares: 'Beauty is but the conscious sum of all our perversions.'[7] Art Nouveau, an aesthetic predicated, in André Breton's words, on 'a ceaseless borrowing (to the point of nausea) of subjects, adventitious or not, from the vegetable world', would be responsible for a massive rehabilitation of botanical imagery and metaphor at the end of the nineteenth century. We can certainly see this intertwining of plants and perversion as nourishing the sudden efflorescence of Narcissus in art, literature and medicine. Émile Gallé, whose name is almost synonymous with the style, had studied botany in Nancy before becoming a glassmaker, and his erudition is evident in the scientifically-correct depiction of flowers and other botanical motifs. In addition, this was the period when sexology took off as a field of medical and forensic study. In the 1963 *The Birth of the Clinic*, Michel Foucault remarks that: 'The old dream of Boissier de Sauvages of being the Linnaeus of diseases was not entirely forgotten in the nineteenth century: doctors long continued to botanize in the field of the pathological.'[8] Such a description is eminently applicable to the German sexologist Richard von Krafft-Ebing and his brethren, the pioneers of a science of sexual aberrations; in the words of Foucault, once again, 'they made up a herbal of them and established a system of classification'. Plants and perversity become even more tightly entwined. Arnold Davidson specifies that the normative concept of sexuality, which forms at this moment, is coterminous with the definition of the field of the perversions: 'our experience of sexuality, was born at the same time that perversion emerged as the kind of deviation by which sexuality was ceaselessly threatened.'[9]

The aesthetic corollary of this science of perverse sexuality was the Decadent movement. Duc Jean Floressas des Esseintes, the hero of Joris-Karl Huysmans's 1884 novel *A rebours* (Against Nature), a veritable manifesto of the movement, had always been 'excessively fond of flowers.'[10] In order to satisfy this penchant, Des Esseintes fills a hothouse with exotic species of plants, but such is his taste for morbidity, that the sickly blooms he amasses resemble patients in a medical ward. Within the Decadent credo, illness and disease are positive markers of aesthetic value. Huysmans continues:

> The gardeners brought in still more varieties, this time affecting the appearance of factitious skin covered with a network of counterfeit veins. Most of them, as if ravaged by syphilis or leprosy, displayed livid patches of flesh mottled with roseola.[11]

Declaring that horticulturalists are the only true artists remaining, Des Esseintes insists that Nature alone would be incapable of producing 'such depraved, unhealthy species' – terms of approbation in this reverse, wilfully perverse, aesthetic discourse. Huysmans resurrects the pornographic imagination of Philogynes Clitorides to express the sexual insecurities of his dandyish hero, whose excessive interest in flowers can be taken as an index of his effeminacy. At the conclusion of a chapter in which he indulges his botanical passion, his mind morbidly overfilled with images of flowers, Des Esseintes has a frightening dream in which he is pursued by a woman, until finally: 'pale with horror, he saw the savage Nidularium [one of his new acquisitions] blossoming between her uplifted thighs, with its swordblades gaping open to expose the bloody depths.'[12] Freud, in one of his attempts to explain male homosexuality, remarks upon cases where the 'compulsive longing for men has turned out to be determined by their ceaseless flight from women.'[13] The against nature of Huysmans's title reverberates, albeit ambiguously, with the concept of unnatural vice. 'Decadence lingers trembling on the brink of homosexuality', writes Alan Sinfield pithily in a sentence that evokes the narcissus flower itself, solitary and leaning over the edge of a stream.'[14]

The French journalist Octave Mirbeau's extraordinary 1899 *Le Jardin des supplices* (The Torture Garden) is another testament to the fevered *fin de siècle* botanical imaginary.[15] The narrator is accompanied by the hysterical Clara on a visit to a Chinese prison, at the heart of which is a torture garden. Descriptions of exotic blooms are interspersed with tales of almost indescribable horror. A Chinese torturer whom they encounter proudly relates a uniquely cruel punishment involving a cage of rats affixed to a victim's backside – reading this was enough to induce a neurosis in Freud's 'Ratman' (a case involving a man with obsessional thoughts about such punishment being meted out to himself and his loved ones). As it happens, the narrator of Mirbeau's novel turns out to know his Linnaeus. Pausing from his storytelling, the torturer spreads apart the petals of the flower, counts the stamens laden with pollen, and speaks:

> 'See milady; one, two, five, ten, twenty. See how they quiver! Look! Sometimes twenty males are required for the delight of a single female! He! he! he! sometimes it's the opposite'. One by one he tore off the petals, before remarking to his eager interlocutor: 'Make love, milady ... make love ... like the flowers!'[16]

The lasciviousness of the kingdom of Flora, discovered in the eighteenth century and forgotten during the nineteenth, is recalled in the executioner's lewd suggestion.

Another theme that occupied Decadent writers, and that again has a connection with perverse sexuality, is the paradox of a flower being nourished by filth and rottenness. Writing in 1895 at the time of the Oscar Wilde trials, Mirbeau muses: 'why is the flower so beautiful that has roots plunged in abject manure'?[17] Mirbeau is responding to the opprobium that was heaped on Wilde as a result of the trial. The image of the beautiful flower with its roots in excremental matter contests the segregation of the pure from the impure on which the moral condemnation, and eventual incarceration, of Wilde was based. Indeed, to the contrary, it goes so far as to infer a necessary conduit between beauty and perversion. One of the sources fuelling these botanical reflections was Charles Baudelaire's *Une Charogne* (A Carcass), a poem from the 1857 volume *Fleurs du mal* (The Flowers of Evil), which conflates beauty and putrescence in a delirious metaphor of a bloated corpse in the sun split open like a blossoming flower.[18] If there is a connection with the myth of Narcissus, it maybe concerns his death and the beautiful flower nourished by his blood. *The Torture Garden's* Clara extols: 'Putrefaction in which the eternal heat of life resides / In which the eternal renewal of metamorphoses unfolds!'[19]

In a surrealist milieu, these ideas were taken up by Georges Bataille in a 1929 essay on 'Le Langage des fleurs' (The Language of Flowers). Bataille's title alludes sarcastically to the prim Victorian language of flowers that replaced the eighteenth-century study of botany when the latter came to be seen as too risqué, but the whole thrust of Bataille's article is aimed at promoting a return of the repressed. More powerfully seductive than the etiolated vision of ideal beauty, Bataille asserts, is the 'impossible and fantastic vision of roots swarming under the surface of the soil, nauseating and naked like vermin'.[20] Like Mirbeau's executioner, Bataille wishes to strip away the adornment of the petals and expose the hairy sexual organs beneath – a brutal defloration. Mocking Kant's idealizing account of beauty, which sets aside the reproductive functions of the flower, Bataille writes there are 'plants so shady one is tempted to attribute to them the most troubling human perversions.'[21]

Only the briefest sketch can be presented here of a cross-pollination, so to speak, with this eighteenth- and nineteenth-century predilection for associating human and plant sexuality, and the art of the twentieth century. The Cubist-inspired paintings of Marcel Duchamp and Francis Picabia in the period 1912–14 are replete with allusions to the reproductive parts of flowers as well as to the more commonly-recognised mechanical forms, doubtless reflecting the fact that both artists were thoroughly steeped in the literature of symbolism. Adopting a longer perspective, however, one can see La Mettrie as licensing an art form that unites *l'homme plante* with *l'homme machine*. Picabia's enigmatic *I See Again in Memory My Dear Udnie* (1914), a picture that relates to a secretive tryst with a dancer on a transatlantic liner, brilliantly demonstrates the capacity for hybridization of these two metaphoric systems in a quasi-abstract composition. However it is Duchamp's series of Bride pictures, culminating in the 'desiring apparatus' of *The Bride Stripped Bare by Her Bachelors, Even (The Large Glass)* (1915–23), that alludes most insistently to correspondences put in place by Linnaean botany. The word Duchamp uses repeatedly in his notes for the bride when she reaches 'the goal of her desire' is 'blossoming'. Deflowering, as a term for the passage from virgin to bride, belongs to everyday parlance but where, aside from Linnaeus, is one likely to find a bride attended by nine bachelors?

It is necessary to insist upon the perversity of Duchamp's non-functioning dada apparatus. The operative terms in *The Large Glass* are suspension and delay. Duchamp spoke of the work as 'a delay in glass'. The consummation of the marriage is definitively thwarted as the bride is left literally hanging in mid-air. The bachelors fire their shots randomly in her direction, recalling the release of pollen more than coupling in the human world. Gilles Deleuze identifies deferral/suspension as fundamental tropes of masochistic perversions and they signify a refusal of genital finality.[22] Dada is against all teleologies. The eschewal of reproductive sexuality is connected with a dada critique of the values of efficiency and productivity enshrined in a modernist machine metaphor and, more broadly, with the deconstruction of an Enlightenment project of rationality. It is within this context that the botanical metaphor and its baggage of associations with polymorphous eroticism comes into its own.

In surrealism, as noted, botanical imagery is more widespread among female artists, not surprising given the entrenched gendered connotations of flower painting. That the surrealist milieu offered these women a propitious environment for the exploration of sexuality is evident from the work of Georgia O'Keeffe, Dorothea Tanning, Ithell Colquhoun, Leonora Carrington, Frida Kahlo and others.[23] A number of these artists, O'Keeffe most famously, use the flower as a symbol for the vagina to celebrate female sexuality. An Arcimboldesque substitution of fruit and plant reproductive parts for the human organs enables Kahlo, who was informed about botany through her friendship with the American botanist Luther Burbank, to find an avenue for the expression of her bisexuality in a metaphorical form.

In the early 1930s, Max Ernst produced a cluster of collages and paintings with found botanical images that play on the anthropomorphic and erotic potential of pistils and stamens. For over a decade, Ernst had utilised scientific diagrams culled from encyclopedias and other popular sources, however the explicitness of

Max Ernst *The Nymph Echo*, 1936, oil on canvas

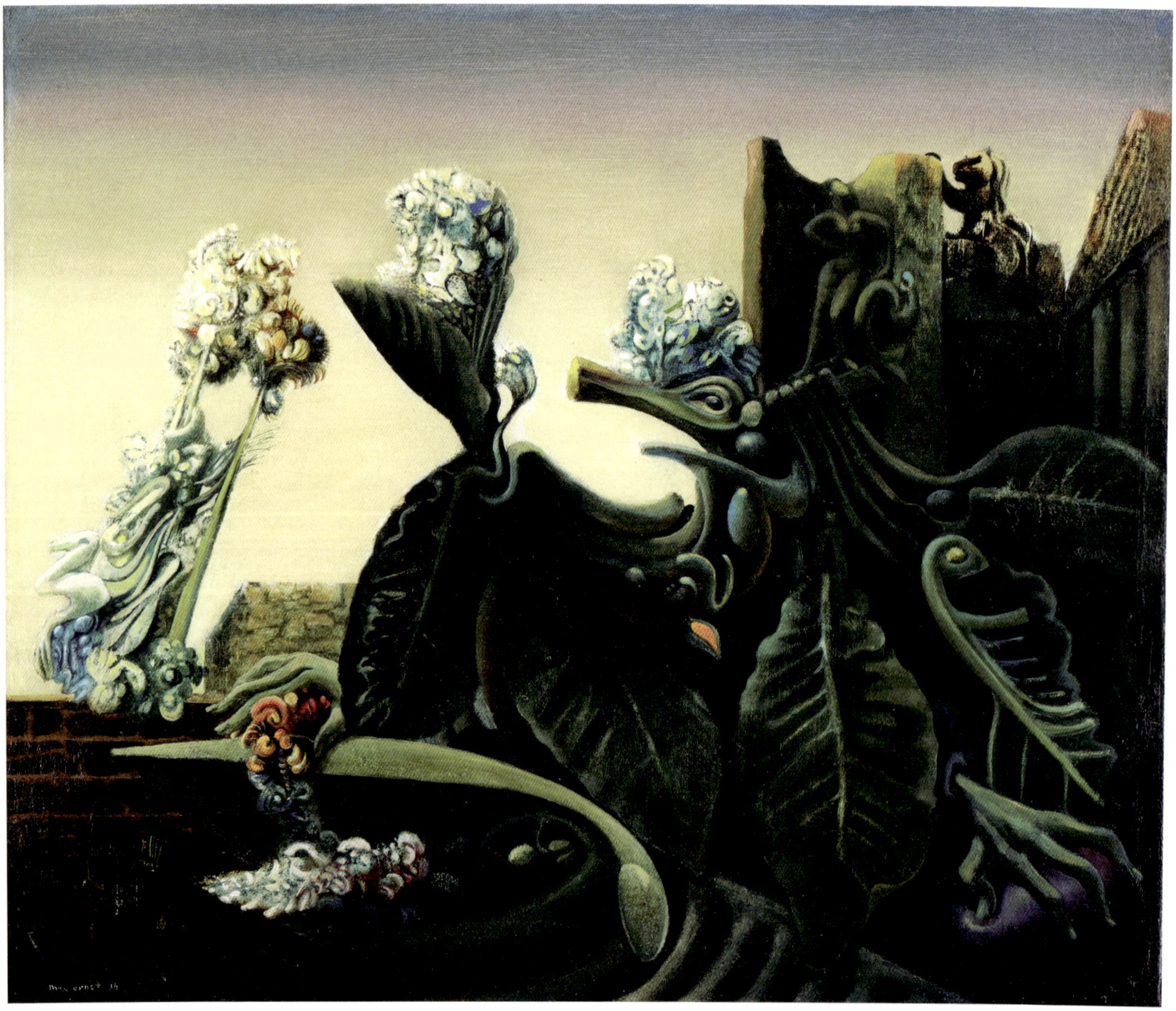

his allusion to the reproductive parts of plants may suggest that these works should be seen as in a dialogue with Georges Bataille – in particular, Bataille's provocative contention in 'The Language of Flowers' that 'even the most beautiful flowers are spoiled in their centres by hairy sexual organs'. Around 1935–36, Ernst produced another series of works titled *The Nymph Echo* that consist of fantastical vegetation, and engage themes of camouflage and mimicry, though oddly none correspondingly of Narcissus. Referencing Ovid's *Metamorphoses*, the sheer abundance of vegetation and the strange blossoming flowers provide cover for, and analogies with, human games of pursuit and sexual couplings of all kinds that transpire in the undergrowth. In these works, it seems that Ernst illustrates Herbert Marcuse's yet to be formulated notion of an expansive and expanded Eros.[24]

In December 1933, the surrealist journal *Minotaure* carried an article by de Sade scholar Maurice Heine, which purported to present a new classification of the perversions.[25] The inciting event, to which this essay can be seen as responding, was the extremely belated publication in 1931 of a French translation of Krafft-Ebing's classic study *Psychopathia Sexualis*, first published in German in 1886.[26] Heine's article mimics the positivist science of sexology in its pseudo-scientific style and classificatory impulse, though it seeks to purge the field of the normative and moralistic assumptions that had blighted the study of sexuality. My interest lies in a diagram which accompanies the article, a tree whose luxuriant foliage is, if not exactly in the manner imagined by Mirbeau, nourished by the perversions. A notable feature of Heine's schema, by contrast with a typical genealogical tree, is the absence of any implied 'normal' development. Heine proposes to analyse the perversions from an entirely amoral point of view; he commends the more neutral term 'paraesthesia' in preference to perversion, as potentially liberating psychobiology from all ethical or religious prejudice. And, indeed, given the surrealist context, the discussion of homosexuality is surprisingly non-judgemental. Of special interest is Heine's attitude to what he terms 'bisexualisme' or 'psychosexual hermaphroditism'. 'This last,' he says, 'far from referring, as Krafft-Ebing and Moll would wish, to an incomplete inversion, realises a complete sexual type, as shown by ontogenesis'.[27] While, in the main, Heine is engaging with a pre-psychoanalytic tradition, he does not ignore psychoanalysis, which he claims adds weight to this interpretation by showing the frequency of repressed homosexual tendencies in even the most clearly heterosexually-identified subjects.

The trajectory of interest in botany and sexuality outlined is one that largely bypasses Freud (whose dream of a botanical monograph contains a reproach to himself for having ignored botany), though its conclusions are consistent with Freud's hypothesis of an innate bisexuality. Freud adopts this notion from his friend the surgeon Wilhelm Fliess and it is in hysterical phantasies that he seeks verification for it. In 'Hysterical Phantasies and their Relation to Bisexuality' (1908), he argues that not only may the hysterical symptom represent a compromise between a libidinal and a repressing impulse, 'it may also represent a union of two libidinal phantasies of an opposite sexual character.' The combination of masculine and feminine impulses in a single hysterical symptom affords evidence of an innately bisexual disposition that is especially visible in psycho-neurotics. Freud refers to hysterical attacks 'in which the patient simultaneously plays both parts in the underlying sexual phantasy. In one case which I observed, for instance, the patient pressed her dress up against her body with one hand (as the woman), while she tried to tear it off with the other (as the man).' Then, in a letter of 1 August 1899 to Fliess, who influenced Freud's views about the innateness of bisexuality, we find the astounding claim: 'Bisexuality! I am sure you are right about it. And I am accustoming myself to regarding every sexual act as an event between four individuals.'[28] After Linnaeus, hermaphroditism becomes the norm in botany and the prospect of four (or even more) 'in a bed' would not even have raised an eyebrow.

Yayoi Kusama *My Flower Bed* (1962–63) at Kusama's studio in New York 1965–66, painted gloves, mattress springs

KUSAMA'S LANGUAGE OF FLOWERS

Flowers and their symbolism have been absolutely pivotal for Yayoi Kusama (b. 1929) from her earliest works, such as *My Flower Bed* (1962–63), through to her most recent, large-scale flower sculptures. A Japanese artist who worked in New York through the 1960s, Kusama's major installation, *Narcissus Garden* (1966), bridges the Oriental symbolism of the narcissus flower and the Western Narcissus myth. Kusama's family had a horticultural business and she grew up surrounded by flowers. As a young painter, she was trained in the traditional techniques of Japanese painting (*nihon-ga*), in which flower painting is a main genre. The surrealist movement was active in Japan until the 1950s and was palpably an influence upon the biomorphic idiom of Kusama's early works. After moving to New York in 1957, she sought out Georgia O'Keeffe, who assumed the role of a mentor and helped her gain a toehold in the art world. This personal connection may have encouraged her to view flowers as a fitting subject for an avant-garde practice and to assert a strong, positive alliance of botany with female sexuality. The 1960s were, moreover, the era of Woodstock and the anti-Vietnam War protests with their slogan of 'flower power' – a potent symbol of peaceful resistance for the counter-culture, of which Kusama counted herself a committed foot soldier.

My Flower Bed shown photographed in her New York studio in 1965–66, illustrates what the feminist critic Lucy Lippard surely meant by Kusama's 'baroque and psychosexual sculpture'. We have from Kusama herself a description of it:

> Filled with loneliness, unable to sleep, I curl up for the night in *My Flower Bed* because flowers are tender and loving. Now I am an insect that returns to its flower during the night; the petals close over me as the mother's womb protects the unborn child … Until dawn, the flowers in *My Flower Bed* will sway in the night breeze and caress me gently, for the night is the time of love and sex.

Kusama creates ambiguous, inherently polymorphous objects that invite a multiplicity of associations. Composed of mattress springs and an accumulation of stuffed fabric gloves, *My Flower Bed* rises up like a prehensile hand or a germinating plant. The encrusted finger-like shapes, generally considered as phallic, with which she also covered pieces of furniture at this time, can also just as easily be read as pistils, that is, the female sexual parts of plants. Kusama taps into the specifically gendered connotations of 'soft' sculpture; indeed the red pigment-soaked cloth of *My Flower Bed* is suggestive of menstrual blood.[29] It is tempting to think that the surrealist 'Eros' exhibition organised by Duchamp and Breton in Paris in 1959, at which Robert Rauschenberg's *Bed* (1955) was exhibited, may have provided a stimulus for Kusama's merger of a surrealist sensibility with an all-pervasive erotic energy that literally gushes like a jet from her body. Certainly, Lippard responded to this, since Kusama was one of the exemplars of a new post-minimalist tendency that she explored in her curating of the influential 'Eccentric Abstraction' exhibition in 1966 which included Kusama alongside Eva Hesse, Louise Bourgeois and Bruce Nauman.

Kusama routinely photographed herself in her installations. These photos are more than just a minor adjunct to the work. The installation functions as the setting for a performative staging of subjectivity, and the photographs (or, indeed, the films that she made in the later 1960s) constitute a form of documentation of the performance, which as a distinct genre dovetails with the politicised body art and Happenings that Kusama participated in during this decade of sit-ins and anti-war protests. One of the most intriguing of the Happenings orchestrated by Kusama was a wedding of two gay men at which she officiated as a 'high priestess' in 1968, the year before the Stonewall riots in New York's Greenwich Village that marked the beginning of gay liberation. Kusama also collaborated with members of the New York gay community filming orgies that were staged in her mirrored installations. In its openness to queer sexuality, Kusama's film and

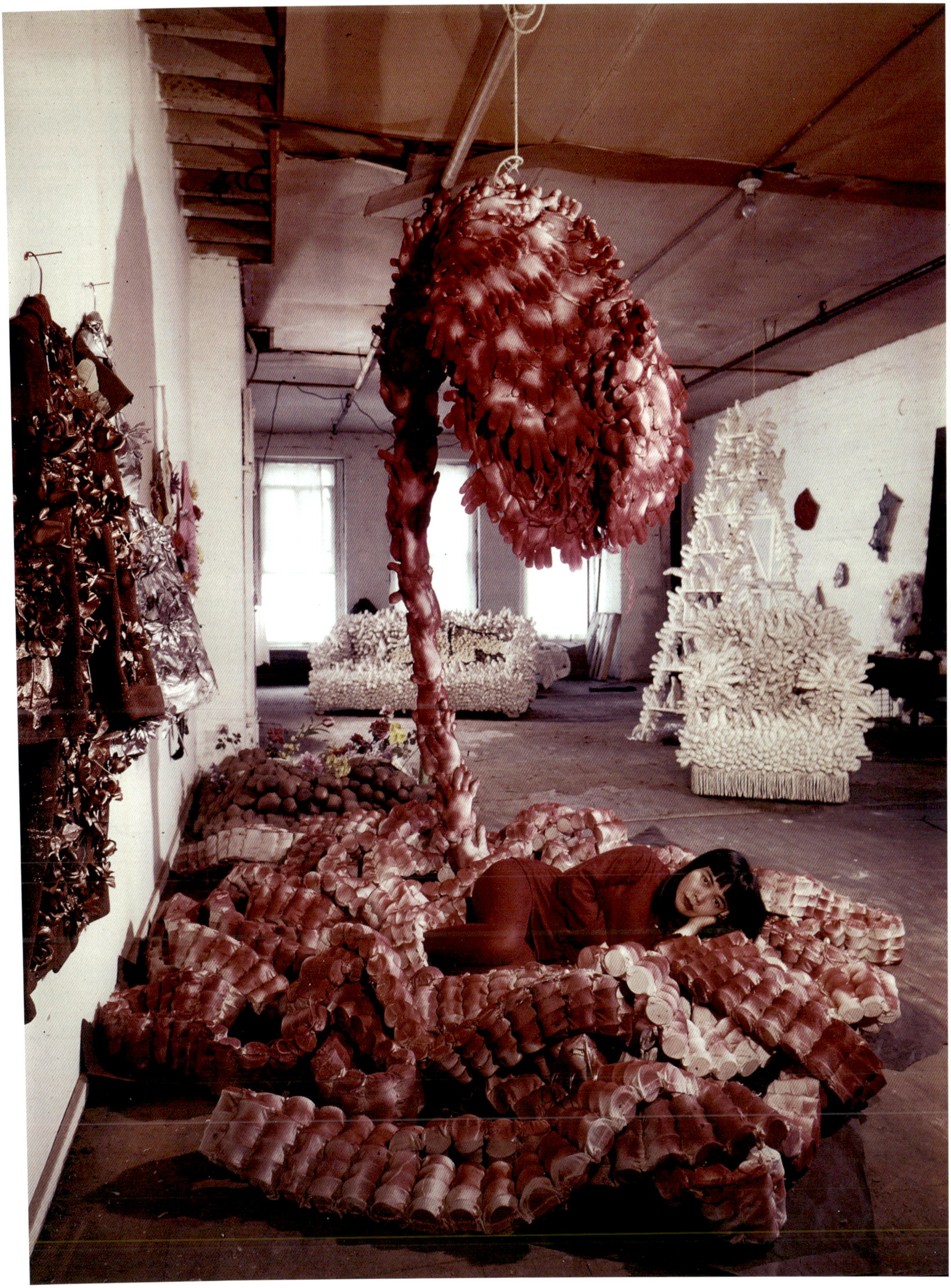

performance work stands apart from other performative work such as Carolee Schneemann's *Meat Joy* from 1964 – an 'erotic rite' in which eight partially nude male and female figures interacted with various foodstuffs and substances including raw fish, sausages, wet paint, plastic and rope – a work that seems more normative in comparison to Kusama's Happenings and films. In a similar fashion to Kusama, the experimental film-maker Warren Sonbert's *Hall of Mirrors* (1966) contained footage of Warhol's assistant Gerard Malanga in Lucas Samaras's *Mirrored Room* (1966, p.127), invoking the idea of Narcissus and co-opting the installation for the performance of a queer subjectivity. Kusama's photographs are all too predictably dismissed as exercises in narcissism and vanity, yet might we not see an even stronger impetus towards dispersion, or what Kusama herself termed self-obliteration?

The camouflaging effect of Kusama's use of coloured and patterned costumes, which cause her to merge bodily with her surroundings, has led some commentators to invoke the idea of mimicry, which was the subject of a now widely-cited article by Roger Caillois in the surrealist magazine *Minotaure* in 1935.[30] Disputing the usual Darwinian explanation that natural mimicry confers a survival advantage, Caillois's essential claim is that it expresses an active desire on the part of the mimetic organism to be assimilated in space.[31] The mania for resemblance which certain species exhibit goes well beyond what is for their own good. He describes a species of leaf insect that is so expert at imitating a real leaf that members of the species indulge in cannibalism without realising they are eating others of their own kind. Caillois compares mimicry to the state of psychasthenia, a condition he characterises as leading to a depletion of energy levels, a sort of subjective detumescence. He refers to studies of schizophrenia in which subjects speak of being 'devoured by space'. The loss of distinction that results from an organism mimicking its inanimate milieu is analogous, Caillois claims, to the operation of the Freudian death drive; life itself, he says, takes a step backwards. Most suggestive apropos Kusama is Caillois's description of the mimetic insect as a sort of 'sculpture-photograph'. Also relevant is the way in which Jacques Lacan took up the concept to describe the narcissistic ego's alienating 'captation' by space. The net effect of inhabiting one of Kusama's reflective environments is not to have one's sense of occupying a unique position in space – of being a centred subject – reinforced, rather, the infinite replication of one's image in many directions simultaneously is like a centrifugal force tugging away at Me. It induces a sort of entropic draining away or dissipation of the self.

It has been a consistent feature of the discourse about her art, fostered by Kusama herself, that it is seen as the manifestation of psychological disturbance. One of the hallmarks of her work is an obsessive tendency towards accumulation. At various times, Kusama has suffered from 'hallucinations' and she has stated that the origin of her trademark polka dots lay in a hallucination of flowers: 'One day I was looking at a red flower-patterned tablecloth on a table, and then when I looked up, I saw the ceiling, the windowpanes and the pillars completely covered with the same red flower patterns.'[32] Recalling this description, the film *Flower Orgy* (1968) simulates a hallucinatory state by projecting flower imagery over footage of naked, writhing bodies. Kusama's 1991 novella *The Foxgloves in Central Park* similarly opens with a delirious vision of a sea of flowers extending to the limit of the horizon. An infinite 'field of sex' was Kusama's own description of the first of her mirrored environments: the very terminology implies a notion of spatial extension, in which a field – of flowers, quite possibly – is conflated with eroticism. From these separate lines of evidence, we conclude that the flower motif has a direct connection with the overriding formal principle of accumulation and with an expanded conception of Eros, one that overflows the individual and permeates the objects and spaces that surround her.[34]

Narcissus Garden is the condensed apotheosis of these various strands. In a sense, it is an ongoing work,

Installation view of Yayoi Kusama with *Narcissus Garden*, 1966

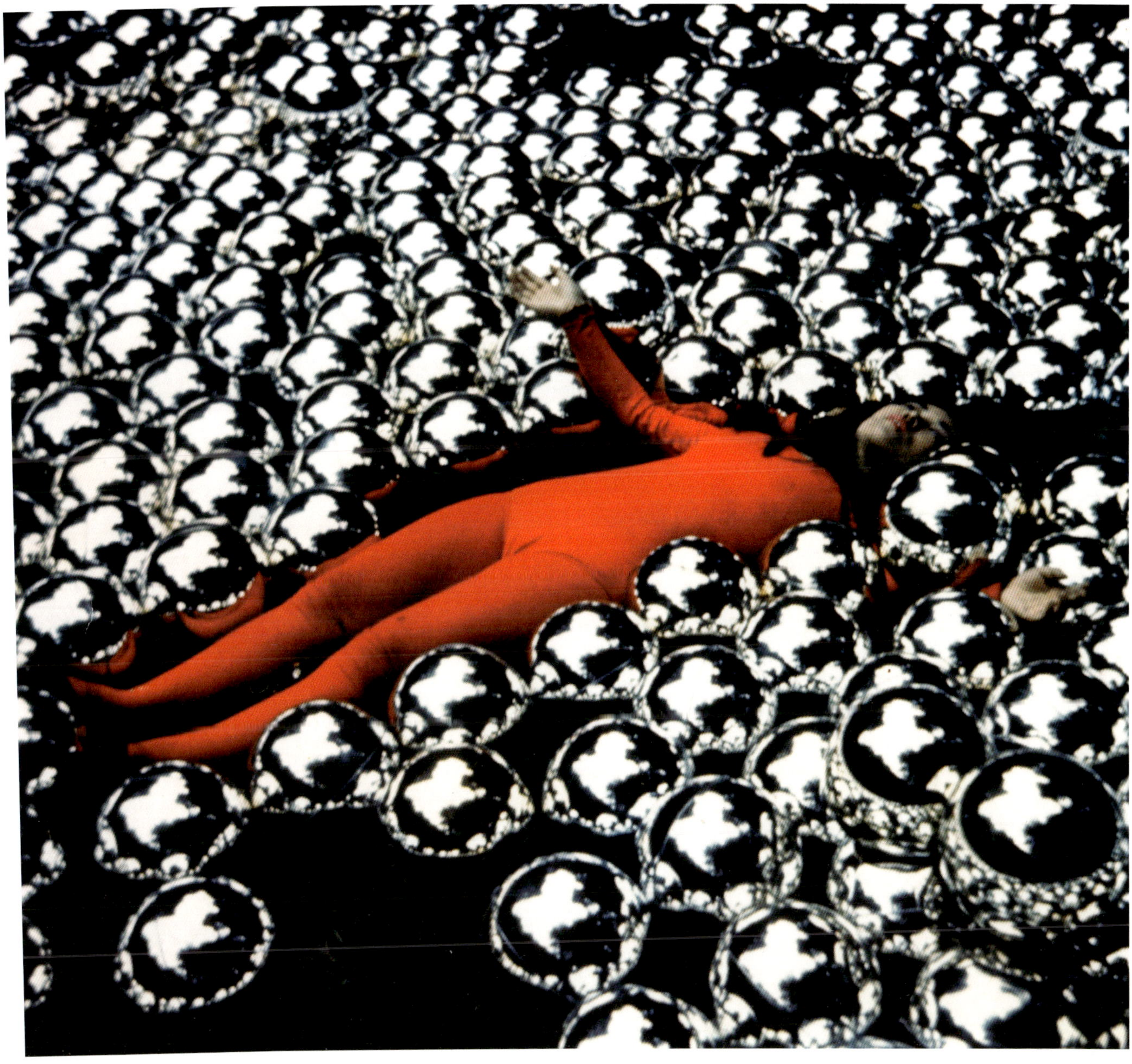

Yayoi Kusama *Fireflies on the Water*, 2000
mirror, metal, electric light bulbs, acrylic plate, water

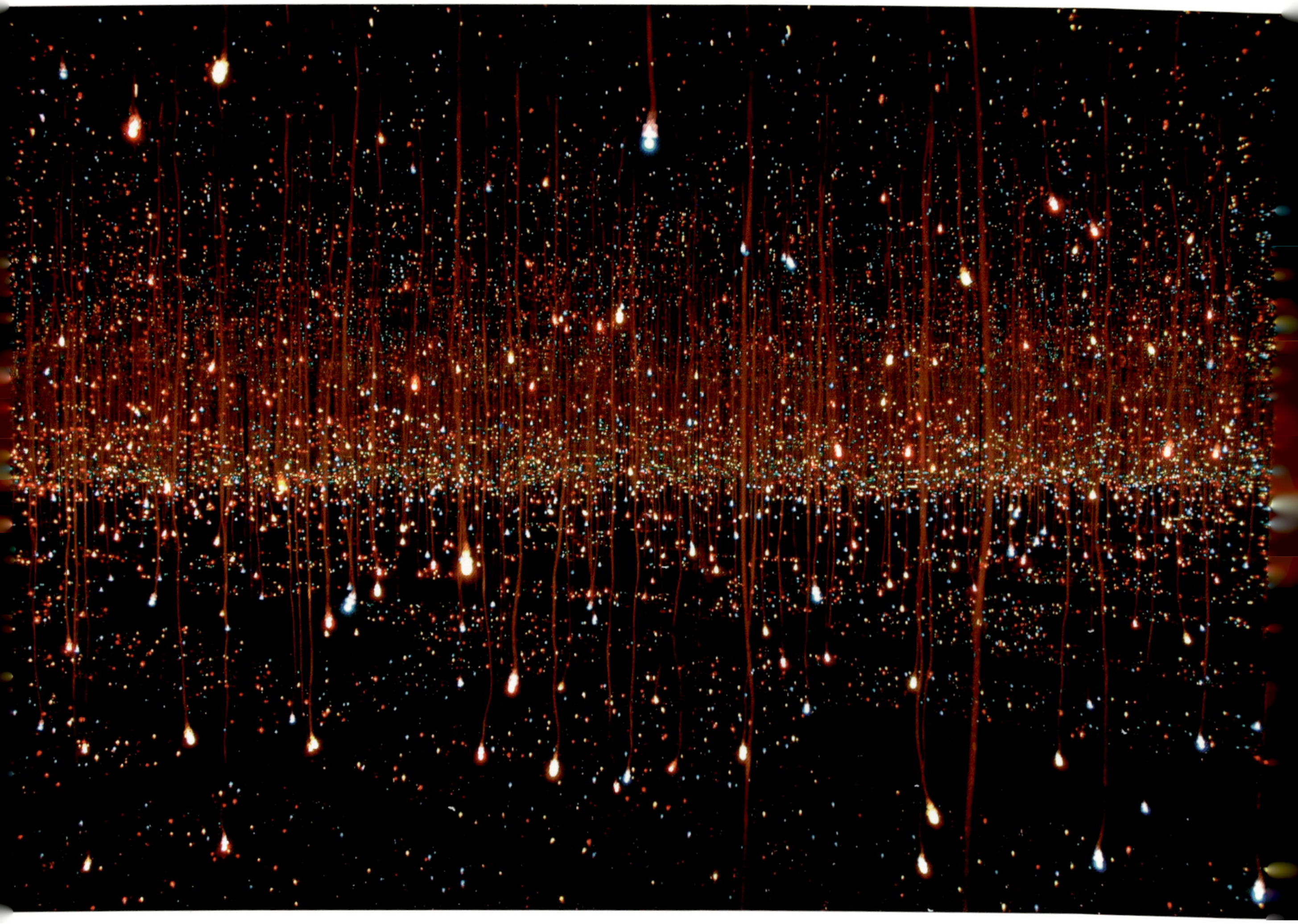

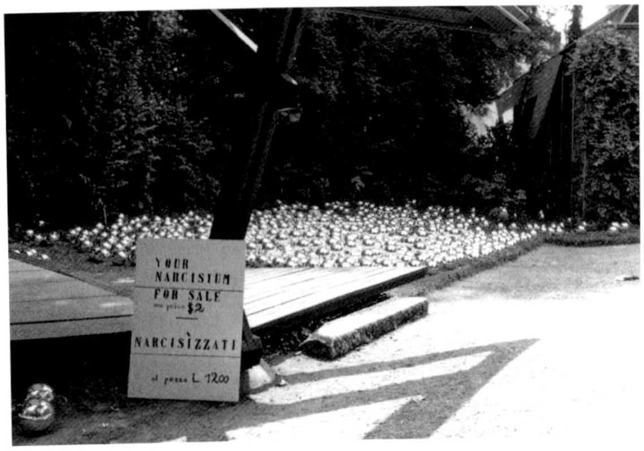

Yayoi Kusama Installation view of *Narcissus Garden* at the Venice Biennale, 1966

with different instantiations in each of the sites where it has been recreated, and thus is susceptible to diverse interpretations. In its original form, it consisted of 1,500 reflective plastic spheres – a 'kinetic carpet' – situated on the lawn in front of the Italian pavilion at the 33rd Venice Biennale. Kusama, who had been denied a place in the official exhibition, mounted the work as a challenge to the commercial ethos of the art world. The balls were on sale to the public for the meagre sum of 1,200 lire ($2) for each bauble. A placard declared: 'YOUR NARCISIUM FOR SALE'. When ordered to stop by the Biennale organisers, Kusama handed out flyers reprinting an appreciation of her work by the doyen of English surrealism, Herbert Read. 'Artists,' she said in a contemporary interview, 'should integrate themselves into economic life by making their work inexpensive and accessible enough to be bought like items in a supermarket.' Accordingly, the Kusama scholar, Midori Yoshimoto, interprets the work as a critique of 'that narcissism that lies in the act of art collecting.'[34] However this by no means exhausts the significance of the Narcissus theme for Kusama, and where *Narcissus Garden* has been shown subsequently, it has been divested of any obvious polemical intent and the accent placed much more upon the work itself as a sculptural installation. The individual spheres that comprise the work are at the mercy of wind, gravity or other forces while the work as a whole is radically dependent on the space in which it is sited. Though the form of *Narcissus Garden* is wholly abstract, the title acts as a touchstone for various poetic and naturalistic associations. Within the conventionalised formulae of traditional Japanese painting, the narcissus flower is ubiquitous as a symbol for spring. One can also easily see how it engages certain aspects of the Western myth, in common with much of her work at the time, through the use of mirrored surfaces. In some of its recreations, such as the Whitney Biennale in New York in 2004, the spheres have been floated on water, adding to this allusion. An extraordinary work of the same date by Japanese artist Sayako Kishimoto titled *Gravestone of Narcissus* (1966) makes one wonder if more than mere coincidence was involved.[35] Was Narcissus 'in the air' at that moment? It also raises a question as to what ties Kusama maintained with the avant garde in Japan during her time abroad.

More recent installations by Kusama, notably *Fireflies on the Water* (2000), continue to suggest naturalistic references to a Japanese garden aesthetic. This extremely lyrical work consists of a myriad of small glowing electric light bulbs suspended over a pool of water with a walkway that allows the viewer to enter into the darkened space. In the manner of Kusama's original 1965 mirrored environment, *Infinity Mirror Room – Phalli's Field*, the individual module is magnified *ad infinitum*. Among her most recent works are massive psychedelic metal sculptures of flowers writhing serpent-like with raw libidinal energies – such as the recent series *Flowers That Bloom Tomorrow* (2010). These pieces, dismissed by some for their brashness and lack of subtlety, have the virtue of laying bare the synergism of plants and polymorphous eroticism that has been a consistent leitmotif of her art from its surrealist beginnings.

MIRRORS AND METAPHYSICS

Kusama's mirrored environments demand to be contextualised in relation to Robert Smithson, Lucas Samaras and other artists who used mirrors in their works in the mid-1960s, while also taking up the explorations of Bauhaus and other interwar photographers. Smithson's *Enantiomorphic Chambers* (1964/65) consisted of two metal frame-and-mirror structures affixed to a wall. The initial idea for it came from a diagram of a stereoscope. Smithson had also read Martin Gardner's 1964 popular science book *The Ambidextrous Universe*, which influenced him to construct the chambers on the principle of enantiomorphic crystals. The resultant interaction of the two mirrored chambers therefore creates an endlessly multiplying concatenation of purely virtual spaces. It is of interest to note that Dalí and Jess had each in different ways seen a connection between stereoptic vision and enantiomorphism with the Narcissus theme. Though the original version of *Enantiomorphic Chambers* is no longer extant, the spatial illusion cannot have been dissimilar to that produced by Kusama's mirrored installations. Smithson spoke of a 'crystalline and collapsible' space 'permuted in a multiplicity of directions.'[36] Vanishing points are inverted by the device in such a way as to heighten an awareness of artifice while the real space that we occupy is simultaneously undermined. As other commentators have noted, mirrors and mirroring continued to play a pivotal role in Smithson's work thereafter. It was around this time also that Lucas Samaras created his *Mirrored Room* (1966), which is very like Kusama's *Infinity Mirror Room – Phalli's Field*, giving rise to competing claims and counter-claims as regards priority. Her relationship with Joseph Cornell, who incorporated mirrors in some of his box assemblages, raises yet another question of possible influence.

To what obscure Zeitgeist were all these artists responding? The preoccupation with mirrors and disorienting virtual spaces chimes with Frederic Jameson's classic account in *Postmodernism, or, The Cultural Logic of Late Capitalism* (1984) of the Bonaventure Hotel in Los Angeles as exemplary of a 'postmodern hyperspace' (a term that revealed Jameson's debts to Situationism and Jean Baudrillard).[37] Jameson's description of bodily immersion in an architectural space deprived of spatio-temporal coordinates speaks to the experience of these mirrored installations. Artists can perhaps be thought of as constructing experimental prototypes where one is brought face-to-face with the consequences of a radical and pervasive transformation in the experience of space. Kusama's obsession with the infinite, actually with infinite reproducibility, calls to mind the postmodern sublime that Jameson describes as the aesthetic correlate of the 'unrepresentability' of late capitalism.[38] Alongside these formal attributes, we need to take note of a parodic mimesis (or mirroring) of the 'cultural logic' of capitalist consumerism, starting with *Narcissus Garden* which, as curator Laura Hoptman notes, 'was as much about the promotion of the artist through the media as it was about the dematerialisation of a sculptural object through the selling off of its elements.'[39] A host of commentators on post-war American consumer society identify narcissism as the defining pathology of that culture. In *The Culture of Narcissism* Christopher Summer argued that competitive individualism, distorted by the relentless pursuit of happiness, has degenerated into 'the dead end of a narcissistic preoccupation with the self.' What more effective way than the myth of Narcissus to capture the eclipse of reality, or what Baudrillard terms 'the desert of the real', in the postmodern condition.

Lucas Samaras Interior view of *Mirrored Room*, 1966, mirror on wood

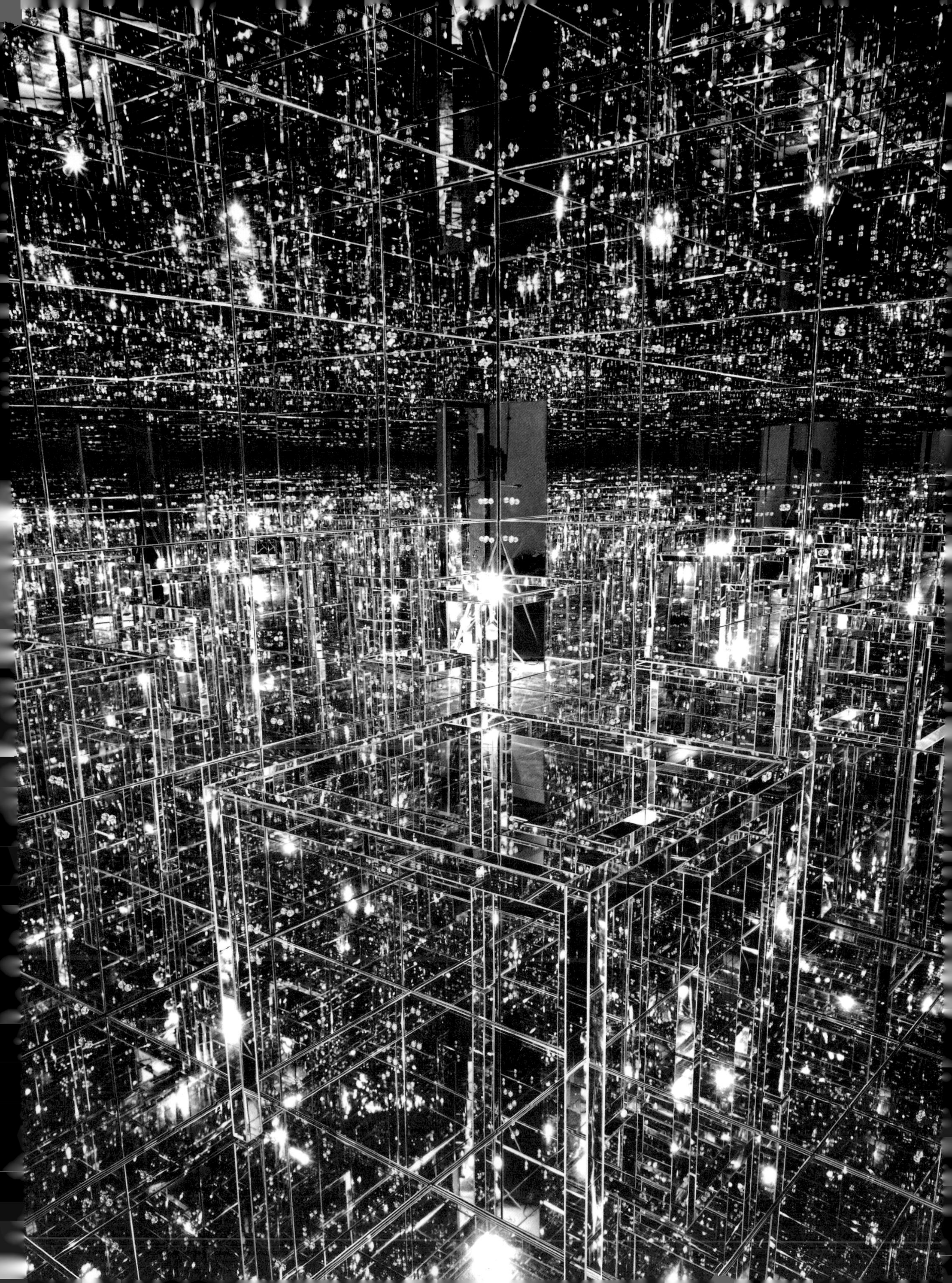

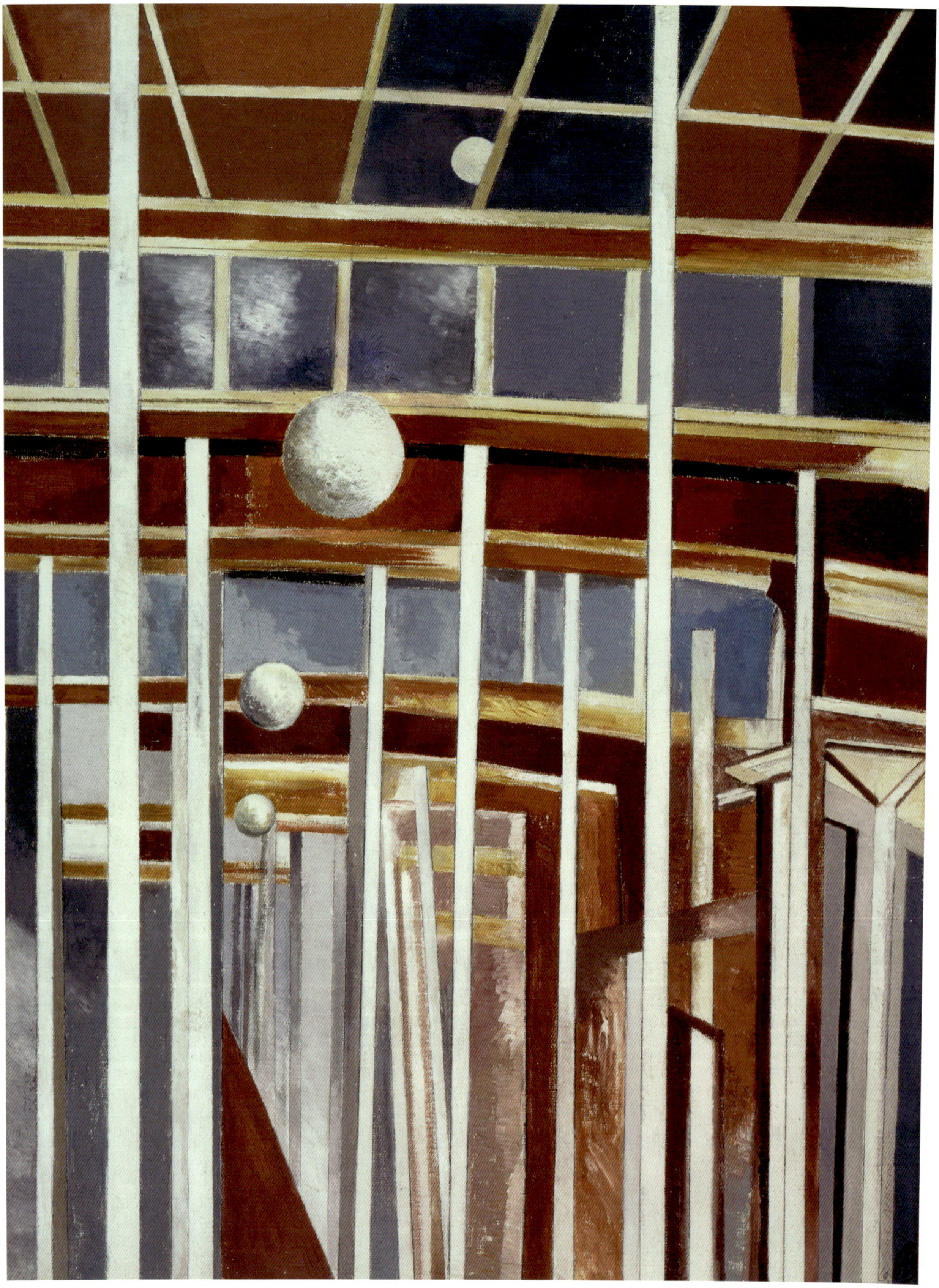

Turning back to the 1930s, one can recognise some striking formal affinities with these 1960s works, despite the differences of means and ends. *Voyages of the Moon* (1934–37), by the English surrealist Paul Nash (1889–1946), had its starting-point in 1930 at Toulon, a naval port in the south of France. It was while holidaying there that Nash first began experimenting with mirror reflections in his painting. Nash's wife, Margaret, recalls a revelation in a French café: 'the long high-walled restaurant, with its entire covering of mirrors that reflected, in a strange astronomical manner, the repeated reflections of large white electric globes which were placed along the ceiling and looked like moons receding in the distance'.[40] *Voyages of the Moon* was made in response to this visual impression, as was, more indirectly, the symbolic *Landscape from a Dream* (1936–38).

Significantly, this epiphany in 1930 coincided with Nash's first use of a camera. It is evident from his writing that Nash kept abreast of new developments

opposite: **Paul Nash** *Voyages of the Moon*, 1934–37, oil on canvas
below: **Paul Nash** *Landscape from a Dream*, 1936–38, oil on canvas

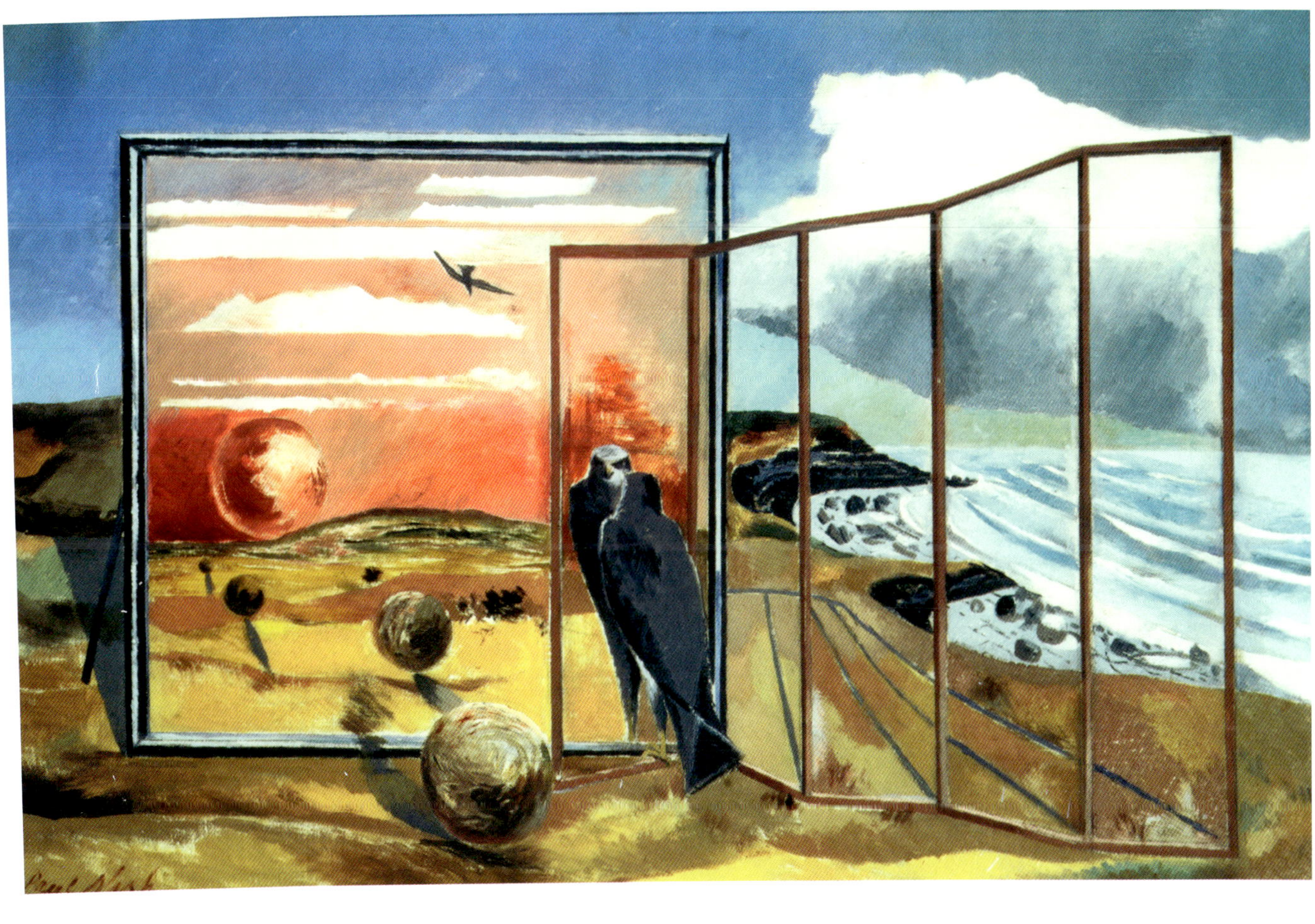

in the medium. In 'Art and Photography', an article for *The Listener* in 1931, he praised Lázló Moholy-Nagy as 'one of the most brilliant of the modern men.'[41] Teaching at the Bauhaus fostered an experimental approach to photography, and often included the use of mirrors, as was seen in the work of Bauhaus-trained Florence Henri (pp.64–67).[42] While none of Nash's extant photographs appear to include mirror

Cecil Beaton *Jean Cocteau, Toulon*, 1930

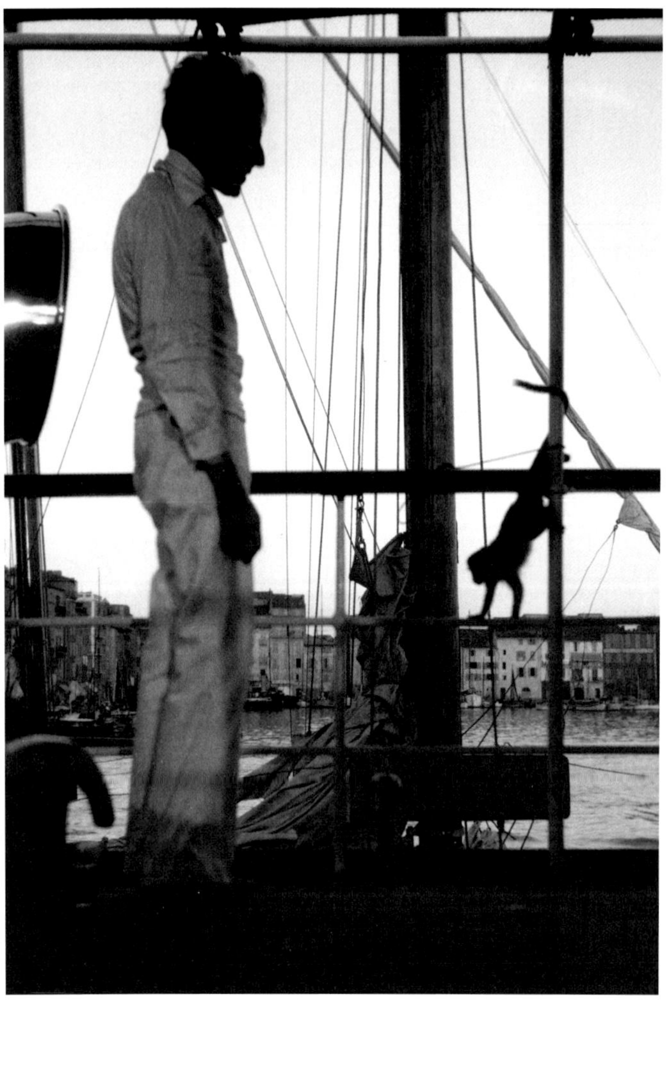

reflections, that does not rule out the idea that he drew inspiration from such avant-garde photography. Examples of Henri's ball and mirror still-lifes were reproduced widely in specialist magazines and yearbooks from the late 1920s onwards as her reputation grew. Where Bauhaus photographers abstract *from* nature, Nash hands their forms back *to* nature. Nash's *Landscape from a Dream* (p.129) can be understood as translating the formal idiom of Henri into a complex metaphysical vision. Art historian Andrew Causey notes Nash's concern at this time with making analogies between spheres of different sorts.[43]A ball of dried grass in the foreground of the picture rhymes with a distant setting sun reflected in a mirror.[44] Nash attributes to the camera lens a special capacity for divining these kinds of formal resemblances. In a review of Karl Blossfeldt's 1928 *Urformen der Kunst* (Art Forms in Nature) for *The Listener*, he observed that: 'here we have an intensely interesting example of the peculiar power of the camera to discover formal beauty which ordinarily is hidden from the human eye.'[45] But what makes the comparison with Henri compelling is the combination in *Landscape from a Dream* of repeated spherical forms with a framed mirror at the centre of the composition, like a picture within a picture.

Nash fuses the abstract concerns of Henri and other artists working in the orbit of 'Abstraction-Création' with the more subjective and symbolic interests of Jean Cocteau and the surrealists. For too long, we have regarded these movements as implacably opposed. At this time the naval port of Toulon was a playground for Cocteau, and a magnet for English artists close to surrealism such as Cecil Beaton and Edward Burra. The British surrealist group, like the Americans, seems to have

Florence Henri *Composition abstraite* (Abstract Composition), 1928

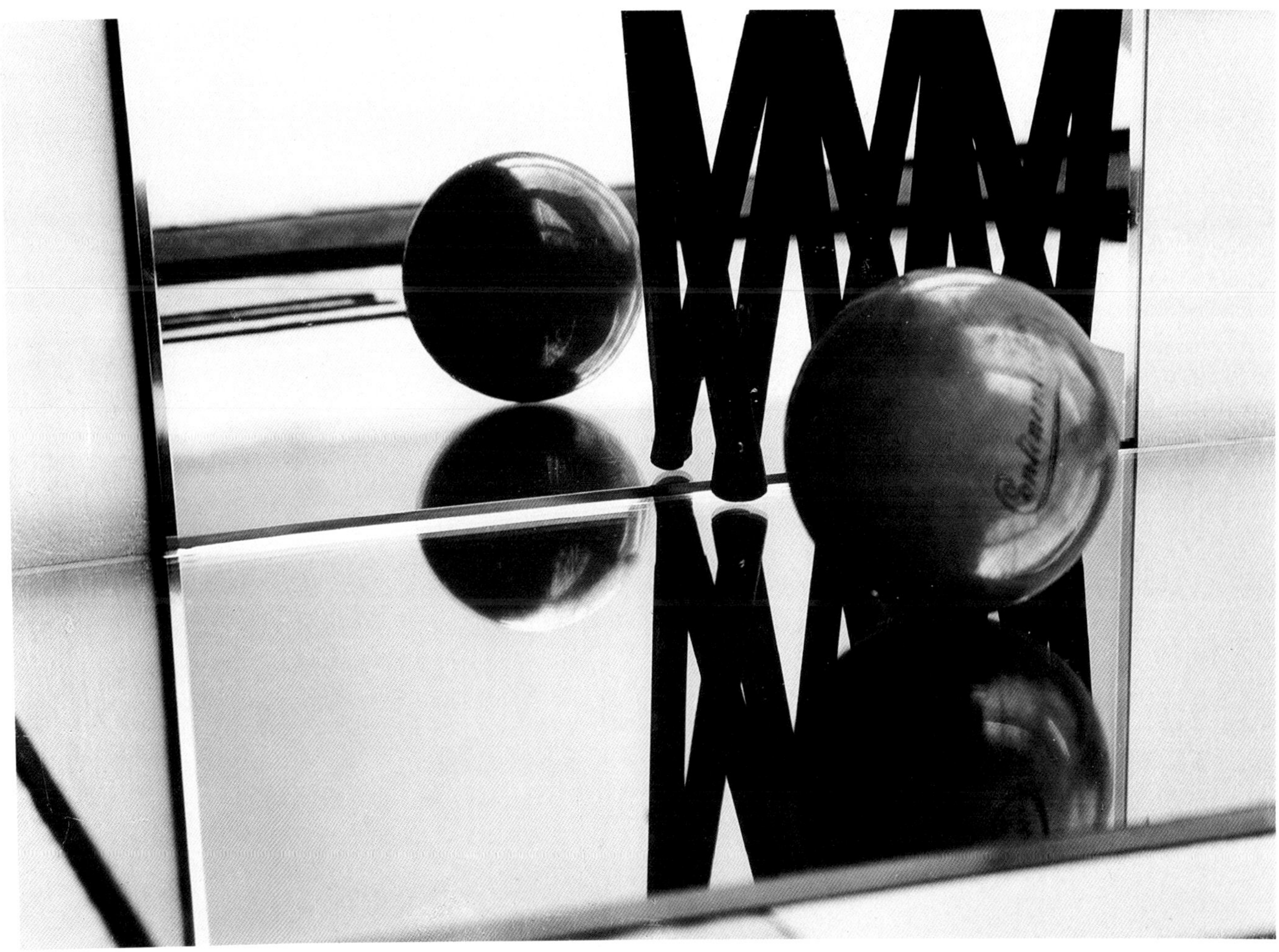

disregarded Breton's attempts to isolate Cocteau from any association with the movement. Nash and his wife were accompanied on their trip to Toulon by Burra, who had spent the previous summer in the company of Cocteau. One supposes that the Nashes had more innocent motives than Burra for wishing to stay there, and while Margaret Nash may have been discomfited by Cocteau's 'strange menagerie', the Cocteau myth must nevertheless be counted as another factor in the development of Nash's work.

Andrew Causey explored the implications for Nash of the original stage version of Cocteau's *Orphée*, which was performed in London in 1931. The omnipresent mirror affords access for *Orphée* (Orpheus) and his attendants to another world as the character Heurtebise (the chauffeur) confides:

> I'm entrusting you with the secret of secrets. Mirrors are the doors through which Death comes and goes. Don't tell anyone. You only have to watch yourself all your life in a mirror, and you'll see Death at work like bees in a glass hive. Good-bye. Good luck![46]

Nash was disposed to take such pronouncements seriously – perhaps more seriously than they were intended by Cocteau. They gelled with the lofty metaphysical ambitions derived from Giorgio de Chirico whose work had a profound influence on Nash's painting at this period. Nash uses a mirror as a device to set off a blood-red sunset against the surrounding blue sky of his local Dorset coastline. A connection with the afterworld may account for why the viewer is inexplicably absent from the reflected scene. But, as is also frequently the case in Cocteau's work, where there's a mirror, Narcissus is not far away. The hawk that gazes transfixed by its reflection in the mirror was imbued with deeply personal associations for the artist. We can assume that the bird has an intimate connection with Nash, as a surrogate possibly, and that the reflected 'double' in this instance has a meaning close to its original one.

Freud, in his 1919 essay on 'The "Uncanny"' refers to Otto Rank's 1914 study *The Double*, which goes into connections of the 'double' with 'reflections in mirrors, with shadows, with guardian spirits, with the belief in the soul and with the fear of death.'[47] These various lines of evidence reveal that the original meaning of the 'double' was 'an insurance against the destruction of the ego, an energetic denial of the power of death'. Freud cites from the language of dreams where doubles or multiples of genital symbols have the function of a denial of castration. He also refers to the funerary practices of the Ancient Egyptians, stating that such superstitious beliefs are a residue of the primary narcissism of the child and primitive man. It is only later in individual and phylogenetic development that the 'double' undergoes a reversal, according to Freud: 'From having been an assurance of immortality, it becomes the uncanny harbinger of death.' The source of Nash's majestic hawk lay in an ancient Egyptian motif, which his biographer tells us he had inscribed upon his gravestone. That the same bird is shown airborne in the space on the other side of the mirror indicates that it probably was meant to symbolise the immortal soul.

This picture, one of Nash's greatest, is an odd amalgam, as befits a dream image. (The literature on Nash does not state whether the picture was based precisely on an actual dream or not.) It is a typical product of English surrealism where nature and a feeling of rootedness in the landscape are often present. But it is not on that account a reactionary image. It was informed by the most progressive avant-garde photographic experiments in the era and the spatial paradoxes that ensue from the placement of a mirror in a landscape anticipate later works of the 1960s, such as Smithson's various installations of groups of mirrors, *Mirror Displacements*, or the self-portrait by the German-born British photographer, Bill Brandt (1904–83) photographed in a mirror in 1966.

Bill Brandt *Self-portrait*, 1966

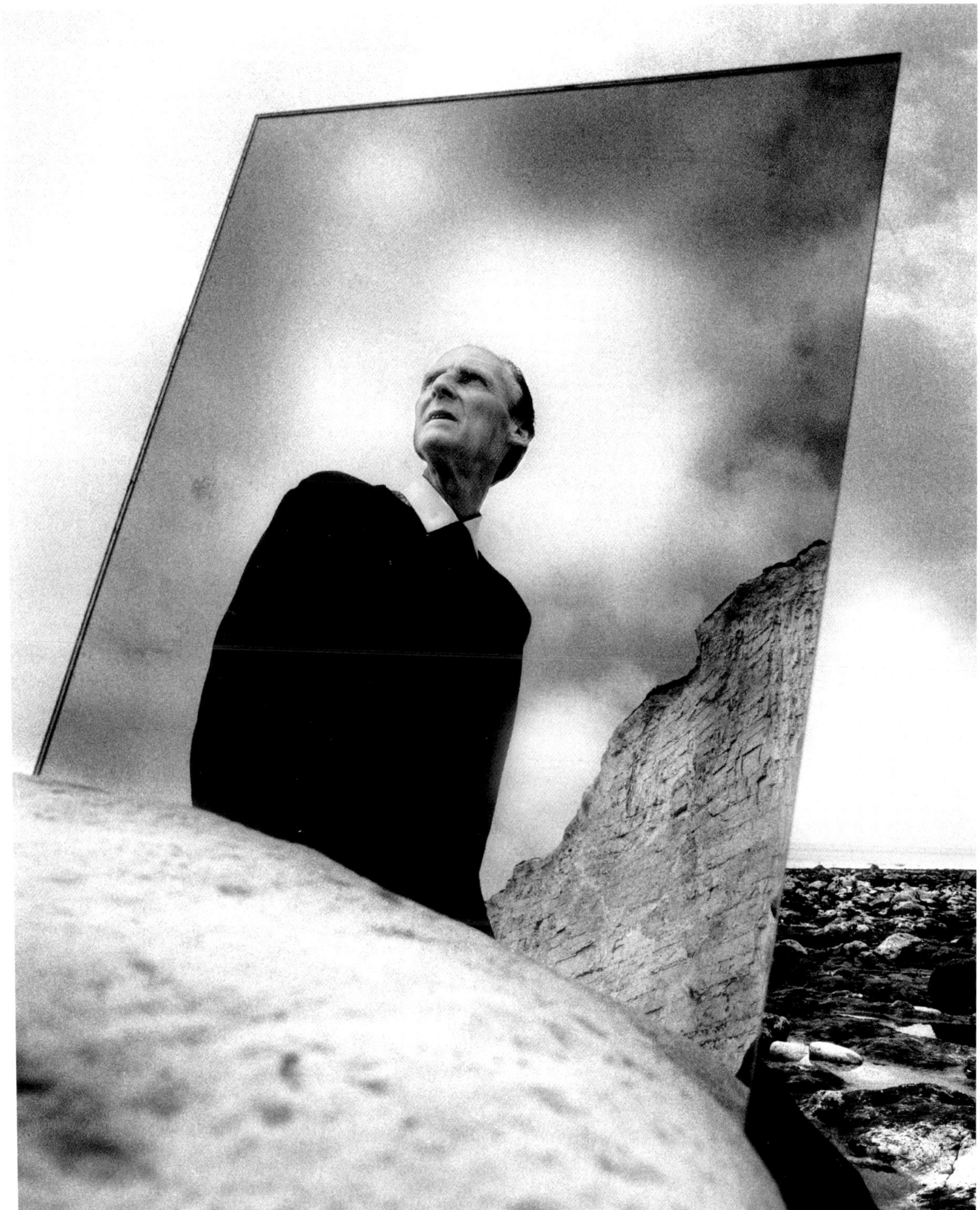

NOTES

1. Larousse, *Grand dictionnaire universel du XIXe siècle*, vol. 11 (Paris, 1866–77), p.838.
2. 'Hardly anyone but a botanist knows the true nature of a flower, and even he, while recognising in the flower the reproductive organ of the plant, pays no attention to this natural end when using his taste to judge of its beauty.' Immanuel Kant, *Critique of Judgement*, (1790), trans. James Creed Meredith (Oxford; Clarendon Press, 1989), p.72.
3. Carl Linnaeus, *Système sexuel des végétaux; Système des plantes* (1735), (Lyon: Chez Bruyset aîné et Buynand, 1804–05).
4. Philogynes Clitorides, *The Natural History of the Frutex vulvaria, or flowering shrub, etc.* (London: W. James, 1732).
5. See Londa Schiebinger, 'The Private Life of Plants: Sexual Politics in Carl Linnaeus and Erasmus Darwin,' in ed. Marina Benjamin, *Science and Sensibility: Gender and Scientific Enquiry 1780–1945* (Oxford and Blackwell, 1991), pp.121–143.
6. Asia Haut, '"Visions bred on sense by fancy": the transvaluation of science, sexuality and polemics in the work of Henry Fuseli and his contemporaries,' PhD thesis, University of Manchester, 2002. I am grateful to Asia Haut for helping to direct my reading.
7. Salvador Dalí, 'De la beauté terrifiante et comestible de l'architecture modern style', *Minotaure* no. 3–4 (12 December 1933), p.76.
8. Michel Foucault, *The Birth of the Clinic*, trans. A.M. Sheridan (London: Tavistock, 1976), p.89.
9. Arnold I. Davidson, *The Emergence of Sexuality: Historical Epistemology and the Emergence of Concepts* (Cambridge: Harvard University Press, 2004), p.57.
10. Joris-Karl Huysmans, *Against Nature* (1884), trans. Robert Baldick (Harmondsworth: Penguin, 1959), p.96.
11. Ibid., p.98.
12. Ibid., p.106.
13. Sigmund Freud, 'Three Essays on the Theory of Sexuality', *Pelican Freud Library*, vol. 7, trans. James Strachey (Harmondsworth: Pelican Books, 1977), p.56.
14. Alan Sinfield, *The Wilde Century: Effeminacy, Oscar Wilde and the Queer Moment* (New York: Columbia University Press, 1994), p.93.
15. See Christina Ferree Chabrier, 'Aesthetic Perversion: Octave Mirbeau's *Le Jardin des supplices*,' *Nineteenth-Century French Studies*, vol. 34, 2006, pp.355–370.
16. Octave Mirbeau, *Torture Garden*, trans. Alvah C. Bessie (New York: JJ Little and Ives Company, 1931), pp.215–217.
17. Octave Mirbeau, *Les Écrivains, 1884–94* (Paris: Flammarion, 1925), pp.2, 52.
18. The term dehiscence covers both these eventualities.
19. Mirbeau, *Torture Garden*, p.235. Translation modified.
20. Georges Bataille, *Visions of Excess: Selected Writings, 1927–1939*, trans. Allan Stoekl (Minneapolis: University of Minnesota Press, 1985), p.13.
21. Ibid., p.12.
22. Gilles Deleuze, *Masochism: Coldness and Cruelty* (New York: Zone Books, 1989).
23. See Nancy Deffrebach, 'Images of Plants in the Art of Maria Izquierdo, Frida Kahlo, and Leonora Carrington: Gender, Identity and Spirituality in Context', PhD thesis, University of Texas at Austin, 2000.
24. A dialogue between Max Ernst and Dorothea Tanning involving flowers could perhaps be demonstrated.
25. Maurice Heine, 'Note sur un classement psycho-biologique des paresthésies sexuelles', *Minotaure* no. 3–4 (12 December 1933), p.36.
26. Bataille wrote a review in *La Critique sociale* in October 1931.
27. The German psychiatrist Albert Moll, one of the pioneers of sexology, was the author of *Die Kontrare Sexualempfindung* (Berlin, 1891) a study of sexual inversion.
28. Judith Butler cautions against confusing gender identification with sexual orientation, arguing that Freud's model of bisexuality preserves a strictly heterosexual orientation of desire.
29. See *Weich und Plastisch – Soft Art*, Kunsthaus Zurich, 1979, p.80.
30. See, for example, Helaine Posner, 'The Self and the World: Negotiating Boundaries in the Art of Yayoi Kusama, Ana Mendieta, and Francesca Woodman,' in Whitney Chadwick ed., *Mirror Images: Women, Surrealism, and Self-Representation* (Cambridge and London: MIT Press, 1998), pp.157–171.
31. Roger Caillois, 'Mimetisme et psychasthénie légendaire,' *Minotaure* no. 7 (10 June 1935), pp.4–10. Translated as 'Mimicry and Legendary Psychasthenia,' *October* (winter 1984): pp.58–74.
32. In Laura Hoptman et al., *Yayoi Kusama* (London: Phaidon Press, 2000), p.119.
33. Jonathan Katz, in a recent paper, analyses Kusama in relation to Herbert Marcuse's *Eros and Civilization: A Philosophical Inquiry into Freud* (1955), (Boston: Beacon Press, 1966).
34. Midori Yoshimoto, *Into Performance: Japanese Women Artists in New York* (New Brunswick: Rutgers University Press, 2005).
35. Ibid.
36. 'A Short Description of Two Mirrored Crystal Structures' (1965), *Robert Smithson: The Collected Writings*, ed. Jack Flam (Berkeley: University of California Press, 1996).
37. Fredric Jameson, 'Postmodernism, or The Cultural Logic of Late Capitalism', *New Left Review* I/146, July–August 1984, pp.53–92.

38. cf. Kant's definition of the sublime: 'the sublime is to be found in an object even devoid of form, so far as it immediately involves, or else by its presence provokes, a representation of *limitlessness*'. Kant, *Critique of Judgement*, p.90.
39. Hoptman, *Yayoi Kusama*, p.63.
40. Quoted in Andrew Causey, *Paul Nash* (Oxford: Clarendon Press, 1980), p.289. I am indebted to Andrew Causey for sharing his unparalleled knowledge of Nash with me.
41. Paul Nash, *Writings on Art*, ed. Andrew Causey (Oxford; Oxford University Press, 2000), p.65.
42. See László Moholoy-Nagy, *Painting, Photography, Film* (London: Lund Humphries, 1969).
43. Causey, *Paul Nash*, p.285.
44. Reputedly, Nash had seen a film with tumbleweed drifting across a prairie. See Anthony Bertram, *Paul Nash: Portrait of an Artist* (London: Faber and Faber, 1955), p.247.
45. Quoted in Andrew Causey, *Paul Nash's Photographs: Document and Image* (London: Tate Gallery, 1973), p.15.
46. Jean Cocteau, *Orpheus, Oedipus Rex, The Infernal Machine*, trans. Carl Wildman (London: Oxford University Press, 1960), p.50.
47. Freud, 'The "Uncanny"', *Pelican Freud Library*, vol. 14, pp.356–357.

Pipilotti Rist still from *Sip My Ocean*, 1996, audio video installation

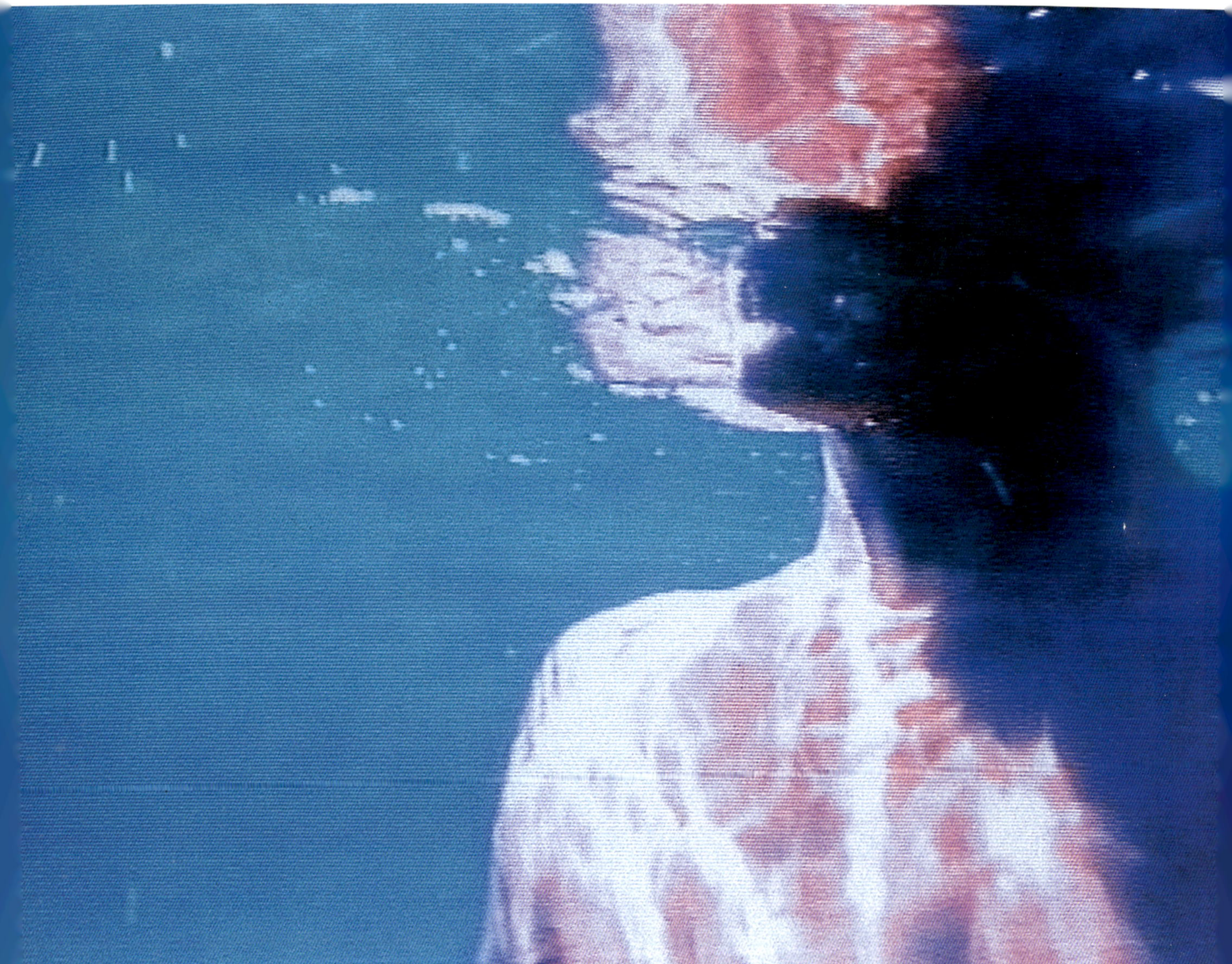

CHAPTER FIVE
THE POOL OF NARCISSUS

When Narcissus died the pool of his pleasure changed from a cup of sweet waters into a cup of salt tears, and the Oreads came weeping through the woodland that they might sing to the pool and give it comfort.
Oscar Wilde, *The Disciple*, 1894[1]

In his poem *The Disciple* (1894) Oscar Wilde retells the death of Narcissus from the perspective of the pool, which mourns the death of Narcissus and is comforted by nymphs known as Oreads. Taking the pool as the basis for my discussion, this chapter will consider a variety of reflections on Narcissus by surrealist and latterday 'disciples' of the myth. The surrealist André Masson represented Narcissus drowning in the pond and, as we shall see, asserted intricate parallels with his treatment of Ophelia. In Ovid's *Metamorphoses*, Narcissus wastes away beside a stream or pool; the idea that he drowns in it was a later accretion to the myth. Pipilotti Rist's immersive audio video installation *Sip My Ocean* (1996) enlarges the pool to an ocean, raising questions about the body and primary narcissism, while Mat Collishaw transposes the pool to a muddy London building site in a work of 1990. Other contemporary artists are concerned with the death of Narcissus as encapsulating the postmodern 'death of the author'. Ovid's description of the tears of Narcissus disrupting the still surface of the pool and causing his reflection to break up affords a productive image for artists seeking to interrogate the 'myth' of a coherent identity.

DROWNING: NARCISSUS AND OPHELIA

André Masson (1896–1987) treated the subject of Narcissus in two paintings from 1934 and 1937 (the latter the same year that Dalí painted *Metamorphosis of Narcissus*). Another drawing on the same theme was chosen as a cover illustration for the special 'Narcissus' issue of the surrealist magazine *View* in 1943 (p.79). Masson's depiction of the Narcissus subject follows his investigations of classical myth, and the Ovidian motif of metamorphosis in particular, as well as reflecting his extensive interest in metaphysics. During this period, Masson was trying to rethink painting as a vehicle primarily for the expression of a complex philosophical vision. Here, I wish to compare *Narcissus* (1937, p.139) with another major painting of the same year *Ophelia* (p.138).

Not coincidentally, Masson was designing stage sets for the theatre in 1937 when he painted *Ophelia*, the tragic heroine of Shakespeare's *Hamlet*. Ophelia's descent into madness in Act IV made her a prototype for portrayals of female insanity. Masson has represented her drowning as recounted by Hamlet's

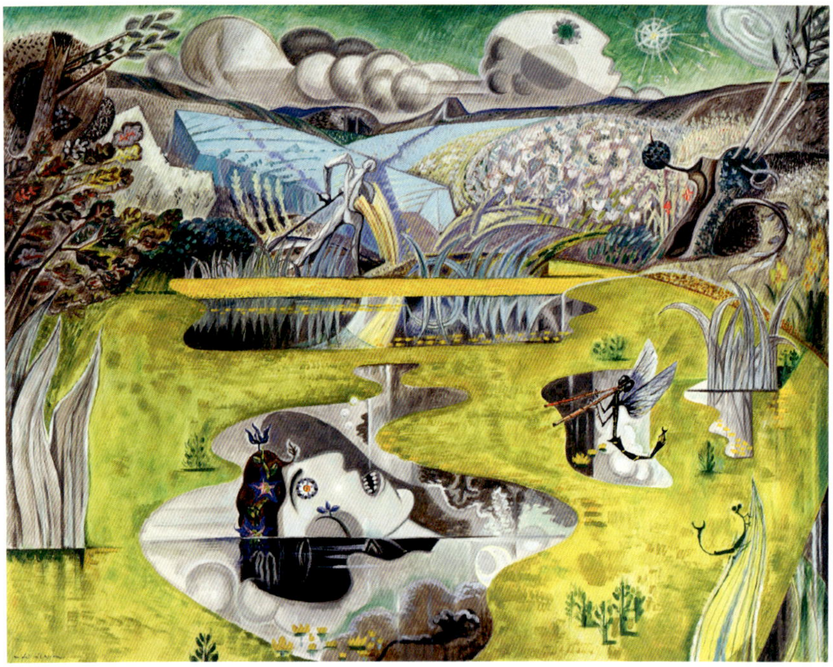

above: **André Masson** *Ophelia*, 1937, oil on canvas
opposite: **André Masson** *Narcissus*, 1937, oil on canvas

mother Queen Gertrude in a monologue that served as a literary source for numerous depictions of Ophelia's death by nineteenth-century artists, such as the Pre-Raphaelite John Everett Millais.[2] Ophelia climbed out on a branch of an overhanging willow ('There is a willow grows aslant a brook') that breaks, causing her to fall in. It is the interlude before she sinks beneath the water, when she is held afloat by her clothes, that Masson depicts. Note the truncated willow at the upper left. Here Ophelia has fallen into a stagnant pool with reeds poking through a layer of algae that will soon close over her. Her pallid profile together with its sombre shadow is reminiscent of Picasso's 'double' heads. Her mouth is open as she sings. She is adorned with a flower garland ('crow-flowers, nettles, daisies, and long purples') and has a daisy in place of her eye. The wild flowers are symbolic of her madness as they recall the earlier scene when Ophelia first appears to the court after having lost her senses, singing songs and handing out wild flowers.

Drowning is also the central motif of Masson's 1937 painting which shows an upended Narcissus tumbling downwards into the pool. The presence of narcissi on the water's edge at the right of Masson's *Ophelia* offers an explicit clue to the correspondence of the two subjects. Ophelia's love is spurned by Hamlet and her madness is interpreted as grief for her murdered father Polonius, but also as lovesickness, just as the nymph Echo suffered in her frustrated desire for Narcissus. Can we say that Ophelia plays Echo to Narcissus? Or that she is his watery reflection? Masson makes another link to the myth of Narcissus through the play of reflections across the water and the visual 'echo' between Ophelia and the head-like form of a distant cloud. Masson may also have taken a cue from the dialogue between Polonius and Hamlet in which they discern the forms of animals in the clouds.[3] Hidden self-portraits (in profile) can be found in other pictures by Masson from this period. Were that so here it would imply a narcissistic 'reflection' of the artist in the image projected in the cloud, and, in fact the upside-down head of Narcissus is quite similar in shape and other features to this cloud-head.

Masson's choice of a Shakespearean theme went hand in hand with his growing preoccupation with German Romanticism – with Goethe especially, and with Novalis. The German Romantics of the late-eighteenth and early-nineteenth century remade Shakespeare in their own image. Goethe undertook an analysis of the character of Hamlet in *Wilhelm Meisters Wanderjahre* (Wilhelm Meister's Apprenticeship, 1795–96), referring to him as: 'An oak tree planted in a precious pot which should only have held delicate flowers'. The sapling at the left of *Ophelia* could be interpreted as alluding in this way to *Hamlet*. It is with the German Romantics, moreover, that a conception of the poet as Narcissus is fully realised. In her study of the Narcissus theme in European literature up to the nineteenth century, Louise Vinge cites August Schlegel's 1798 proclamation *Dichter sind doch immer Narcisse* (The poet is always a Narcissus) as the culmination of this trend.[4] A series of portraits of Goethe from around 1940 attest to Masson's deep interest in the German writer. Masson was particularly interested in Goethe's writings about science and the *Metamorphosis of Lovers* of 1936 reveals an awareness of *Die Metamorphose des Pflanzen* (The Metamorphosis of Plants), Goethe's 1790 treatise on botany. More generally, Masson was receptive to German *Naturphilosophie* that posited the existence of a vital force animating and infusing all of nature. Of course, the Narcissus theme also includes the idea of botanical metamorphosis, which is prominent in Masson's treatment of the subject of both Narcissus and Ophelia.

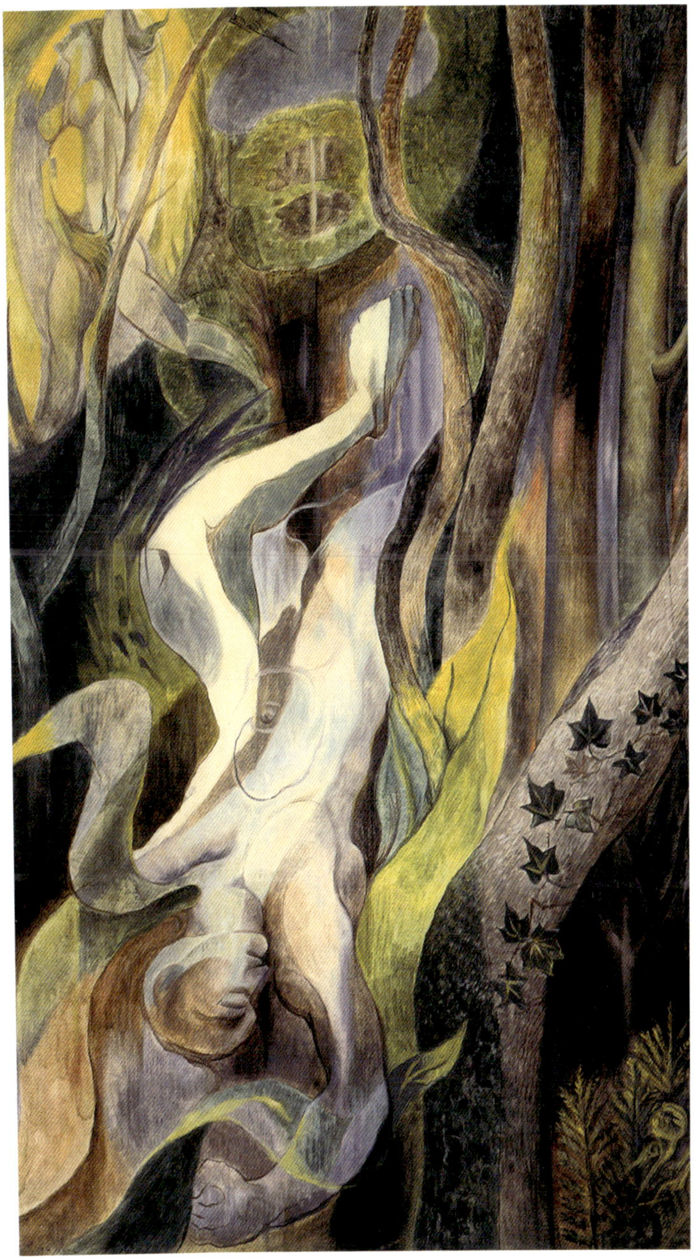

What is the meaning of these subjects for Masson? In the philosopher Gaston Bachelard's instructive analysis of what he terms the 'Ophelia complex', he interprets Ophelia's drowning as the return to an essentially feminine realm.[5] This makes a link with other works by Masson from the period that represent burial in, or return to, the mother earth. Ophelia's fall and death by drowning, like that of Narcissus, can be understood

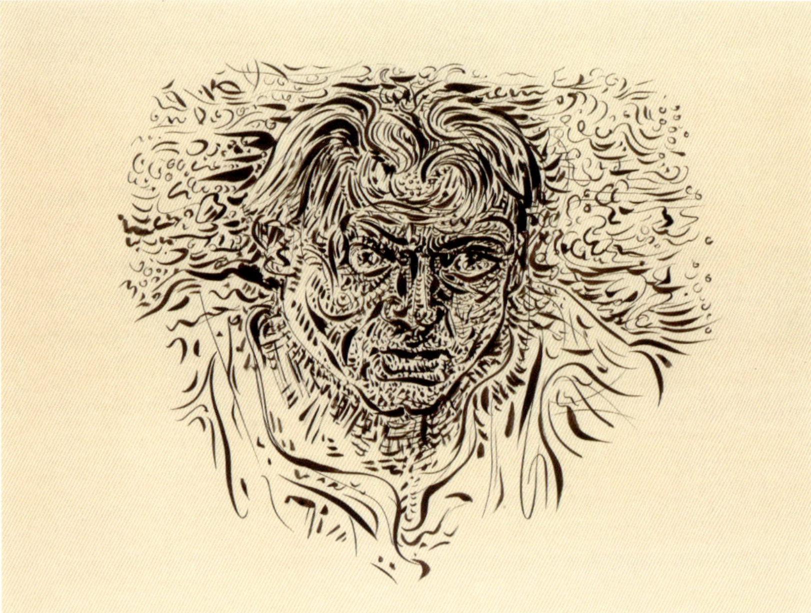

André Masson *Mon portrait au torrent* (Self-portrait in Torment), 1945, ink on paper

in the framework of Neoplatonist thought as the passage of spirit into the sensuous material world.[6] Plotinus took the drowning of Narcissus as an allegory for the error of one who was seduced by mere reflections (as is conspicuous in Masson's *Ophelia*) instead of withdrawing in contemplation of the spirit:

> For if anyone follow what is like a beautiful shape playing over water – is there not a myth telling in symbol of such a dupe, how he sank into the depths of the current and was swept away to nothingness?[7]

For Masson, we have no choice but to go with the flow. Michel Leiris, the surrealist writer who was in many ways closest in spirit to Masson, surmises that 'drowning represents abandonment, disappearance, fusion in the flux of springtime.'[8] Leiris is talking about *Ophelia*, but the narcissus flower is also associated with the spring, and his comments hold equally well for the figure of Narcissus. Like Nietzsche at the end of the nineteenth century, Masson found a kindred spirit in the pre-Socratic philosopher, Heraclitus, who believed that constancy was an illusion and that the universe was in a state of eternal flux. Narcissus's metamorphosis is a visualisation of this universal principle.

In 1945, Masson produced a sort of sequel to his painting of *Narcissus*, a self-portrait drawing in pen and ink that portrays his face reflected on the surface of a fast-flowing stream, the coherence of his self-image broken up by eddying currents. It recalls an aphorism of Heraclitus's that one can never step into the same stream twice, a statement about the constantly changing face of reality, while alluding again to the Narcissus myth. In Ovid, the moment that corresponds most closely to Masson's depiction is the point when Narcissus's tears ripple the surface of the pool and his image disperses, a prelude to the death and disappearance of Narcissus himself.

SIP MY OCEAN

Writing in the first issue of the journal *October* in 1976, Rosalind Krauss decried video as a narcissistic medium.[9] This was a decade when narcissism was already getting quite a lot of bad press. It must have seemed odd that a critic positioned at the radical cutting edge should have directed this 'put down' at what was plainly the newest and latest thing on the art scene. However, this stance turns out to have been consistent with the *October* group's reading of Walter Benjamin, who saw in the surrealists' rejection of technological modernity and their attraction to the 'outmoded' – such as cast-offs they found by trawling the flea markets – the possibility of a redemptive experience which he termed 'profane illumination'.[10] At the time that Krauss was writing, the video apparatus she was discussing consisted of a camera connected to a monitor in which video was recorded and transmitted at the same time, a circuit analogous to the solipsistic self-enclosure of narcissism. The other factor was the insistent presence of the body, typically that of the artist him- or herself, in much of the new work produced in video by artists at the time, such as Vito Acconci, as well as the wider genre of body art which grew out of avant-garde performance of the 1960s and was at its height in the 1970s around the same time as video works were gaining prominence. Amelia Jones has shown that body art was anathema to a dominant strand of feminism at the time which was disposed to see any representation of the female body as complicit with the oppression of women. Krauss's reasons for rejecting body art were different, though, and relate more to her preference for the non-figurative. Now, more than two decades on from Krauss's original critique, the video art of Pipilotti Rist (b. 1962) causes us to re-open the question of narcissism and to ask whether feminist theorizations of the state of primary narcissism may offer a basis

Pipilotti Rist still from *Sip My Ocean*, 1996, audio visual installation

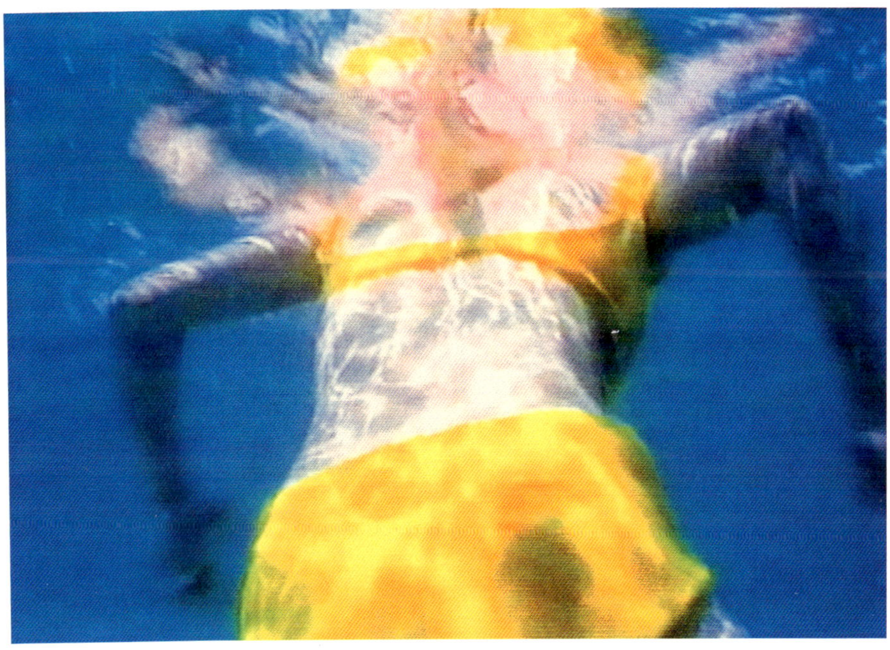

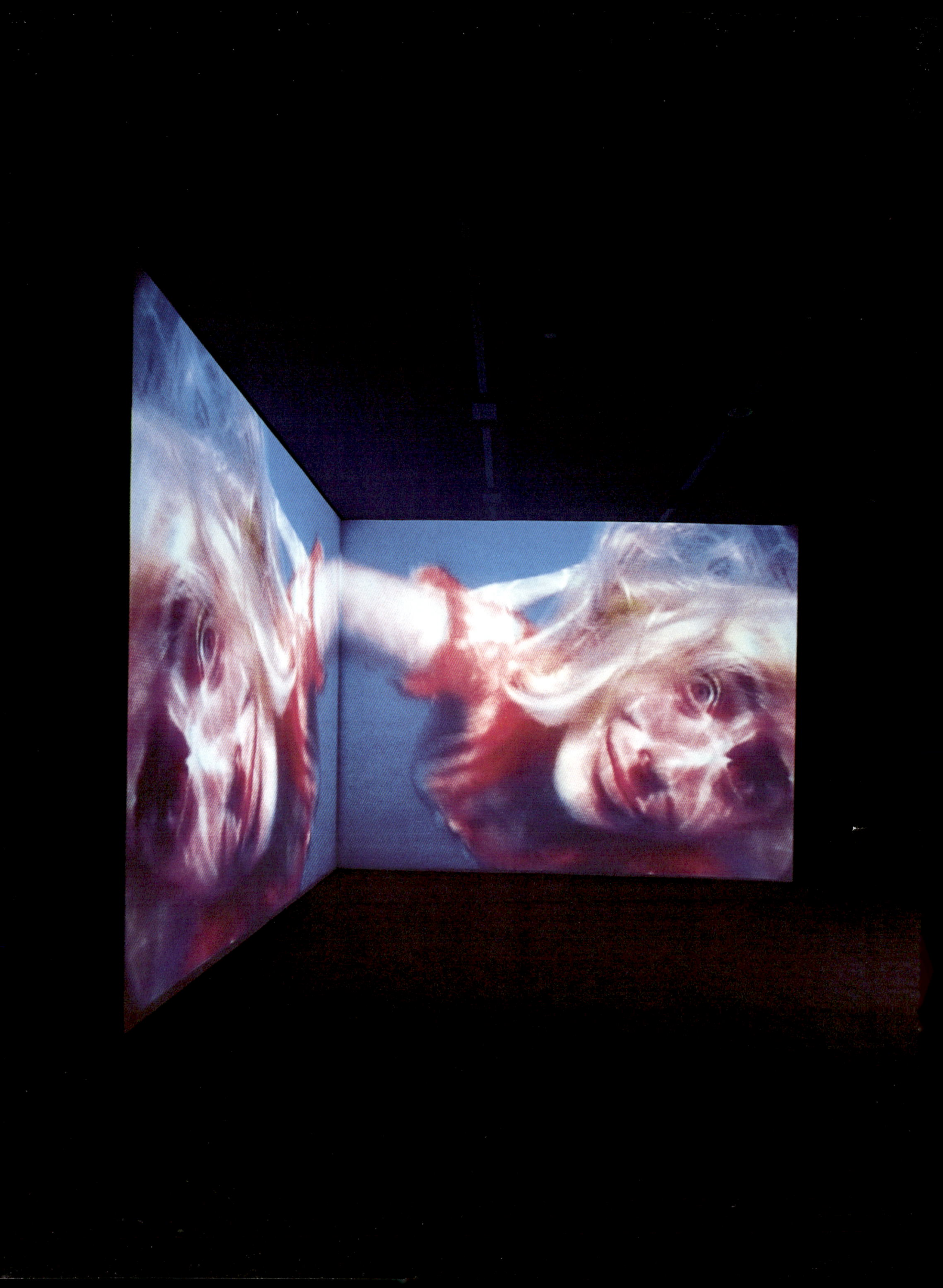

for a more affirmative reading of the body and its pleasures. A consideration of her work's formal and thematic correlations with surrealism is crucial to the argument.

Sip My Ocean, a seminal work in the development of Rist's practice, is a large-scale audio video installation that is projected in duplicate as mirrored reflections on two adjoining walls, with a soundtrack of the artist singing *Wicked Game* by Chris Isaak. Imagery fuses and separates in syncopating rhythm at the corner, which is like a seam between the two screens. The whole film is shot underwater and includes footage of a coral reef in juxtaposition with close-ups of Rist's own body. In common with much of her video work, the projection is considerably larger than human scale. Combined with the technically enhanced, lush colour and computer-generated visual pyrotechnics, it induces a pleasurable sensory satiety and immersive experience as an empathic counterpart to the on-screen aquatic imagery.

Though the derivation of her formal idiom from pop videos is well attested in the existing literature, antecedents for Rist's kaleidoscopic techniques of fusion, duplication and distortion of the body can also be found in surrealist photography. Adopting this longer historical attention span alerts us to a politics of the eroticised body that might otherwise be missed or dismissed as narcissism. Maybe it is over-sensitive to accuse contemporary critics of neglecting surrealism, nevertheless the resurgence of interest in surrealist photography, notably in the influential 'L'Amour fou' exhibition in 1985, co-curated by Dawn Ades and Rosalind Krauss, and its theoretical co-option to a postmodern project, undeniably occurred at a vital, formative moment for many of the current generation of artists.

Considering the purely formal operations in Rist's work, the malleability of the body and its contours can be likened to André Kertész's use of a fairground mirror to produce extreme anamorphic distortions of the body in his photography. Less well-known, though inviting comparison with Rist, is the device invented by the surrealist Léo Malet for creating images that he claimed could reveal a pan-eroticism lurking within the manifest image-world. The simple apparatus consisted of a mirror that stood perpendicular to the plane of an image and was fixed at one side so that it could be swivelled around this axis. As the mirror swept across a randomly-selected illustration from a magazine or other source, the intersection of the image with its

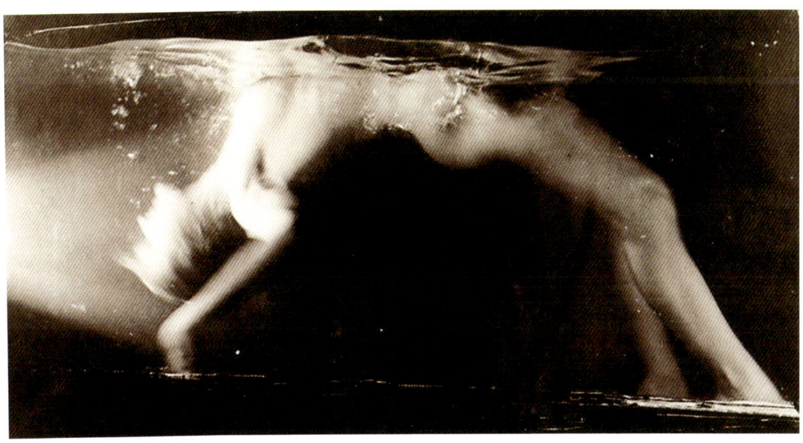

left: **Rogi André** *Jacqueline Lamba dans un aquarium* (Jacqueline Lamba in an aquarium), 1934
opposite: **Pipilotti Rist** installation view of *Sip My Ocean*, 1996, audio visual installation

reflection produced abstracted shapes that were typically vaginal or (less often) phallic.[11] Malet exhibited several of these 'mirror-objects' in the famous exhibition of surrealist objects at the Charles Ratton Gallery in Paris in 1936. Later, the catalogue of the international surrealist exhibition in Brussels in 1945 included a *Personnage narcissique*, a photograph of an image produced with the mirror apparatus. Without pretending there was any direct influence from Malet, it sheds light on Rist's objectives to note that she repeatedly does the same thing at the junction between the two screens of *Sip My Ocean*.

The prevalence of images of the body submerged beneath water in surrealist photography provides another point of contact with Rist's work. The best known of these is a photograph of André Breton's wife, Jacqueline Lamba, in an aquarium in 1934 (p.143). To support her studies at the École des arts décoratifs, Lamba worked as a dancer at the Coliseum, a nightclub in Paris's Pigalle that staged aquatic spectacles. The photograph of Lamba was taken by Rogi André (born in 1905 as Rosza Klein in Hungary), who arrived in Paris in 1925 and learnt photography from her husband, André Kertész, whom she married in 1928.[12] It was published by Breton as one of the illustrations in his book *L'Amour fou* in 1937, which was dedicated to Lamba. Another canonical surrealist photograph in a similar vein by Jacques-André Boiffard is a very foreshortened image of a naked woman whose head and loose hair hang over the edge of a mattress. The image was reproduced in *Documents* no. 8 in 1930 tipped upside down, a simple expedient that creates an illusion of floating in water or flying. Rist has filmed herself in an almost identical pose for the video *Selfless in the Bath of Lava* (1994).

As the German art historian, Horst Bredekamp, has shown, the popularity of aquaria and aquatic spectacles of the kind that Lamba participated in dates from the nineteenth century, at which time there was a growing fascination with the sea.[13] The philosopher Gaston Bachelard, in *L'Eau et les rêves* (Water and Dreams, 1942), chronicles the rise of a new cultural imaginary that supplanted eighteenth-century visions of shipwrecks and of the hidden dangers of the sea with a more comforting fantasy of a nurturing maternal realm. Jules Michelet's *La Mer* (The Sea, 1861) was a mid-century high-water mark for the trend to conflate the sea with the maternal body ('la mer' / 'la mère').[14] Gustave Moreau's *Galatea* (c.1880), which depicts the sea-nymph Galatea isolated in an artificial underwater grotto surrounded by corals with the jealous Cyclops looking in, taps into the vogue for mermaid women disporting themselves in aquaria whose extensions into surrealism would include Salvador Dalí's *Dream of Venus* pavilion for the World's Fair in New York in 1939.

The persistence of this set of cultural meanings naturalises the juxtaposition of the body with coral reefs and other marine imagery in *Sip My Ocean*. The 'oceanic feeling', a notion proposed by the writer Romain Rolland, was attributed by Freud to the persistence of an earlier unbounded state of the ego, a state corresponding to primary narcissism. 'Our present ego-feeling is', Freud conjectures, 'a shrunken residue of a much more inclusive – indeed, an all-embracing – feeling which corresponded to a more intimate bond between the ego and the world about it.'[15] It is an enticement that Rist's *Sip My Ocean* offers to the spectator.

The Argentinian-born painter Leonor Fini's *Narcisse incomparable* (Incomparable Narcissus) of 1971 is a very peculiar treatment of the Narcissus subject by a female surrealist that, in its concentration on the body and its immersion in water, suggests affinities with Rist. Two thirds of the picture is taken up by a pool with water lilies, and virtually the entire canvas is bathed in aqueous blue. Perched on the poolside, Narcissus, a naked youth with a mass of auburn hair, dangles his legs in the water. Next to him stands another figure cut off at thigh level by the picture frame, rendering their gender indeterminate. The upside-down reflection is female and hovers Ophelia-like just beneath the surface of the water. Undeniably, there is 'a climate of ambiguous androgyny' suffusing the image, as critic Georgiana Colville notes.[16]

Leonor Fini *Narcisse incomparable* (Incomparable Narcissus), 1971, oil on canvas

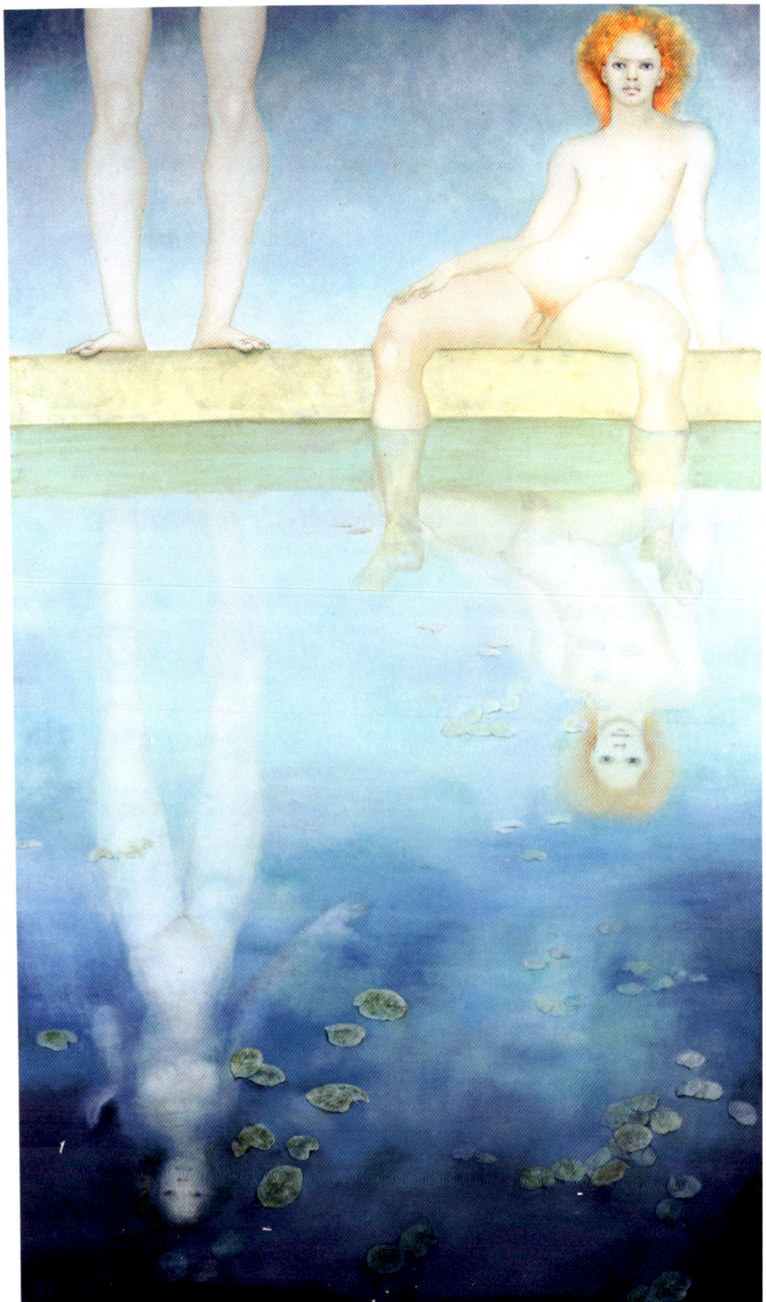

The openly-displayed genitalia of Narcissus, that at first sight we took to be male, could be read as female labia or as being in the process of becoming so. Colville believes that the artist has illustrated Pausanias's version of the myth in which Narcissus falls in love with the image of his dead twin sister rather than his own reflection. Another possibility may be that Fini has combined the myths of Narcissus and Hermaphroditus. There are many overlaps between the stories as told by Ovid. Hermaphroditus is a beautiful youth who comes to rest by a pool of water where he encounters a nymph called Salmacis who desires him. Hermaphroditus dives into the pool and, more forward than Echo, Salmacis leaps after him, wrapping herself around him until their bodies fuse in a single form 'possessed of a dual nature'.[17] When Hermaphroditus emerges from the water he realises that he is but half a man and his limbs have been 'enfeebled by its touch', and he prays to his parents to grant him the wish that the pool be given a magical power to make any man 'suddenly grow weak and effeminate at the touch of these waters'.[18] Does Fini's Narcissus, nonchalantly gazing in our direction, know what is in store for him? Our interest lies in the water, not just as a support for the reflected image, but now also as a medium in which gender differences are dissolved.

'I'm for sure a feminist', states Rist, though it is a claim some would dispute. How might the narcissism of video be construed as a positive feminist strategy? This is a question that revolves around the status of the female body in or outside of representation. Rist describes her work as 'very concentrated imagery put into a concentrated loop', a structure Krauss saw as defining the video medium. Excessive proximity of the body to the camera results in a self-enclosed circularity that effectively brackets out the mediation of another viewer. The nearest comparison one can find is with surrealist images such as Ithell Colquhoun's *Scylla* (1938) or Frida Kahlo's *What the Water Gave Me* (1938). Both artists have portrayed their lower body as it would appear to them lying in a bath; a familiar enough sight, but an unusual subject for painting, it implies a direct contiguity between the viewer and the body (re)presented. Rist filmed similar shots of her own body for *Pour Your Body Out (7354 Cubic Meters)*, which filled the New York Museum of Modern Art's central atrium in 2008–9 and included a sequence where a stream of menstrual blood trickled upwards over her stomach.[19] Colquhoun's metaphorical imagination transforms the body sunk beneath the water into a marine landscape bringing into play the symbolic equivalences of the sea with the maternal body. Her thighs are raised up out of the water, like two massive rocky promontories that join to form a vaginal-shaped passage through which all who wish to enter or leave must pass. Kahlo, from the same starting point, travels in another direction, backwards to the blissful solitude of the foetus *in utero*, bathed in amniotic fluid. Recalling Freud, the state is one of 'total narcissism, in which libido and ego-interest, still united and indistinguishable, dwell in the self-sufficing ego.'[20] Kahlo gives her own endearing yet poignant slant to the allied themes of doubling and mirror reflection. Her toes jutting above the bathwater combine seamlessly with their own reflections to form two islands possessed of a neat enantiomorphic symmetry, one to another, but the perfection of this body image is visibly ruined by vestiges of the accident that left her crippled and eventually would lead to the amputation of her right leg.

Women, according to psychoanalysis, have a more difficult time entering into the symbolic order of language than men. In a kingdom ruled by the phallic signifier, woman can only be figured as 'lacking'. Kahlo depicts her body sliding beneath the reflective surface of the water, a plane that corresponds to the picture plane, and by extension, the symbolic order. She makes a virtue of being exiled from representation. After all, representation necessitates distance and separation; it turns the world (and one's body) into a picture, objectifies it. Narcissus despairs that he cannot be united with himself, even though 'only a little water keeps us apart.'[21] These artists are content being alone with themselves in the self-sufficing plenitude of the body and its autoerotic-cum-narcissistic pleasures. Rist says: 'There's something very childish to play around with your own body without needing another. You're happy being with your own body …' In all these cases, we as beholders must inhabit the body we see, which thereby avoids the worst objectifying and alienating consequences of representation. In common with these surrealist precursors, and as their worthy successor, Rist short-circuits representation.

Any discussion of video narcissism would be incomplete without reference to Bill Viola, one of the pioneers in the artistic use of video. From the beginning of photography, technological media have been held to spell the end of painting. It is somewhat paradoxical, therefore, that Viola's video practice engages intensively with the history of Western painting. Despite coming *after* 'the end of art', Viola's video work meditates reflexively upon this tradition.[22] In recent years, Viola has shown a preference for projecting video on flat plasma screens placed onto the wall like pictures. He has slowed down movement in order to approach the static condition of painting. Since 2003, Viola has also created a series of video pieces called *The Passions*, referencing one of the central themes of Western art, and his works have been displayed in the National Gallery, London among some of the greatest paintings from this tradition. It is as though he endeavours to keep painting alive in an alien medium – the very medium accused of bringing about its demise. Viola explicitly invoked Narcissus in a conversation about *Surrender* (2001), one of the works belonging to his *The Passions* cycle, but the concept of narcissism is more generally applicable to his work. Reflections on water, and immersion in it, are Viola's preferred subjects. Like Alberti, for whom Narcissus was the first artist, Viola weaves an originary story concerning the production of images around the figure of Narcissus gazing at his reflection (Viola is invested, nostalgically perhaps, in beginnings):

> That's a very primordial image … If you consider that as human beings, our ancestors back in the prehistoric world, the first time they saw their own image would have been in water, kneeling over a side-pool in a stream. Reaching to cup your hands and drink it you would have seen yourself, and that's why this idea of the mirror, why the myth of Narcissus, is so powerful. It's one of the first real deep stories and expressions in humankind of the notion of the self-image and what that means.[23]

Surrender is a two channel work on plasma display screens showing a man and a woman expressing anguish or grief. It is a 'moving image' in more than one respect, though we are deprived of any explanation as to the cause of their intense emotion. Both figures bow forwards until their faces touch a pool of water. As they do so, our image of them becomes more and more distorted by a wave pattern. With this comes the realisation that what we had been watching all along was a reflection of the figures on water rather than the actors themselves. The video comes to an end at this point when the illusion which sustains Narcissus is shattered.

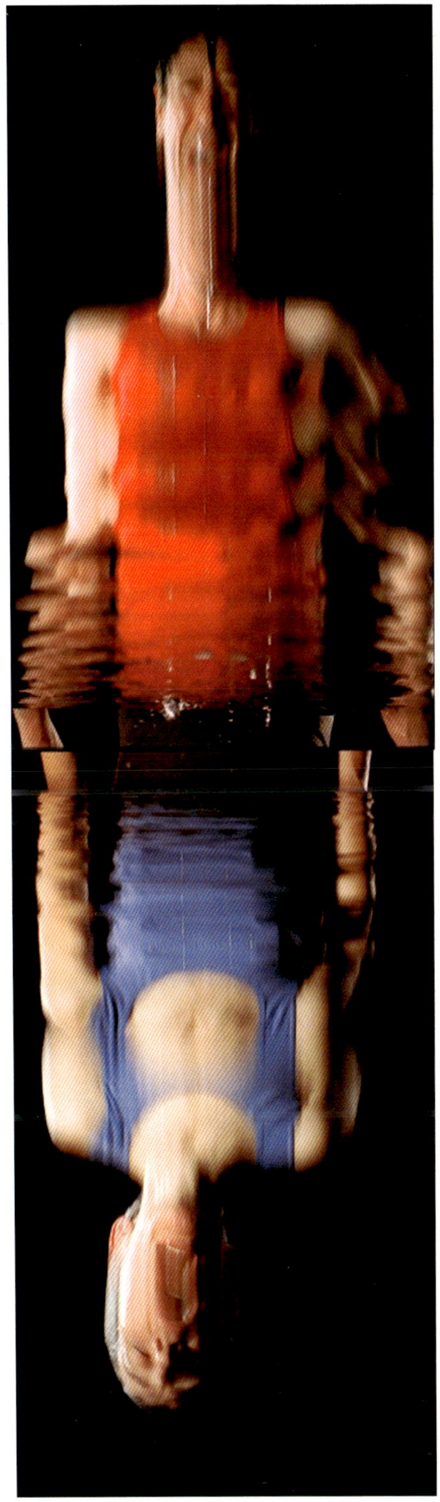

Bill Viola *Surrender*, 2001, colour video diptych on two plasma displays mounted vertically on wall

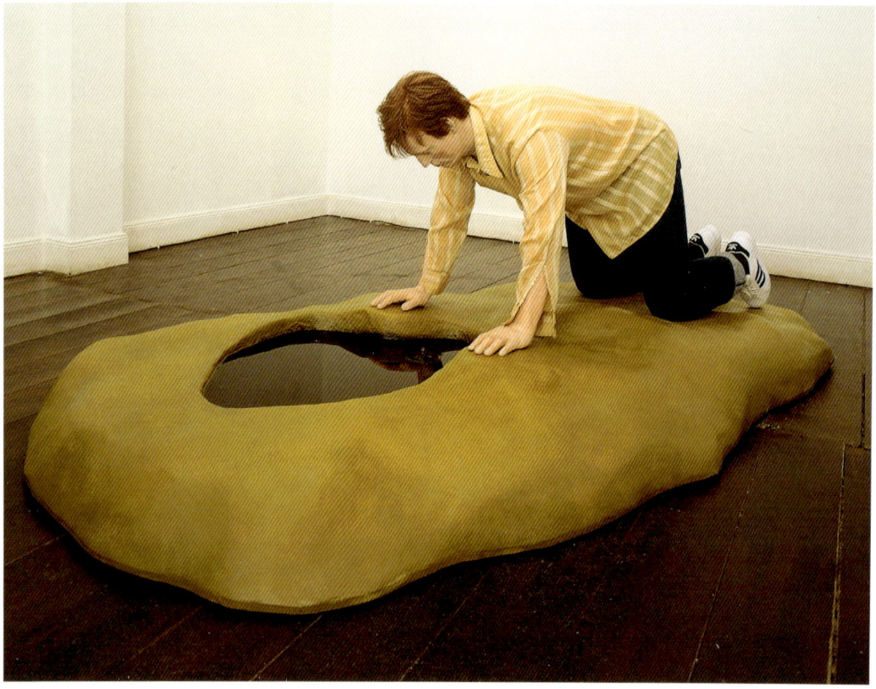

Olaf Nicolai *A Portrait of the Artist as a Weeping Narcissus*, 2000
polyester, textiles, water, electronic pump

PERTURBATION OF NARCISSUS

The German conceptual artist Olaf Nicolai, in *A Portrait of the Artist as a Weeping Narcissus* (2000), revisits a Romantic topos of the artist as a self-absorbed Narcissus, but in an ironic mode stripped of picturesque illusions. A life-size, hyper-real cast of the artist in shirtsleeves is bent over a pond. A motor produces tears that fall into the water – a deliberately kitschy visual paraphrase of Ovid: 'His tears disturbed the water, so that the pool rippled, and the image grew dim.'[24] The realisation that he can never be united with the elusive object of his desire causes Narcissus to cry out in despair; it is a moment of great pathos in Ovid's narration, even more so than the actual death that it foretells. The postmodern 'death of the author', the event for which Nicolai sheds his tears perhaps, is a death of a wholly different order, more bathos than pathos. For this postmodern, Narcissus is the last artist.

Mat Collishaw's heavily citational photographic practice (another 'echography' like that of Jess's), reflects on the history of the medium and its intimate connection with the theme of Narcissus. Collishaw (b. 1966) startles us with a plausible-looking Narcissus relocated from the woodland of Ovidian myth to the prosaic setting of a North London building site. Stripped down to his waist, Collishaw, holding a remote shutter for the camera, peers intently into a murky puddle in which we see the reflection of the concrete bollard behind him. Myth is forced to collide with banal contemporary reality. The circumstances of the picture's genesis were recounted by the artist in an interview in the *Guardian* newspaper, in the course of which, incidentally, he acknowledged the formative influence of surrealism on his photographic practice:

> Back in 1990, I was walking, holding my son, who was then about six months old, through a building site in Finsbury Park in north London. I flew him down towards this little puddle on the ground and showed him his face in it, and as I did so his mother said: 'Oh, he's like Narcissus!' It was such a bizarre observation to make in this filthy, degraded environment that I thought this might be a really good place to restage that myth.[25]

Mat Collishaw *Narcissus*, 1990

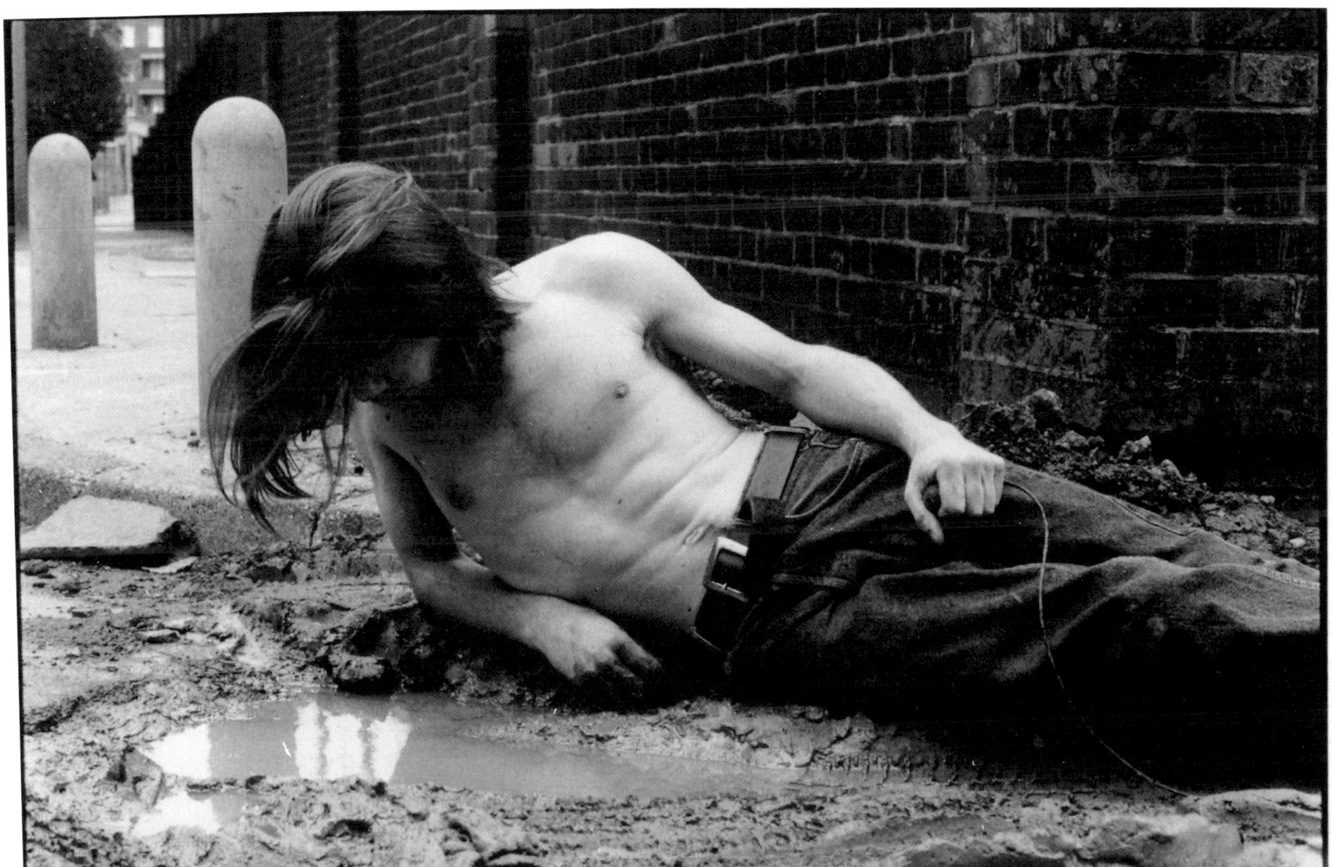

Jake and Dinos Chapman *Black Nazissus*, 1997
fibreglass, mixed media, resin and artificial blood

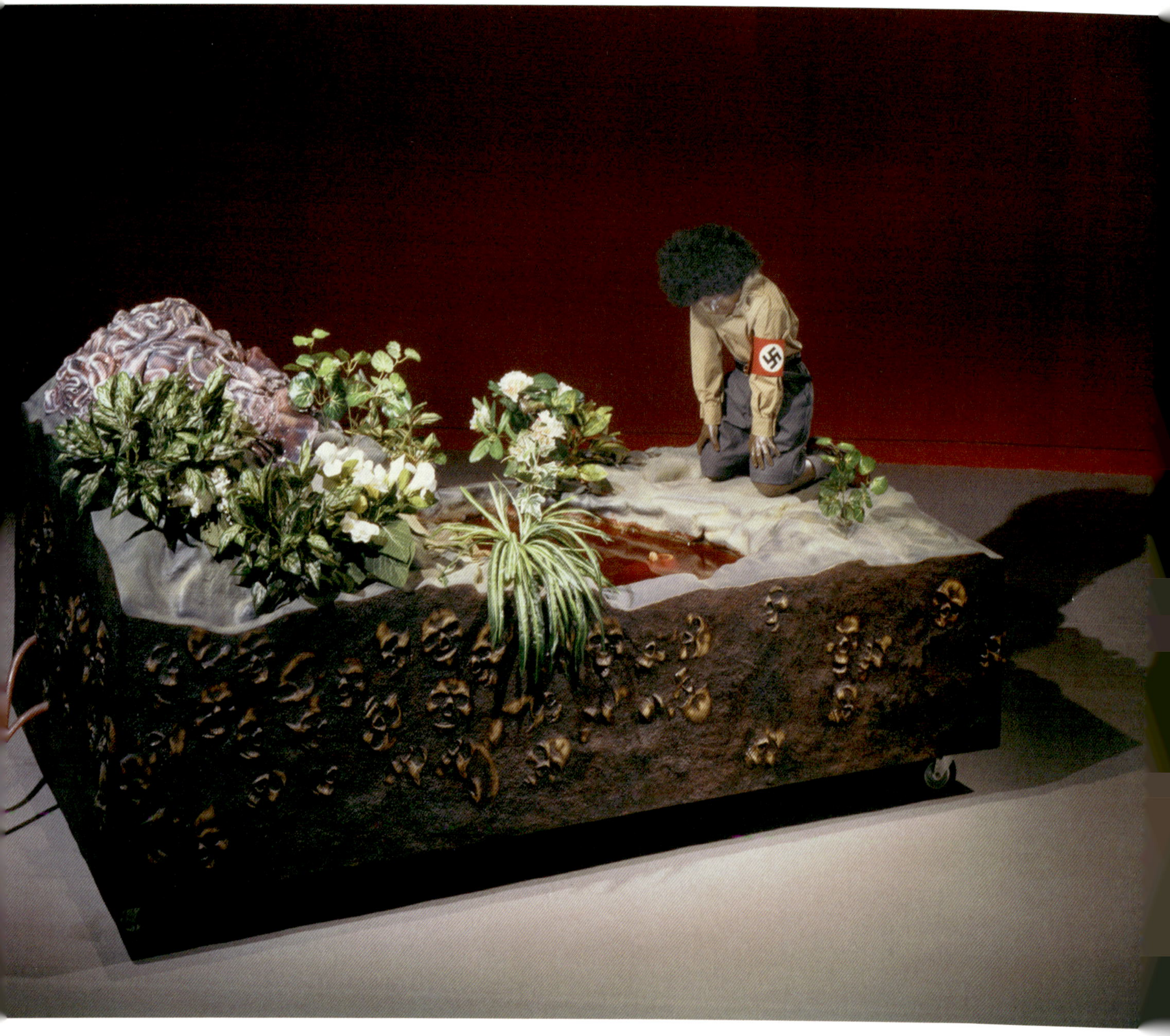

Jake and Dinos Chapman's *Black Nazissus* (1997) belongs to the same anti-idealist counter-tradition as Collishaw's *Narcissus.* The Chapman brothers are de-mythologisers, make no mistake about it. This fiercely rebarbative work is quite hard to describe let alone explain. A black gollywog-style doll dressed in Nazi regalia crouches at the edge of a blood-red pond. His gaze is returned not by a beautiful reflection but a gross 'fuck face' that emerges from beneath the surface of the pool – one of the Chapmans' trademark dysmorphic bodies which have penises and vaginas grafted onto facial features. The figure is equipped with a setting of fake vegetation that mocks the more usual pastoral imagery associated with the Narcissus subject. A motor hidden inside the apparatus is responsible for circulating water, which oozes out of a pustular boil atop a putrid mound before running down into the pool. The plinth itself is constructed in the manner of a cross-sectional model exposing layers of earth beneath the surface, a sort of repressed underbelly of the Narcissus iconography. Bits of human skeletons poke out of the soil, like a mass grave, at the very spot where Narcissus has chosen to kneel down and gaze upon his reflection. Perhaps the Chapman brothers imagined theirs as the last in a long line of Narcissi all of whom lie buried beneath the not-so-tranquil pool? The whole installation is mounted on casters, presumably so that it can be moved quickly to wherever it is needed.

A popular film from the 1940s called *Black Narcissus* has been identified as a possible source for the work, though its story about a group of nuns setting up a convent in the Himalayas bears little resemblance to the myth apart from the title.[26] Curiously, another British artist duo, Tim Noble and Sue Webster, have also created a work called *Black Narcissus* (2006), which is made up of a series of black silicone casts of the artists' hands and penis, that, when configured, cast a shadow of two heads in profile onto the wall.[27] One is reminded that in antiquity a reflection (like that of Narcissus) was thought of as a shadow cast by the object. Ovid tells us that Narcissus fell for 'an insubstantial hope, mistaking a mere shadow for a real body.'[28] The Chapmans veer further away from the original myth by dressing their Narcissus in a Nazi uniform with a swastika armband. The rationale for this is evidently a play on the sound of the word 'nar-ci-ssus' or a pun maybe on the German spelling of Narcissus as 'Narzissus.'

Tim Noble and Sue Webster *Black Narcissus*, 2006
black poly-sulphide rubber, wood, light projector

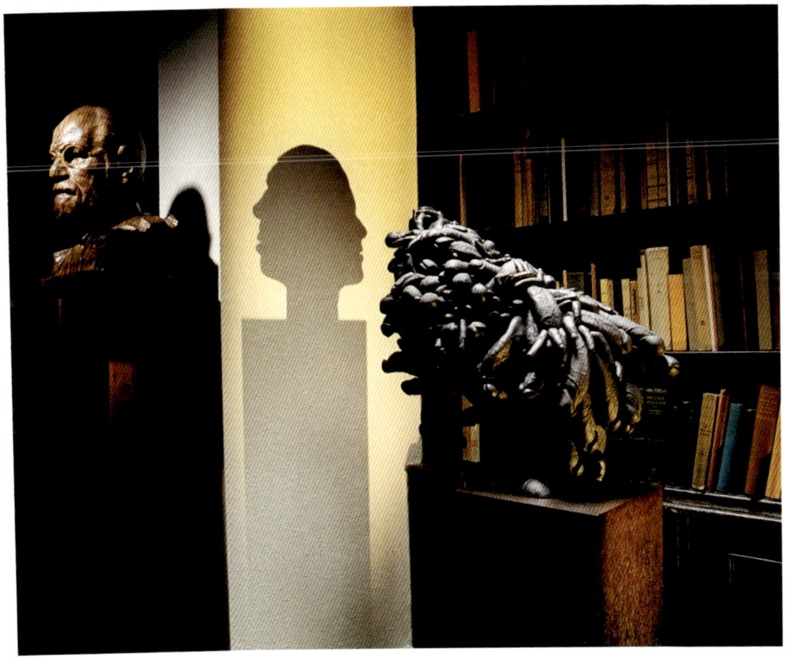

The Chapmans were anticipated in this line of dubious humour by Dalí in his response to a famous case of patricide in Paris in the early 1930s. Violette Nozière was a young woman who poisoned her parents (her mother survived but her father did not) and afterwards claimed in her defence that her father had repeatedly raped her over a number of years. The surrealists rallied to her cause, producing a book of poems and drawings dedicated to her. Dalí's contribution played gratuitously on the name Nozière, relating it to 'Nazière' and making a punning connection between 'nazi' and 'nez' or nose – his portrait of Nozière has a ridiculously elongated nose. There is no reason to think the Chapmans would have known about this drawing, though their 'black Nazi' brings to mind certain other works by Dalí from the later 1930s, such as his painting of a Hitlerian wet-nurse, which even the surrealists regarded as beyond the pale. In more general terms, Dalí may have provided them with a model for how art can be made from a perversely tendentious black humour. This was perhaps of more immediate relevance to them than the fact that Dalí was responsible for what is certainly the best-known twentieth-century image of Narcissus. The obscene face that peers up at Narcissus from the pool likewise has a solid surrealist pedigree behind it. While Freud's 1905 essay 'On the Sexual Theories of Children' may have been a source of inspiration, it is inconceivable that the Chapman brothers weren't also aware – and possibly rather envious – of René Magritte's *The Rape* (1934), which shockingly combines a woman's face and torso, substituting breasts for eyes and pubic hair for a mouth.

It would be a mistake to try to rationalise too far a work that revolves around the oxymoronic notion of a black Nazi. We can say with a degree of certainty, however, that *Black Nazissus* comprehensively negates the various idealizing tropes connected with images of Narcissus in Western art. Most obviously, the Chapmans confront the 'whiteness' of Narcissus: Ovid, evoking the youth's chaste purity, refers to Narcissus as 'white as marble'. Since they acknowledge Georges Bataille as a major influence upon their work, it is very likely the Chapmans would have known Bataille's essay on 'Base Materialism and Gnosticism', which appeared in English translation in *Visions of Excess*. In that article, Bataille, who was a specialist in numismatics at the Bibliothèque Nationale in Paris, discusses the grotesque figures represented on Gnostic coins: headless gods and others that are ass-headed or duck-headed. In these monstrous caricatures of the Hellenistic ideal of the human form, Bataille discerns 'a bizarre but mortal subversion of the ideal and of the order expressed today by the words "classical antiquity".'[29] Transforming the virulent transgressions of an embattled and oppositional second-century religious sect into a recipe for avant-garde success, the Chapmans' 2006 retrospective at Tate Liverpool was provocatively titled 'Bad Art for Bad People.'[30] One suspects that the mordant satire the Chapmans direct at the figure of Narcissus stems from the recognition that they share with Nicolai, namely that the post-Romantic tradition of the artist, as represented by the figure of Narcissus, is over. What is left but to pour scorn on the toppled idol?

Christoph Grunenberg, curator of the Tate Liverpool retrospective and the ICA Boston exhibition 'Gothic: Transmutations of Horror in Late-Twentieth-Century Art' exhibition, which included the Chapmans *Black Nazissus* – its first and only public outing – analyses the work through the lens of Kristevan abjection, arguing that it should be understood as representing a 'narcissistic crisis.'[31] The abject corresponds to a maternal element from which the infant is at first undifferentiated, and from which it must separate in order to constitute itself as an autonomous being. Since it pertains to a moment prior to the existence of a discrete human subject, the abject is a highly ambiguous object. Kristeva states. 'The abject is not an ob-ject facing me, which I name or imagine.'[32] In the vulgarisation of the notion within the art world, however, it became synonymous with a catalogue of bodily effluvia, secretions and excretions that arouse disgust. Kristeva usefully notes the kinship of the abject to perversion. The unruly drives of the pre-Oedipal polymorphously-perverse infant disturb the stillness of the pond, clouding its waters, she writes. Only after the narcissistic ego has formed does the abject come to be retrospectively designated as a threat to identity. Kristeva again:

> Abjection, with a meaning broadened to take in subjective diachrony, *is a precondition of narcissism*. It is coexistent with it and causes it to be permanently brittle. The more or less beautiful image in which I behold or recognize myself rests upon an abjection that sunders it as soon as repression, the constant watchman, is relaxed.[33]

If there is any problem with such a reading, it is that it is all too plausible. *Black Nazissus* is one helluva narcissistic crisis! What this reading overlooks is parody, the Chapmans' secret weapon for 'bringing things down in the world' (Bataille). Nothing, not even the loftier reaches of Kristevan theory, is exempt from it. We must assume that the Chapmans are every bit as well versed in such theory as any art historian since the London art world in the 1990s was abuzz with it. The Chapmans' *mise-en-scène* of abjection, which is an inventory of everything that was defined as disgusting (not excluding blood) by the abject 1990s, is predicated on caricatural excess. Looking about them, they cannot fail to have been impressed by the ease with which so-called 'abject art' was devoured by a rapacious and ever-expanding art market. Crisis, what crisis? The abjection that they serve up like *hors d'oeuvres* for the delectation of the earnest critic turns out to have been well and truly pre-digested.

> Our topic deals with the giving and taking away of faces, with face and deface, *figure*, figuration and disfiguration.[34]

The Narcissus myth, we have seen, encompasses two contrasting narrative moments: the youth's captivation by his perfectly reflected image versus the dispersion of that image when the surface of the pool is disturbed by his tears, prefiguring Narcissus's death and dissolution. It may be possible to map these consecutive moments onto a distinction between the terms gay and queer, with the moment of specular recognition corresponding to a gay identity-politics versus the subsequent moment of 'unbinding' as queer. With respect to the latter moment, the psychoanalytic term unbinding ('Entbindung') enables us to view the dispersion of the coherent subject as a function of the death drive. These considerations are relevant to certain recent engagements with the Narcissus theme. A dialogue with surrealism is discernible in the work of transgender photographer and performance artist, Del LaGrace Volcano. Like Claude Cahun, with whom s/he claims affinity, Volcano evokes Narcissus and related themes of reflection, doubling and twinning (also recalling Cecil Beaton's obsessive fascination with photographing twins), while at the same time critiquing the narcissism of visual representation. Exploring an in-between zone of gender transitivity, Narcissus is updated by Volcano as a gender-ambiguous punk wearing an ACTUP T-shirt. The suicidal Narcissus of Greek myth has become politicised and the language of AIDS activism permeates the space of a queer subjectivity. In another work, the photographer, whose face and upper body are covered in shaving cream, presses frantically against a glass shower screen that is smeared and sullied. It is as though we are shown Narcissus from the other side of the mirror. This image is comparable to Rist's *Open My Glade (Flatten)* (2000), a close-up video of the artist's face compressed by a pane of glass which was projected on a giant screen in New York's Times Square. Narcissus as a signifier for the queer also persists in photographs by

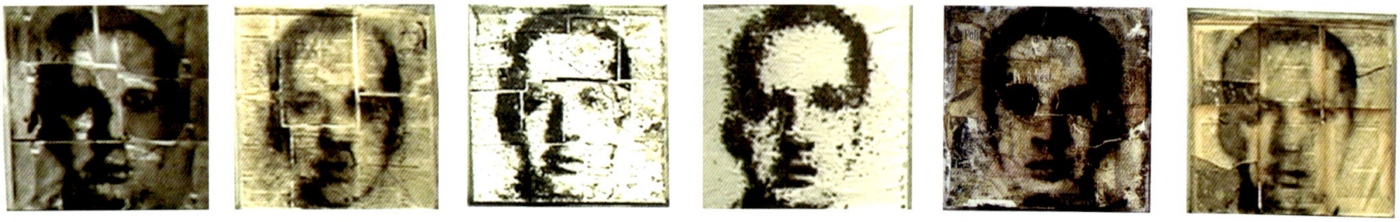

Robert Mapplethorpe that allude to the poses of classical statuary, as well as in French writer Hervé Guibert's self-portrait photographs cataloguing his bodily disintegration due to AIDS, a poignant reprise of the Dorian Gray motif.[35]

In Ovid's *Metamorphoses*, when the nymphs come to collect Narcissus's body they find it has mysteriously disappeared; in its place they discover a flower as a sort of memorial to him. The Colombian artist Oscar Muñoz has staged his own disappearance in a piece titled *Narcisos en proceso* (*Narcissi in Process*), which he began in 1994 and remains ongoing. Muñoz's work has dealt with the conflict in Colombia and with the elimination of political opponents of the regime – the so-called 'disappeared' who have been murdered by secret police. He confronts issues of memory and memorialization using the media of drawing, photography and film to convey impermanence. In *Proyecto para un memorial* (Project for a Memorial), a five-screen projection shown at the Venice Biennale in 2005, Muñoz draws on a hot pavement in Cali, the Colombian city where he lives, copying photographs from newspaper obituaries. The portraits are traced in water and quickly evaporate under the sun. As one image fades, he starts over again. In *Aliento* (Breath, 1996–2002), mirrored discs are mounted on a wall. The condensation from breathing onto the glass reveals etched faces from photographs in Colombian newspapers that disappear as the moisture diminishes. Recent installation works shown in London at the Institute for Visual Arts as part of 'Mirror Images', his first solo exhibition in the UK, include facsimiles of the front pages of the two leading newspapers in Colombia (*El Pais* and *El Tiempo*) on which the artist has burned the portrait images and text onto the front page of an album. As each page is turned, the image gradually becomes less and less distinct. Photography lies behind Muñoz's art practice in a variety of media and affords him a powerful metaphor for the operations of memory and forgetting. In *Narcisos en proceso*, Muñoz uses a photo-booth portrait of himself which is screen-printed with charcoal powder on pieces of paper floating on water in a Plexiglas vitrine. Over the course of the exhibition, the powder gradually disperses. This is comparable to what Lacanian theory has called *aphanisis*, an inevitable 'fading' of the subject. Muñoz creates transient but eloquent monuments to absences. In a sense, that is what 'Narcissus Reflected' intends to do by resurrecting the traces of desires that have been left out of official histories of surrealism.

opposite: **Oscar Muñoz** *Narcisos en proceso* (Narcissi in Process), 1994–
screenprinted charcoal powder on water, paper, Plexiglas vitrines
below: **Oscar Muñoz** *Narciso* (Narcissis), 2001, video still

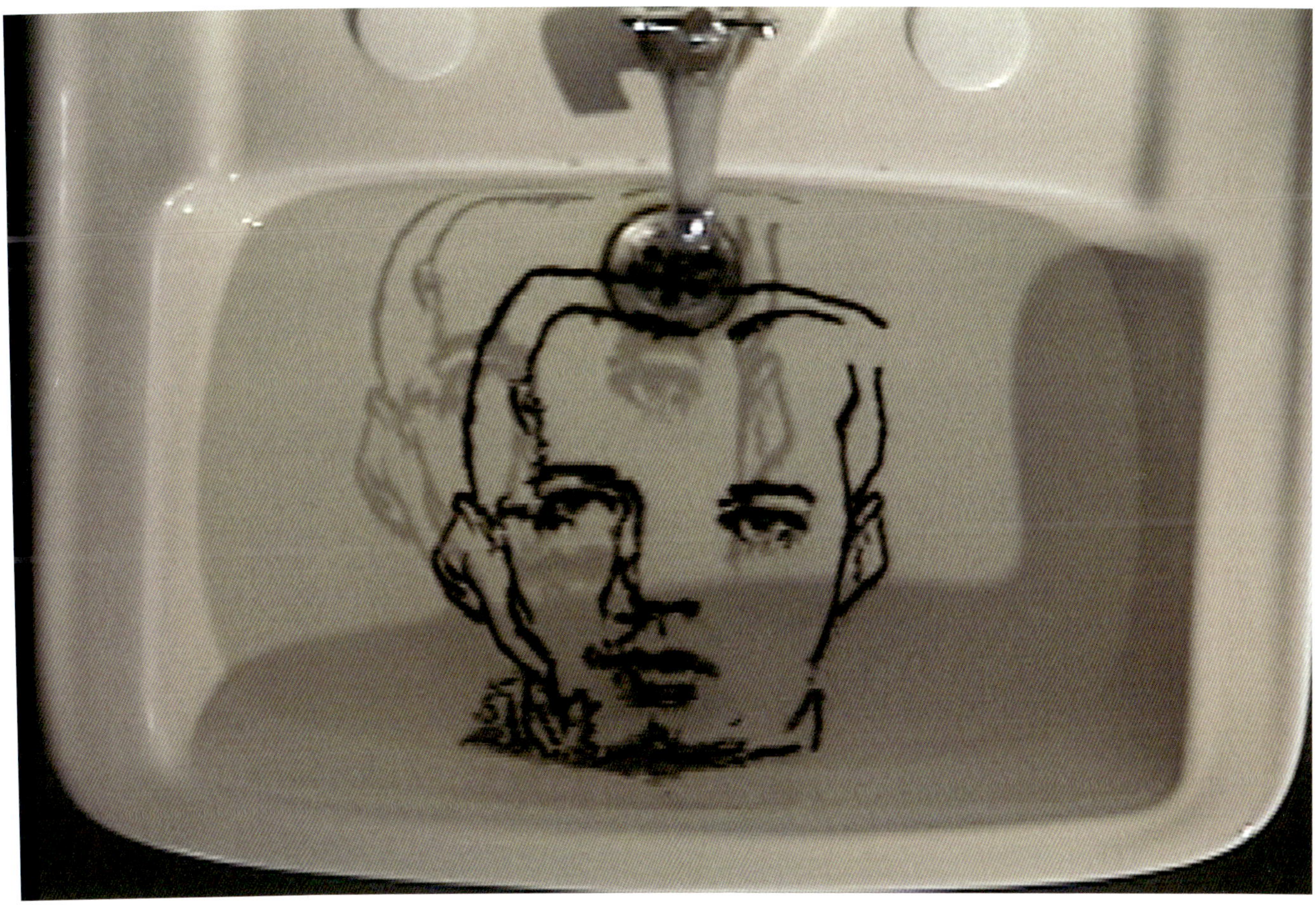

NOTES

1. Oscar Wilde, *Essays and Lectures* (Rockville, MD: Arc Manor, 2008).
2. See Kimberly Rhodes, *Ophelia and Victorian Visual Culture* (Aldershot: Ashgate, 2008).
3. This kind of vision is analogous to Dalí's 'double images', of which the *Metamorphosis of Narcissus* (1937) affords a notable illustration.
4. Vinge describes Schlegel as adapting the myth in order to express an idea of self-reflection of the poet in his work – a belief that holds true for much post-Romantic art. Louise Vinge, *The Narcissus Theme in Western European Literature up to the Early Nineteenth Century* (Lund: Gleerups, 1967), p.304.
5. Gaston Bachelard, *L'Eau et les rêves* (Paris: José Corti, 1942), pp.109–123.
6. The theme of mirroring, especially prominent in *Ophelia*, is indicative of Masson's interest in Neoplatonism. For Plotinus, as was noted previously, the material world is the reflection of a higher spiritual reality.
7. Plotinus, *The Enneads*, trans. Stephen MacKenna (Harmondsworth: Penguin, 1991).
8. Michel Leiris, 'Mythologies', in *André Masson and his Universe* (Genève-Paris: Ed. des Trois Collines, 1947), pp.128–129.
9. Rosalind Krauss, 'Video: The Aesthetics of Narcissism,' *October*, vol. 1 (spring 1976), pp.50–64.
10. Walter Benjamin, 'Surrealism: The Last Snapshot of the European Intelligentsia', in *Reflections*, trans. Edmund Jephcott (New York: Schocken Books, 1986), pp.177–192.
11. Malet explained: 'The mirror moved perpendicularly over an illustrated page from whatever source reveals a secret domain of omnipresent eroticism within images.'
12. See *La Subversion des images: Surréalisme, Photographie, Film* (Paris: Centre Pompidou, 2009), pp.368–369.
13. Horst Bredekamp, *Les coraux de Darwin*, trans. Christian Joschke (Paris: Les Presses du réel, 2008).
14. Bachelard, *L'Eau et les rêves*, p.161. 'Michelet's poetry of the sea is a reverie … The sea is maternal, the water is fantastical breast milk.'
15. Sigmund Freud, 'Civilisation and its Discontents' (1930), *Pelican Freud Library*, vol. 12, trans. James Strachey (Harmondsworth: Pelican Books), p.255.
16. Georgiana Colville, 'Leonor Fini', in *Dictionary of Women Artists*, vol. 1 (London, New York: Routledge, 1997).
17. Ovid, *Metamorphoses*, trans. Mary M. Innes (Harmondsworth: Penguin, 1955), book IV.
18. Ibid.
19. Menstrual blood has central symbolic importance in Pipilotti Rist's 2009 feature film, *Pepperminta*.
20. Sigmund Freud, 'The Libido Theory and Narcissism,' *Introductory Lectures on Psycho-Analysis, Pelican Freud Library*, vol. 1, trans. James Strachey (Harmondsworth: Pelican Books, 1973), p.466.
21. Ovid, *Metamorphoses*, book III.
22. The Italian philosopher Gianni Vattimo insightfully characterises this situation as the 'end yet continuation' of art. Art continues to be made but with a constant awareness of its belatedness. See *The End of Modernity: Nihilism and Hermeneutics in Post-modern Culture* (London: Polity Press, 1991).
23. Catriona Black, 'An Interview with Bill Viola,' *Sunday Herald* (7 December 2003).
24. Ovid, *Metamorphoses*, book III.
25. 'Mat Collishaw's Best Shot,' *The Guardian* (17 April 2008), p.29.
26. Christoph Grunenberg made this suggestion, in *Jake and Dinos Chapman: Bad Art for Bad People* (London: Tate Publishing, 2006).
27. Noble and Webster have made a later version since titled *Bloody Haemorrhaging Narcissus*, an allusion possibly to the newly discovered version of the myth attributed to Parthenius of Nicea in which the boy kills himself with a sword. News of this discovery among papyri held at Oxford was splashed widely across the internet.
28. Ovid, *Metamorphoses*, book III.
29. Georges Bataille, *Visions of Excess: Selected Writings, 1927–1939*, trans. Allan Stoekl (Minneapolis: University of Minnesota Press, 1985), p.46.
30. Hans Jonas, in *The Gnostic Religion*, describes the typical Gnostic use of biblical material in terms that could scarcely be bettered as a characterisation of the Chapman brothers: 'vilification, parody, caricature, conscious perversion of meaning, wholesale reversal of value-signs, savage degrading of the sacred, and gleefully shocking blasphemy.' (London: Routledge, 1992).
31. See Christoph Grunenberg ed., *Jake and Dinos Chapman: Bad Art for Bad People*, p.19.
32. Julia Kristeva, *Powers of Horror: An Essay on Abjection* (New York: Columbia University Press, 1982), p.1.
33. Ibid, p.13.
34. Paul de Man, 'Autobiography as De-Facement,' chapter 4 in *The Rhetoric of Romanticism* (New York: Columbia University Press, 1984), p.76.
35. Will Self's *Dorian: An Imitation* (2002) transposes the Wildean fable to the gay culture of the 1970s and 1980s.

APPENDIX

A note on Salvador Dalí's poem, *Metamorphosis of Narcissus*

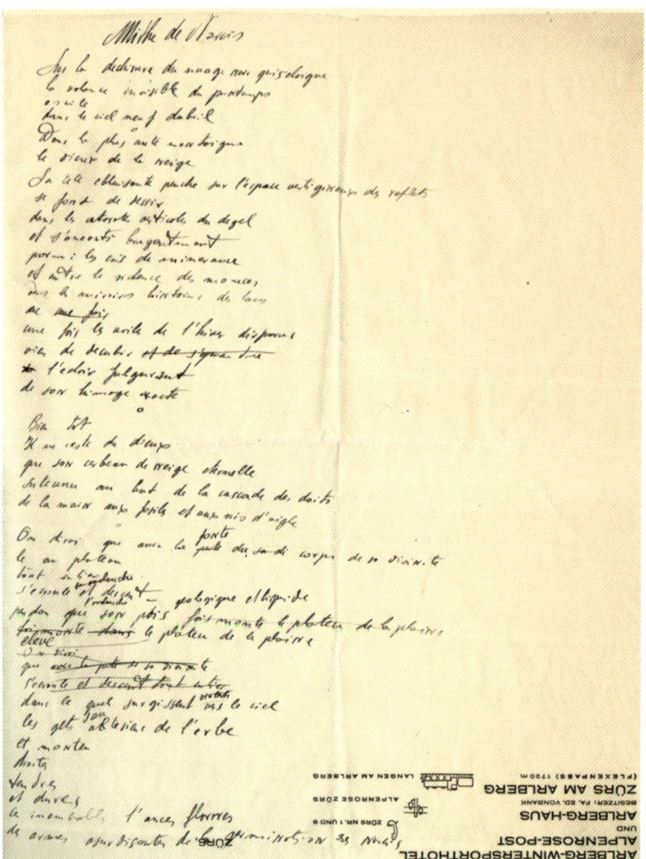

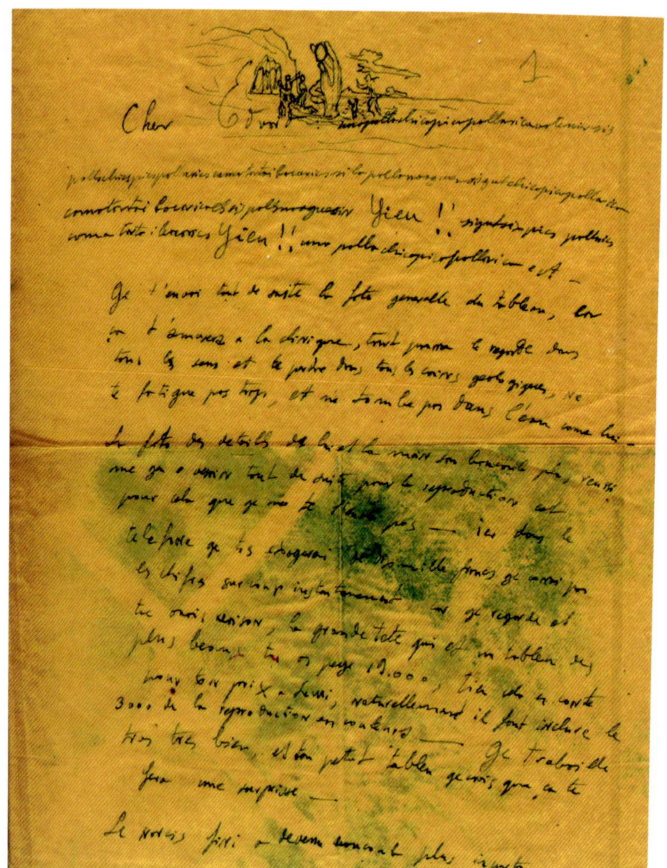

Métamorphose de Narcisse / Metamorphosis of Narcissus was published by Éditions surréalistes and the Julian Levy Gallery in separate French and English editions on 25 June 1937. Adorning the cover is a photograph of Gala by Cecil Beaton (part of a series of photographs by Beaton, see also p.160). The English translation of Dalí's poem is by Francis Scarpe. The original manuscript held at the Fundació Gala-Salvador Dalí is in French, as was Dalí's custom with writings intended for publication, and is titled simply *Le mithe de narcisse* (The Myth of Narcissus). It is hand-written on sheets of headed writing paper from the Arlberg-Wintersporthotel, Zürs am Arlberg. The manuscript stops short of the poem's final stanzas that describe the metamorphosis, which suggests Dalí may have added this ending at the same time as the change of title.

All the evidence points to the picture having been executed in April 1937. The poem seems to have been written at roughly the same time as well. Edward James, a midwife to their creation, relates the circumstances in a letter of 12 October 1938:

> The subject of the poem is the myth of Narcissus and he wrote it contemporaneously with the very extraordinary and remarkable picture that he was then painting. Both poem and picture represent the metamorphosis of Narcissus. Being April when he was at work, and the time when these flowers bloom in the Austrian Alps where we then were, the air happened to be full of that keen diamond-like lucency which comes with the melting snows. There is this feeling of rigorous spring both in the picture and the poem.[1]

In a letter to Julian Levy on 12 June 1937, James boasts: 'I was there when the canvas had its first pencil mark put on it, and even saw the preliminary sketches for the picture before the big canvas was begun at all.'[2] A photograph at the Fundació Gala-Salvador Dalí shows Dalí poised before the picture apparently in the hotel where it was painted (p.36). In April, Dalí addressed a letter to Paul Éluard from Zürs with a commentary on his poetic activity and an explanation of his aims – material that found its way into a prologue to the published poem. He also appended the poem itself, which, at that point, was still titled 'le mithe de narcisse.'[3] A letter from Dalí to James on 15 June 1937 – a *terminus ante quem* for the painting – announced its completion and contained photographs for use in the publication. He gently mocks James who was taking a rest cure in Switzerland, warning him not to spend too long looking at the picture lest he fall in like Narcissus. The picture was exhibited under the present title *Métamorphose de Narcisse* at the Galerie Renou & Colle in Paris from 6 to 30 July 1937.

To an extent, scholarship has only begun to recognise that Dalí is as significant for his writing – funny and brilliant – as for his painting and myriad other pursuits. The exhibition 'Narcissus Reflected' hopes to contribute to the recovery of his literary activity by re-uniting the poem with the picture.

NOTES

1. Letter to Mr. Kornfeld, 12 October 1938, Edward James Foundation. James made a translation of the poem, which however was not the one used in the published English version.
2. Letter to Julian Levy, 12 June 1937, Edward James Foundation.
3. Paul Éluard, *Lettres à Gala 1924–1948*, ed. Pierre Dreyfus (Paris: Gallimard, 1984), 277, pp.476–477. Éluard wrote in response to Gala: 'The Narcissus-hand is amazing. I will reproduce it in my book. However the commentaries of Dalí on his poetry aren't much use to me.'

opposite left: **Salvador Dalí** Page from Dalí's notebook showing poem *Mithe de Narcis* (Metamorphosis of Narcissus) c.1936–37 notebook page
opposite right: **Salvador Dalí** Letter to his patron Edward James 15 June 1937, ink on brown paper

SALVADOR DALI

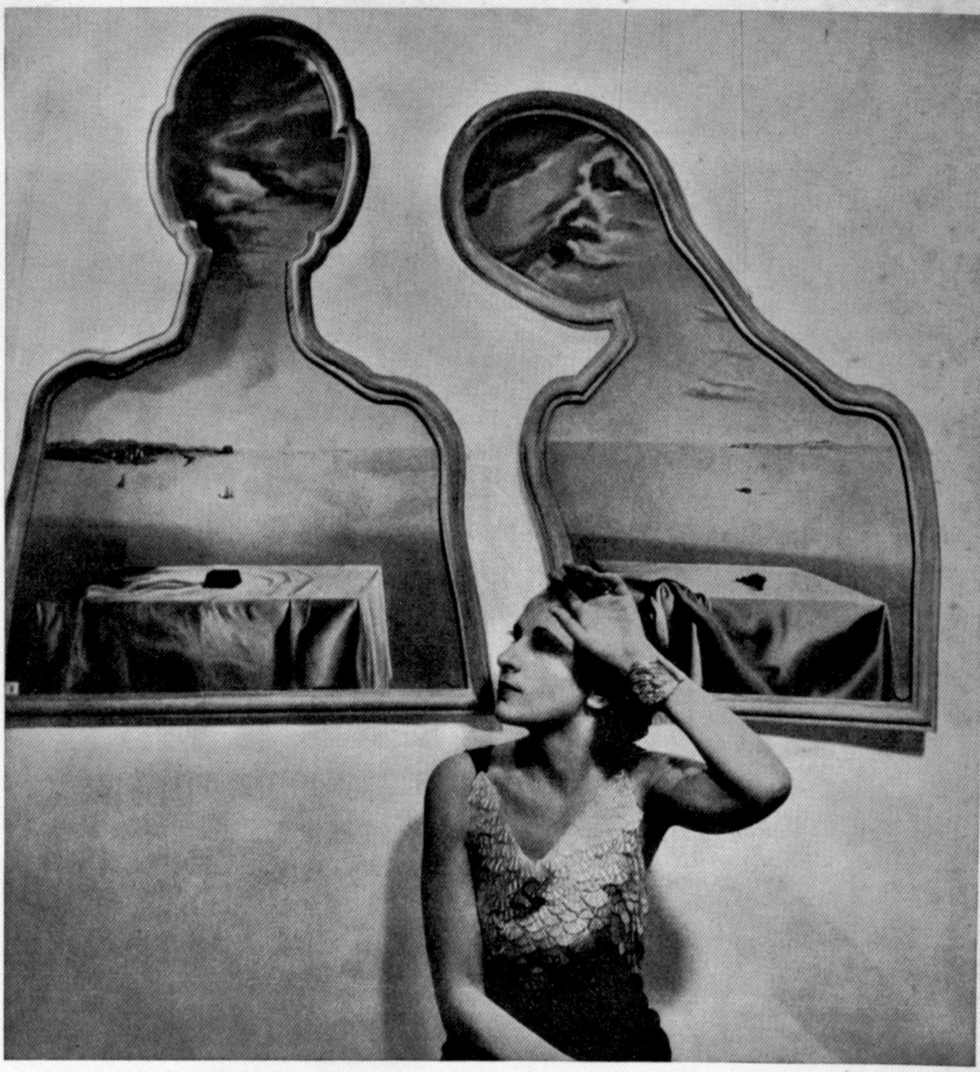

METAMORPHOSIS OF NARCISSUS

METAMORPHOSIS OF NARCISSUS

SALVADOR DALÍ

Of this volume, issued the twenty-fifth of June nineteen hundred and thirty-seven from the presses of the master printer Henri Jourde, five hundred copies were printed for the French edition and five hundred and fifty copies for the English edition.
The cover photograph is by Cecil Beaton.

WAY OF VISUALLY OBSERVING THE COURSE OF THE METAMORPHOSIS OF NARCISSUS REPRESENTED IN THE PRINT ON THE OPPOSITE PAGE:

If one looks for some time, from a slight distance and with a certain 'distant fixedness', at the hypnotically immobile figure of Narcissus, it gradually disappears until at last it is completely invisible.

The metamorphosis of the myth takes place at that precise moment, for the image of Narcissus is suddenly transformed into the image of a hand which rises out of his own reflection. At the tips or its fingers the hand is holding an egg, a seed, the bulb from which will be born the new narcissus – the flower. Beside it can be seen the limestone sculpture of the hand – the fossil hand of the water holding the blown flower.

'Dalí has endowed surrealism with a first-rate instrument, to wit the paranoiac-critical method, which he immediately proved himself capable of applying equally well to painting, to poetry, to the film, to the construction of typical surrealist objects, to fashions, to the history of art and even, if needs be, to all kind of exegesis.'
(André Breton: *What is Surrealism?*)

THE FIRST POEM AND THE FIRST PAINTING OBTAINED ENTIRELY THROUGH THE INTEGRAL APPLICATION OF THE PARANOIAC-CRITICAL METHOD:

For the first time, a surrealist painting and poem objectively allow the coherent interpretation of a developed irrational subject. The paranoiac-critical method is beginning to establish the indestructible pudding of the 'exact details' that Stendhal demanded for the description of Saint Peter's Church in Rome, and it is doing this in the domain of the most paralysing surrealist poetry.

The lyricism of poetic images is philosophically important only when it has attained, in its operation, the same exactness as mathematics do in their operation.

The poet must, before anyone, prove what he says.

FIRST PORT-LLIGAT FISHERMAN. – What's wrong with that chap, glaring at himself all day in his looking-glass?

SECOND FISHERMAN. – If you really want to know (lowering his voice) he has a bulb in his head.

'A bulb in the head', in Catalan, corresponds exactly with the psycho-analytic notion of 'complex'. If a man has a bulb in his head, it might break into flower at any moment, Narcissus!

Under the split in the retreating black cloud
the invisible scale of Spring
is oscillating
in the fresh April sky.
On the highest mountain,
the god of the snow,
his dazzling head bent over the dizzy space of reflections,
starts melting with desire
in the vertical cataracts of the thaw
annihilating himself loudly among the excremental cries
  of minerals,

or
between the silences of mosses
towards the distant mirror of the lake
in which,
the veils of winter having disappeared,
he has newly discovered
the lightning flash
of his faithful image.
It seems that with the loss of his divinity the whole high
plateau
pours itself out,
crashes and crumbles
among the solitude and the incurable silence of iron oxides
while its dead weight
raises the entire swarming and apotheosic
plateau from the plain
from which already thrust towards the sky
the artesian fountains of grass
and from which rise,
erect,

tender,
and hard,
the innumerable floral spears
of the deafening armies of the germination of the narcissi.

Already the heterosexual group, in the renowned poses
of preliminary expectation, conscientiously ponders
over the threatening libidinous cataclysm, the
carniverous blooming of its latent morphological
atavisms.

In the heterosexual group,
in that kind date of the year
(but not excessively beloved or mild),
there are
the Hindou
tart, oily, sugared
like an August date, [1]

the Catalan with his grave back
well planted
in a sun-tide,
a whitsuntide of flesh inside his brain,

the blond flesh-eating German,
the brown mists
of mathematics
in the dimples
of his cloudy knees,

there is the English woman,
the Russian,
the Swedish women,
the American
and the tall darkling Andalusian,
hardy with glands and olive with anguish.

Far from the heterosexual group, the shadows of the
avanced afternoon draw out across the countryside,
and cold lays hold of the adolescent's nakedness
as he lingers at the water's edge.

When the clear and divine body of Narcissus
leans
down to the obscure mirror of the lake,

when his white torso folded forward
fixes itself, frozen,
in the silvered and hypnotic curve of his desire,
when the time passes
on the clock of the flowers of the sand of his own flesh,

Narcissus loses his being in the cosmic vertigo
in the deepest depths of which
is singing
the cold and dyonisiac siren of his own image.

The body of Narcissus flows out and loses itself
in the abyss of his reflection,
like the sand glass that will not be turned again.

Narcissus, you are losing your body,
carried away and confounded by the millenary reflection
  of your disappearance
your body stricken dead
falls to the topaz precipice with yellow wreckage of love,
your white body, swallowed up,
follows the slope of the savagely mineral torrent
of the black precious stones with pungent perfumes,
your body…
down to the unglazed mouths of the night
on the edge of which
there sparkles already
all the red silverware
of dawns with veins broken in "the wharves of blood".[2]

Narcissus,
do you understand?
Symmetry, divine hypnosis of the mind's geometry,
  already fills up your head,
with that incurable sleep, vegetable, atavistic, slow
Which withers up the brain
in the parchment substance
of the kernel of your nearing metamorphosis.

The seed of your head has just fallen into the water.

Man returns to the vegetable state
by fatigue-laden sleep
and the gods
by the transparent hypnosis of their passions.
Narcissus, you are so immobile
one would think you were asleep.
If it were question of Hercules rough and brown,
one would say: he sleeps like a bole
in the posture
of an herculean oak.
But you, Narcissus,
made of perfume bloomings of transparent adolescence,
you sleep like a water flower.
Now the great mystery draws near,
the great metamorphosis is about to occur.

Narcissus, in his immobility, absorbed by his reflection with the digestive slowness of carnivorous plants, becomes invisible.

There remains of him only
the hallucinatingly white oval of his head,
his head again more tender,
his head, chrysalis of hidden biological designs,
his head held up by the tips of the water's fingers,
at the tips of the fingers
of the insensate hand,

of the terrible hand,
of the excrement-eating hand,
of the mortal hand
of his own reflection.

When that head slits
when that head splits
when that head bursts,
it will be the flower,
the new Narcissus,
Gala –
my narcissus.

1. August day – day in August, considered as a *substance.*

2. Federico García Lorca.

LIST OF WORKS

listed in chronological order

George Minne *Kneeling Youth*, 1898
bronze sculpture, 78 x 20 x 47 cm
Museum voor Schone Kunsten, Gent (p.103)

Cecil Beaton *Nancy and Baba Beaton*, c.1927
modern silver gelatin print, 25.4 x 20.3 cm
Courtesy of the Cecil Beaton Studio Archive
at Sotheby's (p.68)

Florence Henri *Autoportrait*, 1927–28
vintage silver gelatin print, 8 x 5.5 cm
Private collection. Courtesy Galleria
Martini & Ronchetti, Genova (p.64)

Florence Henri *Double portrait*, 1927–28
silver gelatin print from 1977, 25.2 x 18.5 cm
Private collection. Courtesy Galleria Martini
& Ronchetti, Genova (p.65)

Cecil Beaton *Paula Gellibrand*, 1928
modern silver gelatin print, 25.4 x 20.3 cm
Courtesy of the Cecil Beaton Studio Archive
at Sotheby's (p.69)

Claude Cahun *Self-portrait*, 1928
modern silver gelatin print, 11.8 x 9.4 cm
Courtesy Jersey Heritage Trust (p.60)

Claude Cahun *Self-portrait*, c.1928
modern silver gelatin print, 17.6 x 12.7 cm
Courtesy Jersey Heritage Trust (p.62)

Claude Cahun *Suzanne Malherbe/Marcel Moore*, 1928
modern silver gelatin print, 12 x 9.4 cm
Courtesy Jersey Heritage Trust (p.61)

Florence Henri *Autoportrait*, 1928
silver gelatin print from 1974, 25.2 x 18.5 cm
Private collection. Courtesy Galleria
Martini & Ronchetti, Genova (p.66)

Florence Henri *Composition abstraite*, 1928
silver gelatin print, 17.4 x 24 cm, Private collection.
Courtesy Galleria Martini & Ronchetti, Genova (p.131)

Florence Henri *Double portrait*, 1928
vintage silver gelatin print, 23 x 17.6 cm
Collection Centre Georges Pompidou.
Courtesy Galleria Martini & Ronchetti, Genova (p.67)

George Platt Lynes *Portrait of René Crevel*, 1928
modern silver gelatin print, 20.3 x 25.4 cm
Collection of The Kinsey Institute for Research
in Sex, Gender and Reproduction.
© Estate of George Platt Lynes (p.54)

Cecil Beaton *Jean Cocteau, Toulon*, 1930
modern silver gelatin print, 25.4 x 20.3 cm
Courtesy of the Cecil Beaton Studio Archive
at Sotheby's (p.130)

Cecil Beaton *Edward James*, 1931
vintage bromide contact print, 24.5 x 19.5 cm
Lent by the National Portrait Gallery, London
Given by executors of the Estate of Eileen Hose,
1991 (p.47)

Cecil Beaton *Salvador Dalí and Gala with*
A Couple with Their Heads Full of Clouds, 1937
modern silver gelatin print, 25.4 x 20.3 cm
Courtesy of the Cecil Beaton Studio Archive
at Sotheby's (p.51)

Paul Nash *Voyages of the Moon*, 1934–37
oil on canvas, 71.1 x 57 cm
Tate: Purchased 1951 (p.128)

Salvador Dalí at Punta dels Tres Frares, Catalonia,
1930s, vintage photograph, 9.1 x 8.9 cm
Work lent by the Gala-Salvador Dalí Foundation
(p.32)

Salvador Dalí painting Metamorphosis of Narcissus, c.1936–37, vintage photograph, 6.3 x 6 cm
Work lent by the Gala-Salvador Dalí Foundation (p.36)

Salvador Dalí Page from Dalí's notebook showing a preparatory sketch for *Metamorphosis of Narcissus*, c.1936–37, notebook page, 28.4 x 23.7 cm
Work lent by the Gala-Salvador Dalí Foundation (p.37)

Salvador Dalí Page from Dalí's notebook showing a compositional sketch for *Metamorphosis of Narcissus*, c.1936–37, notebook page, 20.3 x 15.6 cm
Work lent by the Gala-Salvador Dalí Foundation (p.33)

Salvador Dalí Page from Dalí's notebook showing poem *Mithe de Narcis*, c.1936–37
notebook page, 27.8 x 21.1 cm
Work lent by the Gala-Salvador Dalí Foundation (p.158)

Salvador Dalí Letter to his patron Edward James, 15 June 1937, ink on brown paper, 25.5 x 20.5 cm
Edward James Foundation (p.158)

Salvador Dalí *Metamorphosis of Narcissus*, 1937
oil on canvas, 82 x 109.2 x 8.5 cm
Tate: Purchased 1979 (pp.28–29)

Charles Henri Ford *Narcissus*, c.1937
modern silver gelatin print, 40.6 x 50.8 cm
Indra Tamang/Estate of Charles Henri Ford (p.81)

George Platt Lynes *Chester Nielson with J.Ogle (behind glass)*, 1937
modern silver gelatin print, 25.4 x 20.3 cm
Collection of The Kinsey Institute for Research in Sex, Gender and Reproduction.
© Estate of George Platt Lynes (p.78)

View magazine, vol. 3, no. 3, October 1943 'Narcissus' special issue (cover by André Masson), 31 x 23 cm
Private collection (p.79)

Jean Cocteau *Orphée*, 1950
Black and white film, 91 minutes
By arrangement with BFI (pp.83, 84)

Willard Maas *Narcissus*, 1956
16mm film, 59 minutes
Courtesy The New American Cinema Group/ The Film-Makers' Cooperative (p.85)

Jess Notebook for *Narkissos*, 1959–90
looseleaf notebook, 29.5 x 25.4 x 5.7 cm
Courtesy of Odyssia Gallery, New York (p.100)

Jess Compositional drawing for *Narkissos*, 1959
pencil on paper, 10.8 x 7.6 cm
Courtesy of Odyssia Gallery, New York (p.106)

Jess Compositional drawing for *Narkissos*, 1964
pencil on paper, 25.7 x 21.5 cm
Private collection (p.101)

Pierre Molinier *Double autoportrait*, c.1965
collage, 17.8 x 9 cm
Private collection, Paris (p.76)

Pierre Molinier *Mes jambes*, 1965
8mm film transferred to DVD, black and white, 8 minutes
Maison Européenne de la photographie, Paris
Courtesy Comité Molinier, Paris

Bill Brandt *Self-portrait*, 1966
vintage bromide print, 34.5 x 29.5 cm
Lent by the National Portrait Gallery, London.
Bill Brandt Archive. Purchased 1982 (p.133)

Yayoi Kusama *Narcissus Garden*, 1966
700 stainless steel spheres, dimensions variable
© Yayoi Kusama. Courtesy Victoria Miro Gallery London, Ota Fine Arts, Tokyo and Yayoi Kusama Studio Inc. (pp.112, 123, 125)

Pierre Molinier, *Mes jambes*, c.1967
vintage silver gelatin print, 11 x 3.5 cm
Collection Centre Georges Pompidou (p.74)

Pierre Molinier, *Pantomime narcisse*, 1967
vintage silver gelatin print, 15 x 11 cm
Private collection, Paris (p.73)

Cecil Beaton *Gervase Griffiths, Reddish*, 1968
modern silver gelatin print, 20.3 x 25.4 cm
Courtesy of the Cecil Beaton Studio Archive at Sotheby's (p.71)

Pierre Molinier *Le lit et ses commodités*, c.1968
vintage silver gelatin print, 8.8 x 11.5 cm
Private collection, Paris (p.72)

Cecil Beaton *Gilbert and George*, 1974
modern silver gelatin print, 25.4 x 20.3 cm
Courtesy of the Cecil Beaton Studio Archive at Sotheby's (p.70)

Pierre Molinier *Luciano Castelli*, 1975
vintage silver gelatin print, 17.5 x 12.5 cm
Private collection, Paris (p.75)

Françoise Molinier *Pierre Molinier's apartment photographed by his daughter the day after his suicide*, 1976, vintage silver gelatin print, 18 x 12.5 cm
Private collection, Paris (p.77)

Françoise Molinier *Pierre Molinier's apartment photographed by his daughter the day after his suicide*, 1976, vintage silver gelatin print, 17.8 x 11.7 cm
Private collection, Paris

Jess Pinning Board for *Narkissos*, undated
paper, images and texts pinned to board, 147.3 x 106.7 cm
Courtesy of The Jess Collins Trust (p.91)

Jess Study for *Narkissos I*, undated
pencil on paper, 88.9 x 66 cm
Courtesy Gallery Paule Anglim (p.97)

Jess Study for *Narkissos II*, undated
pencil on paper, 83.8 x 64.1 cm
Courtesy of The Jess Collins Trust (p.102)

Jess Study for *Narkissos III*, undated
pencil on paper, 33 x 26 cm
Courtesy of The Jess Collins Trust (p.105)

Jess Study for *Narkissos IV*, undated
pencil on paper, 30.5 x 24.8 cm
Courtesy of The Jess Collins Trust (p.92)

Jess *Narkissos*, 1976–91
pencil on paper and paste up, 177.8 x 152.4 cm
San Francisco Museum of Modern Art (pp. 88, 93, 95)

Pipilotti Rist *Sip My Ocean*, 1996
audio video installation: 2 projections, 1 player, 1 audio system, blue walls and blue carpet, music after 'Wicked Games' written by Chris Isaak, interpreted and performed by Anders Guggisberg and Pipilotti Rist, dimensions variable
Courtesy the artist and Hauser & Wirth (pp. 136, 141, 142)

All sizes height by width by depth.

SELECTED BIBLIOGRAPHY

Stephen Bann, *The True Vine: On Visual Representation and the Western Tradition*, (Cambridge: Cambridge University Press, 1989).

Steven Bruhm, *Reflecting Narcissus: A Queer Aesthetic*, (Minneapolis and London: University of Minnesota Press, 2001).

Whitney Chadwick, *Mirror Images: Women, Surrealism, and Self-Representation*, (Cambridge and London: The MIT Press, 1998).

Salvador Dalí, *The Secret Life of Salvador Dalí*, (1942), trans. Haakon M. Chevalier (London: Vision Press, 1968).

Bram Dijkstra, *Idols of Perversity: Fantasies of Feminine Evil in Fin-de-Siècle Culture*, (Oxford: Oxford University Press, 1986).

Havelock Ellis, 'The Conception of Narcissism' (1927), *Studies in the Psychology of Sex, vol. 7: Eonism and Other Supplementary Studies* (Philadelphia: F.A. Davis Co., 1928).

Freud's 'On Narcissism: An Introduction', eds Peter Fonagy, Ethel Spector Person, Joseph Sandler (New Haven and London: Yale University Press, 1991).

Julia Kristeva, *Tales of Love*, trans. Leon S. Roudiez (New York: Columbia University Press, 1987).

Christopher Lasch, *The Culture of Narcissism: American Life in an Age of Diminishing Expectations*, (New York: W.W. Norton & Company Inc., 1978).

Tirza Latimer, *Women Together/Women Apart: Portraits of Lesbian Paris*, (New Jersey: Rutgers University Press, 2005).

Steven Z. Levine, *Monet, Narcissus, and Self-Reflection: The Modernist Myth of the Self*, (Chicago and London: The University of Chicago Press, 1995).

Herbert Marcuse, *Eros and Civilization: A Philosophical Inquiry into Freud* (1955), (Boston: Beacon Press, 1966).

Ovid, *Metamorphoses*, trans. Mary M. Innes (Harmondsworth: Penguin, 1955).

Otto Rank, *The Double. A Psychoanalytic Study* (1914), trans. Harry Tucker (Chapel Hill: University of North Carolina Press, 1971).

Rabun M. Taylor, *The Moral Mirror of Roman Art*, (Cambridge: Cambridge University Press, 2008).

Louise Vinge, *The Narcissus Theme in Western European Literature up to the Early Nineteenth Century*, (Lund: Gleerups, 1967).

Friedrich Wieseler, *Narkissos: Eine kunst mythologische Abhandlung*, (Göttingen, 1856).

ACKNOWLEDGEMENTS

Author's thanks: I would like to thank everyone whose commitment has enabled 'Narcissus Reflected', the exhibition and the book, to come to fruition. The origins of my Narcissus obsession lay in an invitation to write about Dalí's *Metamorphosis of Narcissus* for the 1998 exhibition 'Salvador Dalí: A Mythology', curated by Dawn Ades and Fiona Bradley. It has, therefore, been a great pleasure to work once again as guest curator with Director Fiona Bradley, and the rest of her extremely capable staff at The Fruitmarket Gallery especially Stacy Boldrick, Elizabeth McLean, Armida Taylor and Samantha Woods. As befits a largely surrealist show, they have been a 'dream team' to work with. Discussions with colleagues on the AHRC surrealism and sexuality project – Dawn Ades, James Boaden, Jonathan Katz, Silvia Loreti, and Joanna Pawlik – enriched and informed the conception of the exhibition and corrected various of my misconceptions. I am especially grateful to Silvia Loreti for her assistance. Numerous curators and collectors have lent not only their valuable artworks but also their enthusiastic support. In particular, Paule Anglim, Odyssia Skouras, Christopher Wagstaff and John Zarobell have enabled us to present a significant body of Jess's work to UK audiences for the first time. The generosity of Montse Aguer, Director of the Fundació Gala-Salvador Dalí, has permitted me to realise an aim to reunite the manuscript for Dalí's *Metamorphosis of Narcissus* poem with the picture. And Jean-Luc Mercié willingly shared his unrivalled expertise on the artist Pierre Molinier. At a time of belt-tightening, our funders (AHRC, Terra Foundation for American Art, British Academy, Art Mentor Foundation Lucerne) have voted fulsomely for the show with their back pockets. I hope they will feel vindicated in their support by this exceptionally beautiful exhibition.

Edited by Fiona Bradley and Sam Woods
Designed and typeset by Elizabeth McLean
Assisted by Susan Gladwin

The Fruitmarket Gallery thanks Elizabeth Cowling

Printed by Stewarts of Edinburgh

The Fruitmarket Gallery staff:
Director: Fiona Bradley
Deputy Director: Elizabeth McLean
Development Manager: Armida Taylor

Administrator: Amelia Smith
Bookshop Manager: Matthew Williams
Commercial Opportunities Manager: Iain Morrison
Exhibitions and Publications Organiser: Sam Woods
Finance Manager: Celeste Stamenkovic
Gallery Manager: Jamie Mitchell
Installation Technician: Simon Shaw
Press and Marketing Manager: Louise Warmington
Research and Interpretation Manager: Stacy Boldrick
Senior Installation Technician: Colin MacFarlane

Ovid's *Metamorphoses* translated with an introduction by Mary M. Innes (Penguin Classics, 1955). Copyright © Mary M. Innes, 1955. Reproduced by permission of Penguin Books Ltd.

Picture credits:
pp.28–29: Tate: Purchased 1979. © Tate, London, 2011. © Salvador Dalí, Fundació Gala-Salvador Dalí, DACS, 2011.
p.16: Digital image © 2011. Photo Scala, Florence / Fotografica Foglia – Courtesy of the Ministero Beni e Att. Culturali.
p.20: Courtesy National Museums Liverpool (Walker Art Gallery).
p.26: Philippe Halsman / Magnum Photos. Image rights of Salvador Dalí reserved, Fundació Gala-Salvador Dalí, Figueres, 2011.
p.31: Museum Boijmans Van Beuningen, Rotterdam. © Salvador Dalí, Fundació Gala-Salvador Dalí, DACS, 2011.
pp.32: 33, 36, 37: Work lent by Gala-Salvador Dalí Foundation. © Salvador Dalí, Fundació Gala-Salvador Dalí, DACS, 2011. Image rights of Salvador Dalí reserved, Fundació Gala-Salvador Dalí, Figueres, 2011
p.34: Private Collection / Giraudon / The Bridgeman Art Library. © Salvador Dalí, Fundació Gala-Salvador Dalí, DACS, 2011.
p.35: Alinari Archives – Anderson Archive, Florence.
p.41: ©bpk – Bildagentur für Kunst, Kultur und Geschichte, Berlin / Salvador Dalí, Collection Museum Berggruen und Sammlung Scharf-Gerstenberg. © Salvador Dalí, Fundació Gala-Salvador Dalí, DACS, 2011.
p.42: Museum Boijmans Van Beuningen, Rotterdam. © ADAGP, Paris and DACS, London, 2011.
p.45: Courtesy Fundación Federico García Lorca.
p.47: Collection of the National Portrait Gallery, London. Given by the executors of the Estate of Eileen Hose. © National Portrait Gallery.
p.48: © Salvador Dalí, Fundació Gala-Salvador Dalí, DACS, 2011.
pp.51, 68, 69, 70, 71, 130: Courtesy of the Cecil Beaton Studio Archive at Sotheby's.
pp.54, 78: Collection of The Kinsey Institute for Research in Sex, Gender and Reproduction. © Estate of George Platt Lynes.
p.56: Musée de Saint-Denis, France / Archives Charmet / The Bridgeman Art Library.
pp.60, 61, 62: Courtesy Jersey Heritage Trust.
pp.64, 65, 66, 131: Photograph Florence Henri. © Galleria Martini & Ronchetti, Genoa, Italy.
p.67: Photograph Florence Henri. © Galleria Martini & Ronchetti, Genoa, Italy. Localisation: Paris, Musée national d'Art moderne – Centre Georges Pompidou. © Collection Centre Pompidou, Dist. RMN / Georges Meguerditchian.
pp.72, 73, 75, 76, 77: Private Collection, Paris. © ADAGP, Paris and DACS, London, 2011.
p.74: Photograph Pierre Molinier. © ADAGP, Paris and DACS, London, 2011. Localisation: Paris, Musée d'Art moderne – Centre Georges Pompidou. © Collection Centre Pompidou, Dist. RMN / Georges Meguerditchian.
p.79: Private collection.© ADAGP, Paris and DACS, London, 2011.

p.81: Collection Indra Tamang / Estate of Charles Henri Ford. Images courtesy Indra Tamang.
pp.83, 84: By arrangement with BFI. Image supplied by BFI Stills. © ADAGP, Paris and DACS, London, 2011.
p.85: Courtesy The New American Cinema / The Film-Makers' Cooperative, New York.
p.88: (details: pp. 93, 95): San Francisco Museum of Modern Art. Purchase through the gifts of Phyllis Wattis, Elaine McKeon, Judy and John Webb, Bobbie and Michael Wilsey, Jean and Jim Douglas, Susan and Robert Green, Pat and Bill Wilson, and the Accessions Committee Fund: gift of Frances of John Bowes, Shawn and Brook Byers, Emily L. Carroll and Thomas W. Weisel, Doris and Donald Fisher, Diane and Scott Heldfond, Maria Monet Markowitz and Jerome Markowitz, and the Modern Art Council. © The Jess Collins Trust and reproduced courtesy of the Trust
pp.91, 92, 102, 105: © The Jess Collins Trust and reproduced courtesy of the Trust.
p.94: © Allan Ginsberg / CORBIS.
p.97: Courtesy Gallery Paule Anglim. © The Jess Collins Trust and reproduced courtesy of the Trust.
pp.98, 100, 106: Courtesy of the Odyssia Gallery, New York. © The Jess Collins Trust and reproduced courtesy of the Trust.
p.99: National Gallery of Ancient Art, Palazzo Barberini, Rome. Alinari Archives, Florence
p.101: Private Collection. © The Jess Collins Trust and reproduced courtesy of the Trust.
p.103: Museum voor Schone Kunsten, Gent. © Lukas – Art in Flanders VZW.
p.104: © V&A Images/Victoria and Albert Museum, London.
p.108: Collection of The Art Institute of Chicago
pp.112, 123, 125: © Yayoi Kusama. Courtesy Victoria Miro Gallery, London, Ota Fine Arts, Tokyo and Yayoi Kusama Studio Inc.
p.118: Digital image © 2011. © Photo SCALA, Florence. The Museum of Modern Art, New York / Scala, Florence. © ADAGP, Paris and DACS, London, 2011.
p.121: Collection Musée national d'Art moderne, Centre Georges Pompidou, Paris. © Yayoi Kusama. Courtesy Victoria Miro Gallery, London, Ota Fine Arts, Tokyo and Yayoi Kusama Studio Inc.
p.124: Photograph: Norihiro Ueno. © Yayoi Kusama. Courtesy Victoria Miro Gallery, London, Ota Fine Arts, Tokyo and Yayoi Kusama Studio Inc.
p.127: Albright-Knox Art Gallery, Buffalo, New York; gift of Seymour H. Knox, Jr. © Lucas Samaras, Courtesy The Pace Gallery.
pp.128, 129: © Tate, London, 2011
p.133: Bill Brandt. © Bill Brandt Archive Ltd
pp.136, 141, 142: Video stills. Courtesy the artist and Hauser & Wirth.
p.138: The Baltimore Museum of Art: Bequest of Saidie A. May, BMA 1951.328 © ADAGP, Paris and DACS, London, 2011.
pp.139, 140: © ADAGP, Paris and DACS, London, 2011. Localisation: Paris, Musée national d'Art moderne – Centre Georges Pompidou. © Collection Centre Pompidou, Dist. RMN / Philippe Migeat.
p.145: Private Collection, Basel. © ADAGP, Paris and DACS, London, 2011.
p.147: Photograph: Kira Perov. Courtesy Bill Viola Studio LLC.
p.148: Photograph: Uwe Walter, Berlin. © Olaf Nicolai. Courtesy Galerie EIGEN + ART Leipzig / Berlin. © ADAGP, Paris and DACS, London, 2011.
p.149: © Mat Collishaw and Tate, London, 2011.
p.150: © Jake and Dinos Chapman. Courtesy White Cube.
p.151: Photograph: David Hughes. © Tim Noble & Sue Webster. Images courtesy the artists.
pp.154, 155: Courtesy the artist and Sicardi Gallery
p.158: Courtesy the Edward James Foundation
pp.158, 160: © Salvador Dalí, Fundació Gala-Salvador Dalí, DACS, 2011.

The Fruitmarket Gallery would like to thank all those who supplied photographs and have given permission to reproduce copyrighted material in this book. Every effort has been made to locate and credit copyright holders of the images reproduced in this book and the publisher welcomes communication from any copyright holder from whom permission was inadvertly not gained.